The New
Wider World
Second Edition COURSEMATE

for **AQA A** *GCSE Geography*

Paul Guinness

Skills unit developed by
Simon Ross

Contents

Introduction

About this book

This New Wider World Coursemate matches the content of *The New Wider World* to your own GCSE Geography specification, and follows the same order. It is a pocket companion for your course and provides a summary of the core information you will need to know and revise for your GCSE Geography examinations.

AQA A specification

Scheme of assessment and specification structure

The scheme of assessment comprises three components:

Paper One		1½ hours
Paper 40% of the total marks		70 marks
Paper One		1½ hours

People and the natural environment

Comprises two sections:

Section A: Geographical

This section examines skills related to Ordnance Survey mapwork, photographs, sketch maps, cross-sections, satellite images and other resources. The Ordnance Survey map will always have a UK context. This section is worth 25 marks.

Section B: People and the natural environment

There are seven resource-based, short structured questions, one on each of the topics. Candidates answer any **three** questions. Each question is worth 15 marks.

Topics:

1 Tectonic activity
2 Rocks and landscapes
3 River landscapes
4 Glacial landscapes
5 Coastal landscapes
6 Weather and climate
7 Ecosystems

Paper Two	1½ hours
35% of the total marks	75 marks

People and the human environment

There are three sections, each with two resource-based, structured questions, one on each of the topics. Candidates answer **three** questions, one from each section

Each question is worth 25 marks

Topics:

Section A	1	Population
	2	Settlement
Section B	3	Agriculture
	4	Industry
Section C	5	Managing resources
	6	Development

Coursework

25% of the total marks   **30 marks**

Coursework of approximately 2500 words based on a fieldwork investigation at a local/small scale.

The topics chosen for investigation must relate to some part of the specification content.

Thus, to meet the requirements of Papers One and Two you need to have studied 3 topics from People and the natural environment and 3 topics from People and the human environment (one from each section).

How your Coursemate is organised

Your Coursemate follows the same structure, and order as the topics in your specification. Most of the information is from *The New Wider World*, so your book acts as a companion to both *The New Wider World* and your own specification. Your Coursemate is organised in the following way:

- The **Unit** and **chapter headings** match those used in the specification.
- The **page references to** *The New Wider World* at the beginning of each chapter tell you which pages in the textbook your Coursemate refers to.
- The **Key ideas** relate to those that appear in your specification, and the content of your Coursemate is organised around these.
- **Key words to know** – these are the key geographical words and terms you need to know and be able to use.
- **Check this!...** – doing these questions will check that you know and understand the key concepts in each chapter.
- **Back to...** is a cross-reference to *The New Wider World* for finding more information. It can also be a cross-reference to other information in your Coursemate.
- **Case studies** are based on the case studies and place studies in *The New Wider World*, and **Case study extras** are new case studies written especially for your specification. Where relevant these will: refer you back to the textbook for more information; tell you how to get the best from your case study; provide links to other topics; provide updates to the case study, which may be accessed via a link from the Nelson Thornes website at www.nelsonthornes.com/newwiderworld and include questions that encourage you to learn the case study so that you can use it well in your examination.
- **Exam practice** – these questions are similar to those you will meet in the examination. You can check your answers by going to *The New Wider World Coursemates* website at www.nelsonthornes.com/newwiderworld.
- Each exam practice question is followed by an **exam tip** to provide help and advice on answering the question.

At the end of this book you will find a chapter on **geographical skills**. This gives information on the basic geographical skills you will need for the interpretation, presentation and analysis of geographical information and data throughout your Geography course and in your examinations.

> All references to The New Wider World in your Coursemate are to the Second edition.

Tectonic activity

1 The Earth's crust is unstable and creates hazards

What is tectonic activity and where is it found?

Tectonic activity is caused by the movement of **plates** (segments of the Earth's crust) resulting in earthquakes and volcanic eruptions.

Earthquakes and volcanoes

Figure 1.1a shows the distribution of earthquake activity and major centres of volcanic activity. The map clearly shows that there is a well-defined distribution pattern, with most earthquakes and volcanoes occurring in long, narrow belts. These belts include those that:

- encircle the whole of the Pacific Ocean, the so-called 'Pacific Ring of Fire'
- extend down the entire length of the mid-Atlantic Ocean.

Notice also that earthquake activity stretches across southern Europe and Asia, linking the Atlantic and Pacific Oceans, and that volcanic activity is found in smaller areas in southern Europe, the Caribbean, east Africa and the mid-Pacific Ocean.

Figures 1.1a and b show that earthquakes and volcanic activity occur in narrow **zones of activity**. If the Earth were the size of an apple, its **crust** would be no thicker than the apple's skin. Underneath the crust is the **mantle** where temperatures are so high that rock exists in a semi-molten state. The crust is broken into segments known as plates which float on the mantle. Heat from within the Earth creates convection currents which cause the plates to move, perhaps by a few centimetres a year. Plates may either move away from, towards, or sideways past, neighbouring plates. Plates meet at **plate boundaries** (Figure 1.1c) and it is here that most tectonic activity occurs, and where high mountain ranges are located.

Plates consist of two types of crust.

- Continental crust is older, lighter, cannot sink and is permanent.
- Oceanic crust is younger, heavier, can sink and is constantly being destroyed and replaced.

These differences in crust account for the variation in processes and landforms and level of activity at plate boundaries.

KEY IDEAS

1 The Earth's crust is unstable and creates hazards.

2 The interaction between people and the environments and hazards created by tectonic activity.

Key words to know

Plates
Zones of activity
Crust
Mantle
Plate boundaries

Figure 1.1a Earthquake activity

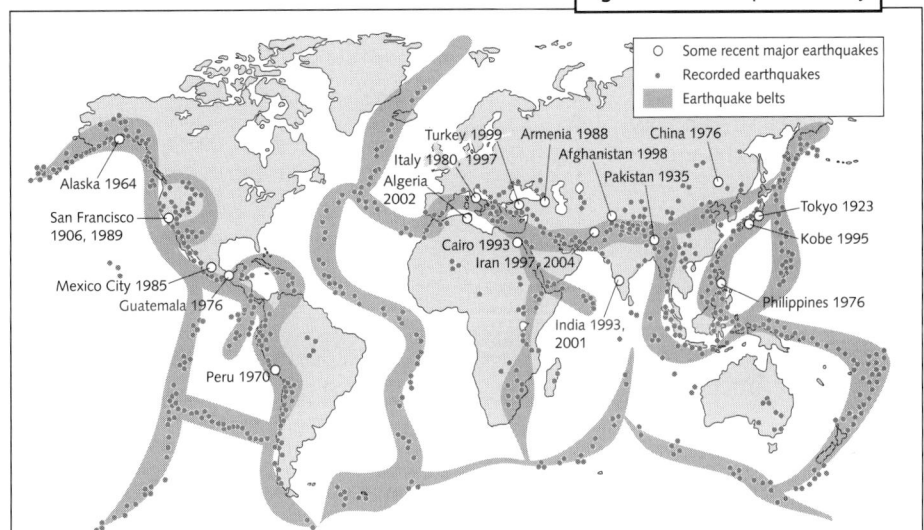

- Some recent major earthquakes
- Recorded earthquakes
- Earthquake belts

Alaska 1964
San Francisco 1906, 1989
Mexico City 1985
Guatemala 1976
Peru 1970
Turkey 1999
Italy 1980, 1997
Algeria 2002
Cairo 1993
Iran 1997, 2004
Armenia 1988
Afghanistan 1998
Pakistan 1935
China 1976
Tokyo 1923
Kobe 1995
Philippines 1976
India 1993, 2001

← **Back to ...**

The New Wider World **p264**
for further information on
the birth of Surtsey.

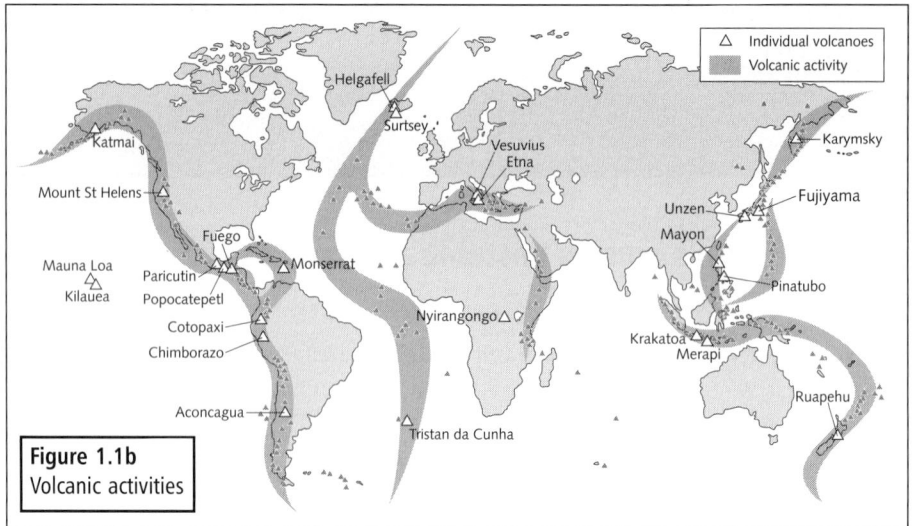

Figure 1.1b
Volcanic activities

1 Earthquakes and
  volcanoes seem to
  occur in long narrow
  belts.
a) Name two belts (areas)
   where both
   earthquakes and
   volcanic eruptions
   occur.
b) Name an area in Europe
   where both
   earthquakes and
   volcanic eruptions
   occur.

2 What type of margin
  can be found between
  the plates listed below?
  ● Nazca and South
    American
  ● North American and
    Eurasian
  ● Nazca and Pacific
  ● Indo-Australian and
    Eurasian
  ● North American and
    Pacific
  ● African and Eurasian
  ● Pacific and
    Indo-Australian

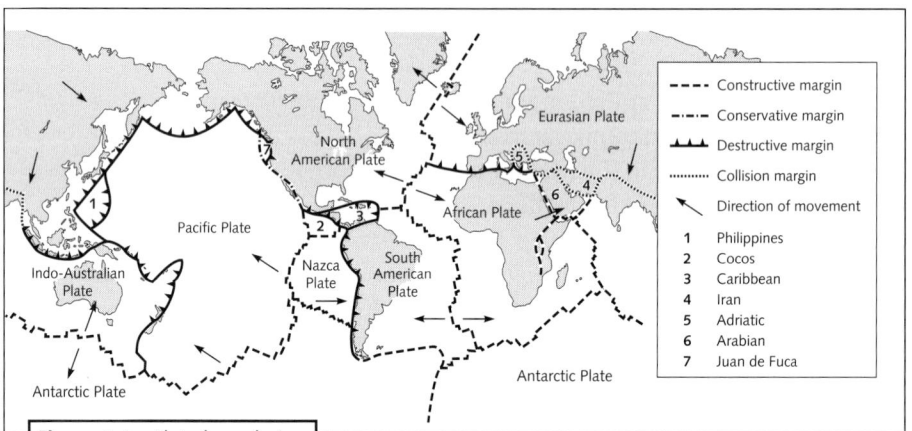

Figure 1.1c Plate boundaries

What happens when plates move?

Constructive margins (tensional)

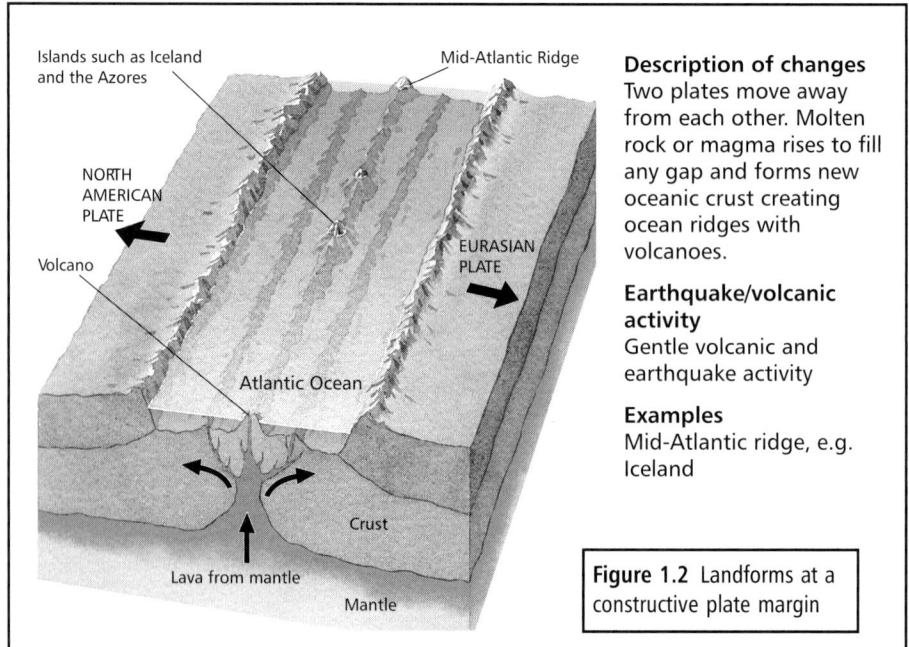

Description of changes
Two plates move away
from each other. Molten
rock or magma rises to fill
any gap and forms new
oceanic crust creating
ocean ridges with
volcanoes.

**Earthquake/volcanic
activity**
Gentle volcanic and
earthquake activity

Examples
Mid-Atlantic ridge, e.g.
Iceland

Figure 1.2 Landforms at a
constructive plate margin

Destructive margins (compressional) and the formation of fold mountains

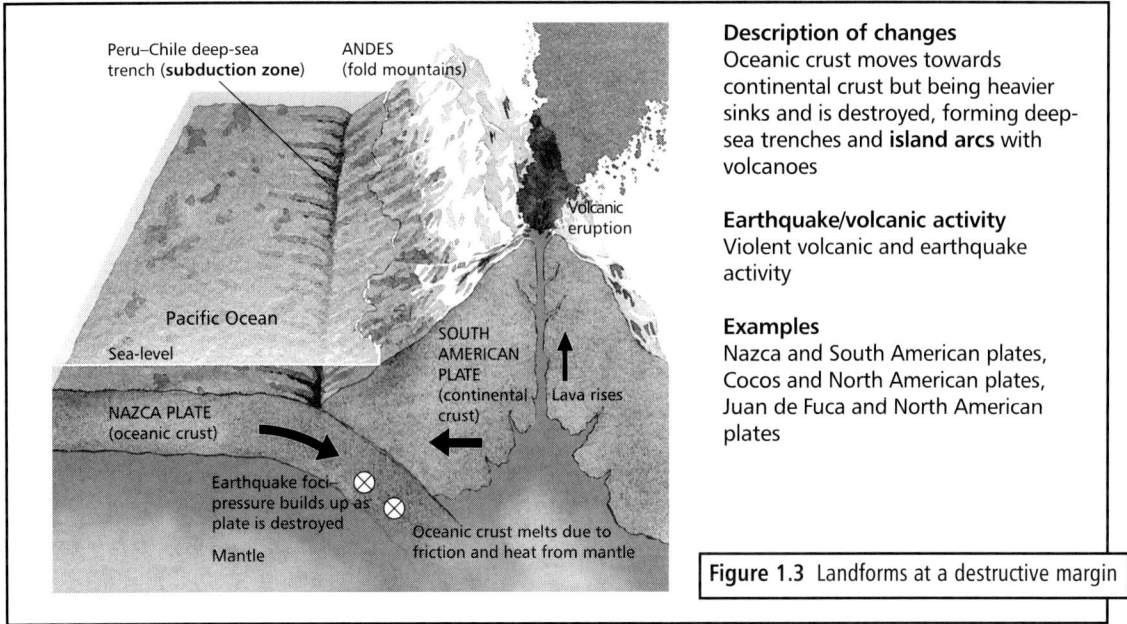

Description of changes
Oceanic crust moves towards continental crust but being heavier sinks and is destroyed, forming deep-sea trenches and **island arcs** with volcanoes

Earthquake/volcanic activity
Violent volcanic and earthquake activity

Examples
Nazca and South American plates, Cocos and North American plates, Juan de Fuca and North American plates

Figure 1.3 Landforms at a destructive margin

Fold mountains often occur at destructive margins but they can also be formed at collision margins. There have been a number of mountain building periods, due to intense folding, in the history of the Earth. The last was the Alpine mountain building period 30 million years ago. Mountain ranges such as the Alps and the Andes, formed at this time, are known as young fold mountains.

Key words to know

Subduction zone
Island arcs
Fold mountains

Collision margins and the formation of fold mountains

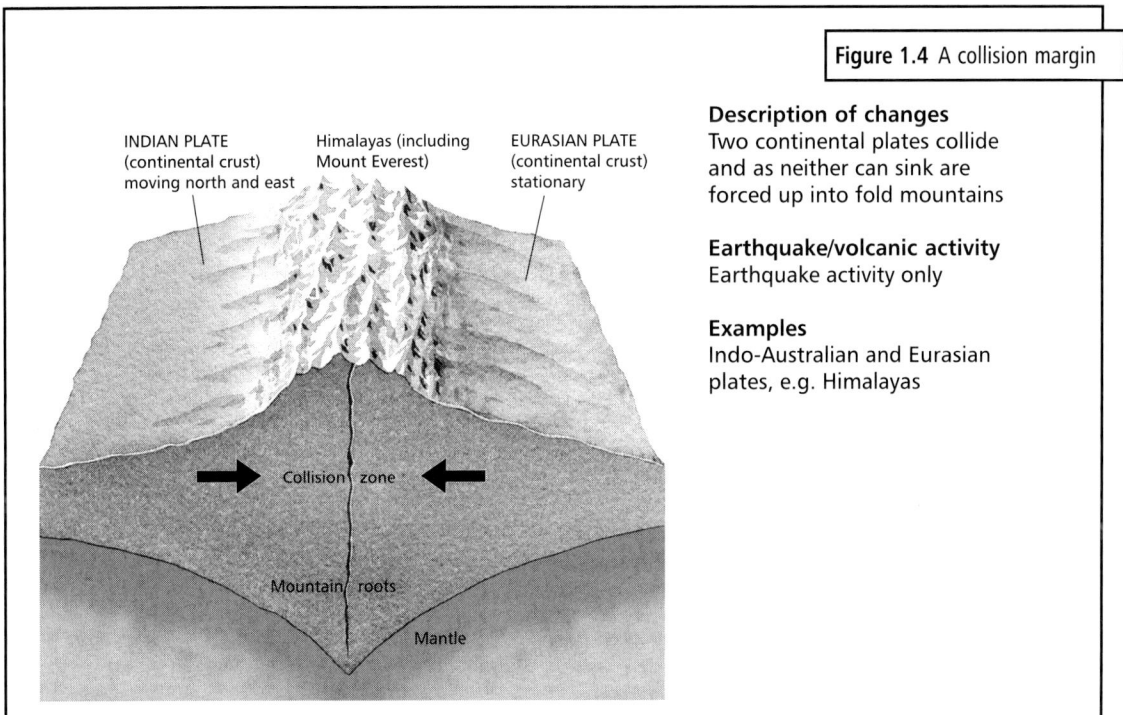

Figure 1.4 A collision margin

Description of changes
Two continental plates collide and as neither can sink are forced up into fold mountains

Earthquake/volcanic activity
Earthquake activity only

Examples
Indo-Australian and Eurasian plates, e.g. Himalayas

Conservative margins

Back to ...

The New Wider World **p265** for further information on the San Andreas Fault in California.

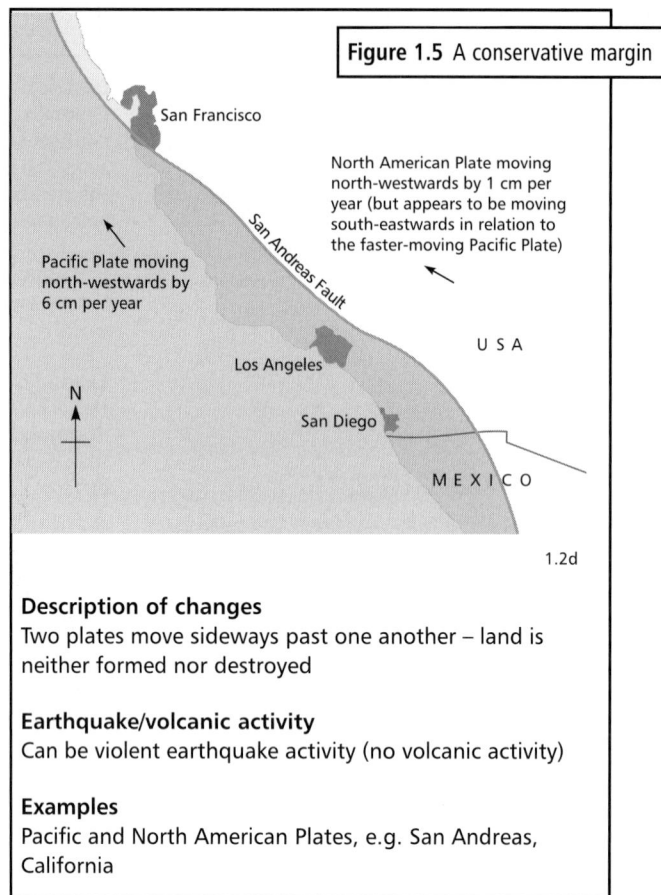

Figure 1.5 A conservative margin

San Francisco

North American Plate moving north-westwards by 1 cm per year (but appears to be moving south-eastwards in relation to the faster-moving Pacific Plate)

San Andreas Fault

Pacific Plate moving north-westwards by 6 cm per year

USA

Los Angeles

N

San Diego

M E X I C O

1.2d

Description of changes
Two plates move sideways past one another – land is neither formed nor destroyed

Earthquake/volcanic activity
Can be violent earthquake activity (no volcanic activity)

Examples
Pacific and North American Plates, e.g. San Andreas, California

Check this!...

1 a) Describe what happens at constructive, destructive, collision and conservative plate margins.
  b) Give examples of each type of plate margin.

2 With the aid of a labelled diagram, explain why:
  a) volcanoes occur at constructive plate margins
  b) volcanoes and earthquakes occur at destructive plate margins
  c) fold mountains and earthquakes occur at collision plate margins
  d) earthquakes occur at conservative plate margins.

Key words to know

Focus
Epicentre
Richter Scale

What are the characteristic features of an earthquake?

The **focus** of the earthquake is the point within the Earth's crust where the earthquake occurs. Seismic shock waves travel outwards from the focus.

The **epicentre** is the point on the Earth's surface immediately above the focus of the earthquake.

How are earthquakes measured?

The **Richter Scale** measures the size of the seismic waves during an earthquake (Figure 1.6). Each level of magnitude on the scale is ten times greater than the level below it.

The Richter scale measures the size of the seismic waves during an earthquake.

Earthquake size (magnitude measured by seismograph)

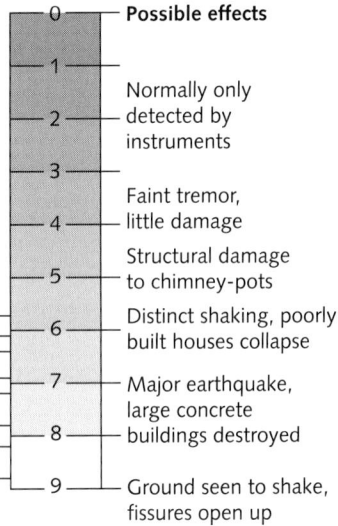

Possible effects

0
1
2 — Normally only detected by instruments
3
4 — Faint tremor, little damage
5 — Structural damage to chimney-pots

Assisi 1997 5.7
Afghanistan 1998 6.1
India 1993 6.4
6 — Distinct shaking, poorly built houses collapse

San Francisco 1989 6.9
Kobe 1995 7.2
7 — Major earthquake, large concrete buildings destroyed

Mexico City 1985 7.8
San Francisco 1906 8.2
8

Lisbon 1755 8.8
(largest estimated modern earthquake)
9 — Ground seen to shake, fissures open up

Figure 1.6 The Richter Scale

What are the characteristic features of volcanoes?

Volcanoes form when magma escapes through a **vent** (fracture or crack) in the Earth's surface. There are two main types of volcano, **composite** and **shield volcanoes** (Figure 1.7).

When lava is fluid (quick flowing) it results in a gently sloping shield volcano, e.g. Mauna Loa (Hawaii). Viscous (thick, slow flowing) lavas result in steeply sloping volcanoes. Often such volcanoes are made up of alternate layers of ash and lava and are called composite volcanoes.

Key words to know

Vent
Composite volcano
Shield volcano

Figure 1.7 (a) Composite and (b) shield volcanoes

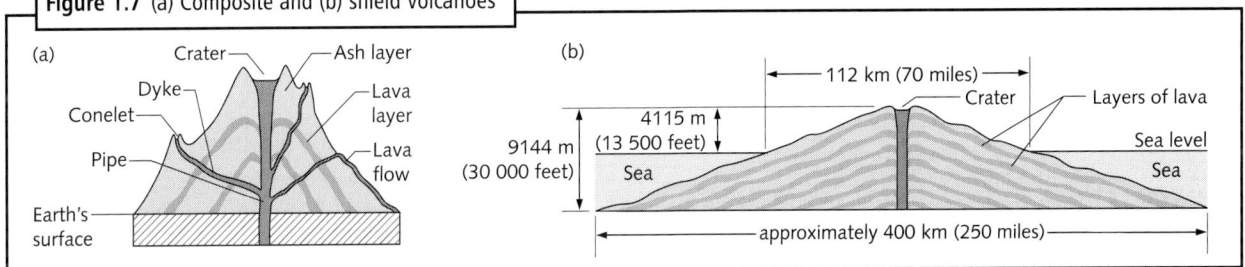

(a) Crater — Ash layer
Dyke — Lava layer
Conelet
Pipe — Lava flow
Earth's surface

(b) 112 km (70 miles)
Crater — Layers of lava
4115 m (13 500 feet)
9144 m (30 000 feet)
Sea
Sea level
Sea
approximately 400 km (250 miles)

Check this!...

1 Explain what the terms 'focus' and 'epicentre' mean, and what the Richter Scale is used for.

2 Name two types of volcano and describe their characteristic features.

What kind of human activity exists in fold mountain areas?

Case Study Extra

Courmayeur (Italy), Alps

Back to ...

The New Wider World p265 on collision margins to find out how fold mountains are formed.

The New Wider World pp166–167 for further information on winter tourism in Courmayeur, and p321 for an alternative case study of human activity in highland areas.

This case study is about human activity in one range of fold mountains (the Alps), and focuses on tourism. Courmayeur is found in the Alps near the head of the Val d'Aosta in the extreme north-west of Italy. It lies at the foot of Mont Blanc, the highest mountain in the Alps. Courmayeur is a mountaineering and winter sports resort. There are benefits and disadvantages as Figure 1.8 shows.

Figure 1.8 Benefits and disadvantages of tourism in a mountain area such as Courmayeur

Benefits	Disadvantages
More and better paid jobs, so less out-migration	At peak times tourists outnumber local people
Improved accessibility	Increase in new buildings and ski lifts, etc. spoil traditional character of village and create visual pollution
Improved services and shopping	Traditional way of life and jobs are lost
New leisure amenities can be used by local people	Houses increase in price and are too expensive for local people
Multiplier effect – success of tourism has led to other jobs	Seasonal unemployment
	Alpine ecosystem is destroyed

Farming in the Alps
- Since the middle of the nineteenth century, tourism has complemented agriculture in the high alpine valleys.
- In this high altitude area, pastoral farming dominates (dairying, goat herding, cheese making, etc.)
- Transhumance is still practiced, with animals moved to higher pastures during summer.
- Because of low incomes from farming, young people have long migrated from farming communities, leaving behind an ageing population and depopulated communities.
- A number of local crafts have developed to supplement farm incomes.
- The number of farms has declined steadily over time.
- Flooding is a hazard to farming and other activities.

HEP in the Alps
- High precipitation, deep and steep-sided valleys, impermeable rock, low population density all make HEP an attractive source of energy.
- HEP meets most of the energy requirements in the Alps.
- The population of the region is against the construction of new large HEP stations but favours the addition of smaller plants and the upgrading of existing ones.

Using your case study
Use this case study to answer questions on human activity in a range of fold mountains. You will need to know about tourism, farming and HEP. Read the question carefully and pick out the key words. Only use the information which is relevant to the question – don't simply include everything you know about the case study.

Case study links
This case study can also be used when answering questions about the effects of human activity, such as tourism, in upland glaciated areas.

Learn it!

a) Where is Courmayeur?

b) Why is Courmayeur such a popular tourist region?

c) Why is HEP the main source of energy in the Alps?

What are the causes and effects of a volcanic eruption in an LEDC?

Case Study

Merapi volcanic eruption, Indonesia, 1994

Back to ...

The New Wider World pp268–269 for the case study of the Merapi volcanic eruption and pp266–267 for a case study of a volcanic eruption in an MEDC – Mount St Helens in the USA.

Using your case study

Use this case study to answer questions on the effects and responses to a volcanic eruption in an LEDC. You will need to know about **primary** and **secondary effects**, and short, medium and long term responses to the eruption. You can use this case study to answer questions on why people continue to live in areas of tectonic activity, the advantages and disadvantages and their values and attitudes. Also use it to compare the effects and responses between tectonic activity in MEDCs and LEDCs.

Update

For up-to-date information on volcanic eruptions use the link on *The New Wider World Coursemate* website.

Key words to know

Primary effect/hazard
Secondary effect/hazard

Learn it!

a) Why is this an area of volcanic activity?

b) Explain the effects of the 1994 eruption.

c) Why do people live around Merapi?

What are the causes and effects of an earthquake in an MEDC?

Case Study

Kobe, Japan, 1995

Back to ...

The New Wider World pp270–271 for the case study of the Kobe earthquake and pp272–273 for a case study of an earthquake in an LEDC – Afghanistan, 1998.

Using your case study

Use this case study to answer questions on the effects and responses to an earthquake in an MEDC. You will need to know about primary and secondary effects, and short, medium and long term responses to the eruption. Also use this case study to compare the effects and responses between tectonic activity in MEDCs and LEDCs.

Update

For up-to-date information on earthquakes use the link on *The New Wider World Coursemate* website.

Learn it!

a) Why is earthquake activity a constant hazard in this region?

b) What were the i) primary effects and ii) secondary effects of the 1995 earthquake?

c) What happened in the months after the earthquake?

How can MEDCs and LEDCs predict and prepare for volcanic eruptions and earthquakes?

	Volcanic eruptions	Earthquakes
Prediction	Easier to predict than earthquakes because: • tremors increase within volcano • as magma begins to rise, so do ground temperatures – detected by satellites using heat-seeking cameras (new technology) • rising magma causes the volcano to swell and bulge. This can be measured by tiltmeters (which measure slope angles) and satellite global positioning systems. • volcano emits an increasing amount of gas and steam.	Far harder to predict the time and location of earthquakes. It is possible to: • install sensitive instruments that measure an increase in earth tremors (seismometers), pressure, and any release of radon gas. • map epicentres and frequencies of previous earthquakes to see if there is a location and/or time pattern. • observe unusual animal behaviour – dogs howling, fish jumping, mice fleeing houses.
Preparation	• Setting up monitoring and warning systems, using new technology. • Preparing an evacuation plan, organising transport, accommodation and food for those who need to be moved. • Training emergency services. • Organising emergency services such as water, food and power. • Organising post-eruption plans including repairing communications and buildings.	• Constructing buildings and roads to withstand earthquakes. • Training emergency services. • Organising emergency services to provide water, food and power. • Setting up a warning and information system for use on TV and radio.
	MEDCs and LEDCs Effects of volcanic eruptions and earthquakes are usually much greater in LEDCs. Human response to volcanic eruptions and earthquakes is usually much quicker and more efficient in MEDCs. LEDCs often have to rely upon, and wait for, international aid.	

Back to ...

The New Wider World **p274** for more information on how buildings can be designed to withstand earthquakes.

Check this!...

1 Why are MEDCs better able to cope with earthquakes and volcanic eruptions than LEDCs?

2 What can be done to predict and prepare for earthquakes and volcanic eruptions?

1 a Name the type of plate margin in Figure 1.9a and give an example. (2)

   b Name the type of plate margin in Figure 1.9b and give an example. (2)

2 Explain the causes and consequences of the plate movement in Figure 1.9b. (5)

3 With reference to examples explain why so many people live near plate margins? (6)

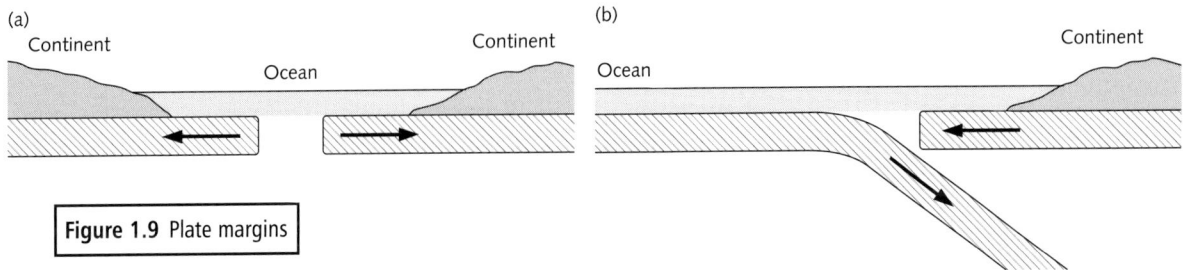

Figure 1.9 Plate margins

EXAM TIPS

For question 3 you should include reference to the lack of choice for most people in LEDCs compared to the more conscious weighing up of the costs and benefits in the safer environment (earthquake-proof buildings, etc.) in MEDCs.

Back to …

The New Wider World website to check your answers to the Exam Practice question.

2
Rocks and landscapes

KEY IDEAS

1 The Earth's crust is composed of different rock types and is modified by weathering.

2 The interaction between people and landscapes produced by different rock types.

Key words to know

Igneous rocks
Sedimentary rocks
Metamorphic rocks
Impermeable
Permeable
Porous

Check this!...

1 Define the terms igneous, sedimentary and metamorphic.

2 What is the difference between a permeable rock and an impermeable rock?

⇨ *The New Wider World*, pp244–251

1 The Earth's crust is composed of different rock types and is modified by weathering

Rocks – types, formation and uses

Rock types

The Earth's crust consists of many different types of rock. It is usual to group these rocks into three main types.

1 **Igneous rocks** result from volcanic activity. They consist of crystals which formed as the volcanic rock cooled down.

2 **Sedimentary rocks** have been laid down in layers. They usually consist either of small particles that have been eroded and transported, or of the remains of plants and animals.

3 **Metamorphic rocks** are those that have been altered either by extremes of pressure, or by extremes of heat.

Rock structure

The structure of a rock can affect its resistance to erosion and its permeability to water.

Resistance

Rocks have different strengths and so produce different landforms. For example:

● The harder a rock is, the more resistant it is likely to be to erosion. Harder rocks are therefore usually found as hills and mountains. Valleys are formed in soft rocks.

● In a drainage basin, the more resistant the rock, the steeper the valley sides.

● On coasts, resistant rocks form steep cliffs and stand out as headlands, whereas softer rocks form bays.

Permeability

An **impermeable** rock is one that does not let water pass through it, in contrast to a **permeable** rock which does allow water to pass through it. Permeable rocks may either:

● consist of tiny pores through which water can pass – such rocks, which include chalk, are said to be **porous**; or

● contain areas of weakness, such as bedding planes, along which water can flow.

Rock structure, therefore, affects the landforms of an area and can produce distinctive types of scenery.

Use of rocks

Many rocks have an important economic value. Such rocks are extracted, usually by mining or quarrying, for specific purposes (Figure 2.1).

Weathering

Rocks that are exposed on the Earth's surface become vulnerable to weathering. Weathering is the disintegration (breaking up) and decomposition (decay) of rocks in situ – that is, in their place of origin.

Figure 2.1 Type, formation and uses of rocks

	Rock	Formation	Uses
Igneous	Granite	Magma rises from the Earth's mantle and slowly cools within the Earth's crust. The slow rate of cooling produces large crystals.	Building (Aberdeen is known as 'the granite city'). Pottery (from kaolin, or china clay). Sites for reservoirs. Grouse moors (granite gives very poor soils). Some tourism.
	Basalt	Magma reaches the Earth's surface as lava from a volcano, and cools very quickly. The rapid cooling creates small crystals.	Weathers into a fertile soil. Foundation material for roads. Some tourism (Giant's Causeway and Fingal's Cave).
Sedimentary	Coal	Fossilised remains of trees and plants that grew under very hot, wet conditions	Thermal energy – power stations, industry, domestic use
	Sandstone	Results from grains of sand being compressed and cemented together	Building material – sites for many settlements
	Limestone	Remains of shells and skeletons of small marine organisms, e.g. coral, which lived in warm, clear seas	Sheep pasture (soils thin and porous), quarried for cement and lime. Stone walls. Tourism.
	Chalk	A form of limestone	Thin soils suited to cereals (wheat and barley). Also cement and lime. Spring line is ideal for settlement.
Metamorphic	Marble	Limestone changes by heat and pressure	Monuments (e.g. Italy)
	Slate	Shales and clays changed by pressure	Building material (roofs)

Weathering, unlike erosion, need not involve the movement of material. There are two main types of weathering:

1 **Physical weathering** is the disintegration of rock into smaller pieces by physical processes without any change in the chemical composition of the rock. It is most likely to occur in areas of bare rock where there is no vegetation to protect the rock from extremes of weather. An example of physical weathering is frost shattering (freeze–thaw).

2 **Chemical weathering** is the decomposition of rocks caused by a chemical change within the rock. It is more likely to occur in warm, moist climates, as these encourage chemical reactions to take place. An example of chemical weathering is limestone solution.

Frost shattering occurs in cold climates when temperatures are around freezing point and where exposed rock contains many cracks.

- Water enters the cracks during the warmer day and freezes during the colder night.
- As the water turns into ice it expands and exerts pressure on the surrounding rock.
- When temperatures rise, the ice melts and pressure is released.
- Repeated freezing and thawing widens the cracks and causes pieces of rock to break off.
- Where broken-off rock collects at the foot of a cliff it is called scree.

Limestone solution is caused by carbonic acid (carbon dioxide in solution) which occurs naturally in rainwater.

- Although it is only a weak solution, carbonic acid reacts chemically with rocks such as limestone which contain calcium carbonate.
- As the limestone slowly dissolves, it is removed in solution by running water.
- Solution widens bedding planes and joints.

Back to ...

The New Wider World **pp244–245** for more information on the types, formation and uses of rock and for photographs showing the landscape features they form.

Key words to know

Physical weathering
Chemical weathering
Frost shattering
Limestone solution

Check this!...

1 Explain the difference between physical and chemical weathering.

2 How does a) frost shattering and b) limestone solution occur?

Limestone

Limestone consists mainly of calcium carbonate. There are several types of limestone including chalk, and Jurassic and Carboniferous limestone.

Carboniferous limestone

Carboniferous limestone was formed on the bed of warm, clear seas. Since its emergence from the sea, Carboniferous limestone has developed its own distinctive type of scenery, mainly due to the influence of three factors:

Structure Carboniferous limestone is a hard, grey sedimentary rock which was laid down in layers on the sea-bed. The horizontal junctions between the layers are called **bedding planes**. **Joints** are lines of weakness at right-angles to the bedding planes (Figure 2.2).

Permeability **Permeability** is the rate at which water can either be stored in a rock or is able to pass through it. Chalk, which consists of many pore spaces, can store water and is an example of a porous rock. Carboniferous limestone, which lacks pore spaces, allows water to flow along the bedding planes and down the joints, and is an example of **pervious rock**.

Vulnerability to chemical weathering Carbonic acid in rainwater reacts with the calcium carbonate of the rock. As a result the limestone is slowly dissolved, by chemical weathering, and is then removed in solution by running water. Chemical weathering, therefore, widens weaknesses in the rock such as bedding planes and joints.

Underground landforms

- Carboniferous limestone areas lack surface drainage.
- A river that has its source on nearby impermeable rock will flow over the surface until it reaches an area of limestone.
- Various acids in the water, including carbonic acid derived from rainfall, begin to dissolve and widen surface joints to form **swallow holes**, or **sinks**.
- The river will, in time, disappear down one of these swallow holes.
- Once underground, the river will continue to widen joints and bedding planes through solution. Where solution is more active, underground caverns may form.

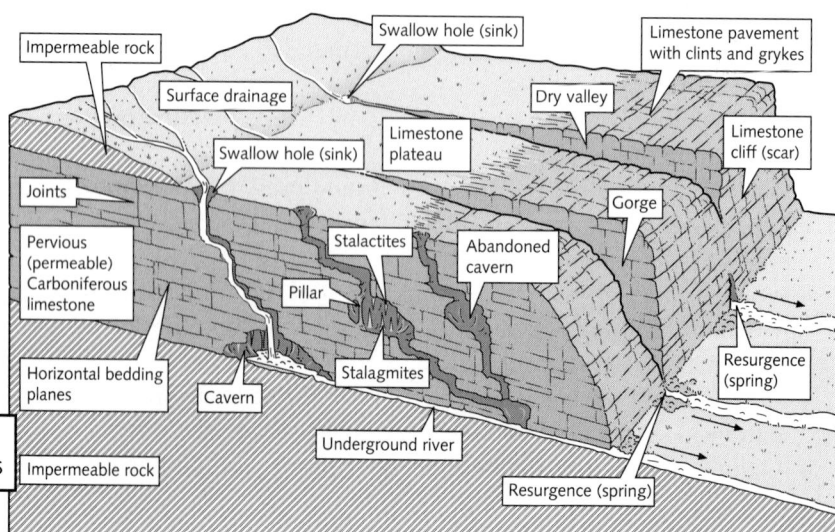

Figure 2.2
Limestone landforms

Impermeable rock — Surface drainage — Swallow hole (sink) — Limestone pavement with clints and grykes — Dry valley — Limestone cliff (scar) — Swallow hole (sink) — Limestone plateau — Joints — Pervious (permeable) Carboniferous limestone — Stalactites — Abandoned cavern — Gorge — Pillar — Horizontal bedding planes — Cavern — Stalagmites — Resurgence (spring) — Impermeable rock — Underground river — Resurgence (spring)

12

- The river will abandon these caverns as it tries to find a lower level. Should the river meet an underlying impermeable rock, it will have to flow over this rock until it reaches the surface as a **spring**, or **resurgence**.

Surface landforms

- **Dry valleys** are evidence that rivers once flowed on top of limestone. This might have occurred during the Ice Age when the ground was frozen and acted as an impermeable rock.
- Limestone areas often have a flat, plateau-like appearance. Where there is no soil, the top bedding plane will be exposed as a **limestone pavement**. Many joints reach the surface along this pavement. They are widened and deepened by solution to form grooves known as **grykes**. The flat-topped blocks between grykes are called **clints**.
- Where limestone collapses over an underground river it creates a gorge.

Deposition landforms

- Water, containing calcium carbonate in solution, continually drips from the ceilings of underground caves.
- Although it is cold in these caves, some evaporation does take place allowing the formation of icicle-shaped **stalactites**.
- As water drips on to the floor beneath the stalactite, further deposits of calcium carbonate produce the more rounded **stalagmites**.
- **Pillars** are the result of stalactites and stalagmites joining together.

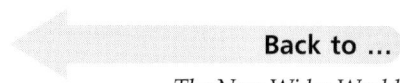

Check this!...

1 Explain how the underground landforms found in limestone areas are formed.

2 What are dry valleys?

3 How is a limestone pavement formed?

For an update on limestone use the link on *The New Wider World Coursemate* website.

For further information see 'Karst scenery in the Yorkshire dales' (GeoActive, April 2000).

Back to ...

The New Wider World
pp248–249 for more information on Carboniferous limestone and for photographs showing landforms found in limestone areas.

Key words to know

Spring
Resurgence
Dry valley
Limestone pavement
Grykes
Clints
Stalactites
Stalagmites
Pillars
Escarpment
Water table

Chalk

Chalk is a soft limestone. However, as the rock is permeable, water is able to pass through it, making it relatively resistant to erosion. Where the rock is horizontal, the landscape is one of gently rounded hills. Where the rock has been tilted, the porous and more resistant chalk alternates with impermeable and less resistant clays to form ridge and vale scenery, e.g. the North and South Downs. The ridges, referred to as **escarpments**, consist of a steep scarp slope and a gentle dip slope (Figure 2.3).

- Rivers and streams are usually absent on chalk, appearing as springs at the junction of the permeable and impermeable rocks.
- Springs occur where the **water table** reaches the surface.
- The water table, below which the ground is saturated, is likely to rise after wet weather and fall during times of drought.

Figure 2.3 A chalk escarpment

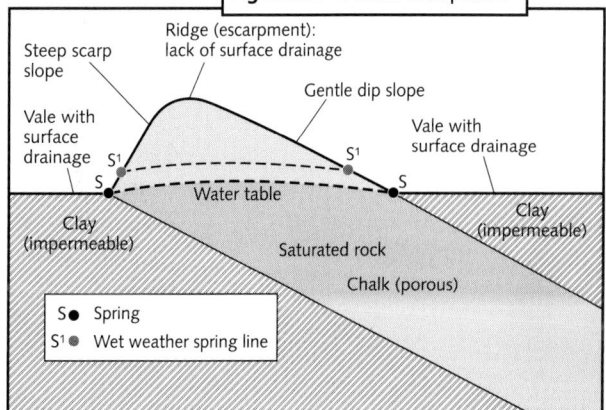

Ridge (escarpment): lack of surface drainage
Steep scarp slope
Gentle dip slope
Vale with surface drainage
Vale with surface drainage
Water table
Clay (impermeable)
Clay (impermeable)
Saturated rock
Chalk (porous)

S● Spring
S¹● Wet weather spring line

Back to ...

The New Wider World **p250**
Figure 15.22 for a diagram
showing the formation of
granite moorlands.

Key word to know

Tor

Back to ...

pp10–11 of this book for
information on the land
uses and economic uses of
granite, Carboniferous
limestone, chalk and clay.

- Dry valleys are another feature of chalk areas. They are believed to have formed during the Ice Age when the ground was frozen and so acted as an impermeable rock.

Granite

Granite forms when magma (molten rock) from inside the Earth rises towards the surface and cools within the crust. The slow rate of cooling allows large crystals to form and large cracks (joints) to develop. Over a lengthy period of time the less resistant rocks that overlie the granite may be removed by erosion. If this removal is by running water, rounded moorlands are formed, e.g. Dartmoor. If it is by ice, then jagged mountains are created, e.g. the Isle of Skye. Granite, being an impermeable rock, has numerous rivers and much surface drainage.

The most distinctive granite landform is the **tor**. Tors are thought to result from the joints within the granite being widened by chemical weathering when the granite is near to, but still underneath, the surface. The weathered rock is only later exposed on the surface.

Check this!...

1   What is an escarpment?

2   Explain the location of the springs in Figure 2.3.

3   What are the characteristics of granite?

4   How are tors formed?

For further information on chalk and clay landscapes see 'Chalk and clay landscapes' (GeoActive, April 2001).

For further information on granite landscapes see 'Granite landscape: physical and human influences' (GeoActive, January 2001).

---

2 The interaction between people and landscapes produced by different rock types

Quarrying of rocks

The extraction of rocks and minerals from the Earth's crust has been important since the earliest of human civilisations. Minerals are a finite, non-renewable resource. Although none of the 80 rocks and minerals needed in the present-day world are expected to become exhausted in the near future, the easiest and cheapest to obtain have often already been used up.

Quarrying and mining in National Parks

National Parks, although created in areas of outstanding natural beauty, are places where people live and have to find work. Quarries are one source of employment. They are still worked in several National Parks in England and Wales including Snowdonia and the Lake District for slate, and the Peak District and Yorkshire Dales for Carboniferous limestone. Working quarries pose a major conflict in National Parks because, although they can bring economic and some social benefits to people living there (Figure 2.4a), they, and more especially disused quarries and mines (e.g. copper and lead), can cause considerable environmental damage and some social loss (Figure 2.4b).

National Park Authorities are responsible for all planning applications, whether it is for a new quarry development or the extension of an existing project. The authorities have to ensure that working quarries and mines are landscaped and screened and that disused quarries and mines are restored, wherever possible, to their pre-quarry appearance.

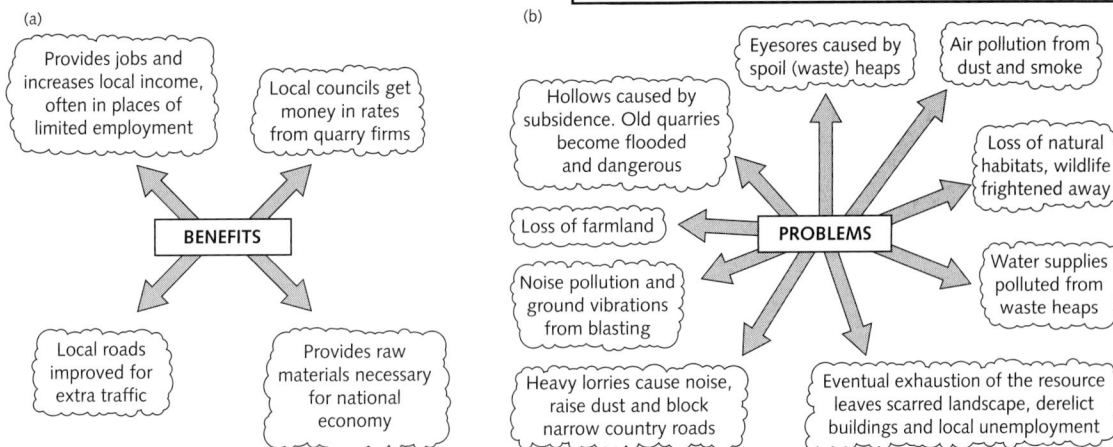

Figure 2.4 The benefits and problems of quarrying and mining

(a)

Provides jobs and increases local income, often in places of limited employment

Local councils get money in rates from quarry firms

BENEFITS

Local roads improved for extra traffic

Provides raw materials necessary for national economy

(b)

Eyesores caused by spoil (waste) heaps

Air pollution from dust and smoke

Hollows caused by subsidence. Old quarries become flooded and dangerous

Loss of natural habitats, wildlife frightened away

Loss of farmland

PROBLEMS

Noise pollution and ground vibrations from blasting

Water supplies polluted from waste heaps

Heavy lorries cause noise, raise dust and block narrow country roads

Eventual exhaustion of the resource leaves scarred landscape, derelict buildings and local unemployment

Case Study Extra

Limestone quarry and Hope cement works near Castleton in the Peak District

The Hope quarry and cement works (Figure 2.5) is the largest single employer in the area around Castleton. The main uses of the quarried limestone are:

1 as aggregate for road-making and for building
2 for cement
3 for agriculture
4 for building stone.

Castleton is at the head of a very popular area for day visitors and tourists. The village is surrounded by spectacular limestone scenery. The supporters of this quarry and others in the Peak District point to:

● the employment created
● the multiplier effect of the industry on the local economy
● the local use of limestone for building.

Those who are concerned about the disadvantages of Hope and other quarries in the area point to:

● unsightly quarry buildings
● ugly spoil heaps
● steep and dangerous cliff faces
● dust and noise from blasting
● the loss of plants and wildlife habitats
● the impact of quarry traffic.

Using your case study

Use this case study as an example of a quarry, which has both advantages and disadvantages for the local community. Make sure that you can:

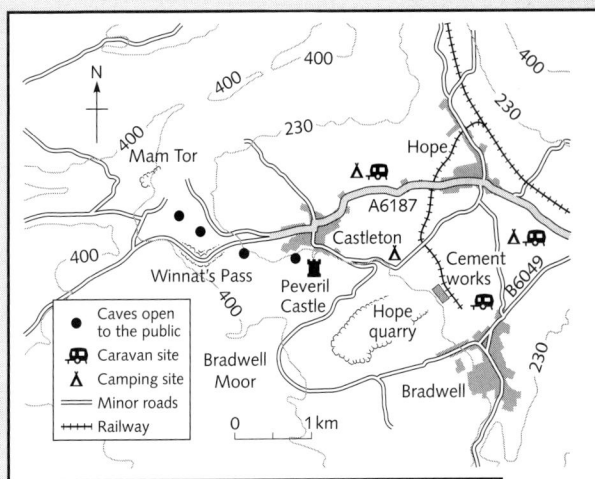

Figure 2.5 Limestone quarry and the Hope cement works near Castleton

1 describe the location of the quarry
2 discuss its benefits
3 explain its disadvantages
4 understand why people's opinions vary about the cost/benefit balance of the quarry.

Update

For an update on quarrying see 'Quarrying in the Peak District' (GeoActive 285, January 2003).

Learn it!

a) Draw an annotated sketch map to show the location of the quarry.

b) List the advantages of the quarry.

c) State the disadvantages of the quarry.

The Issue of abandoned quarries

When a company decides to stop activity at a quarry, the following are the main options:

- The quarry can be filled in, soil laid down and the land returned to farming.
- The site may be landscaped and then used for recreation.
- Near urban areas quarries are useful locations as landfill sites for rubbish.

EXAM PRACTICE

1 Put the following labels in the correct boxes on a copy of Figure 2.6. (4)
  Dip slope
  Water table
  Spring
  Scarp slope

2 What is a porous rock? (2)

3 Why is population density usually low on chalk escarpments? (3)

4 When a new quarry is proposed in an area why might some people be in favour and others against the proposal? (6)

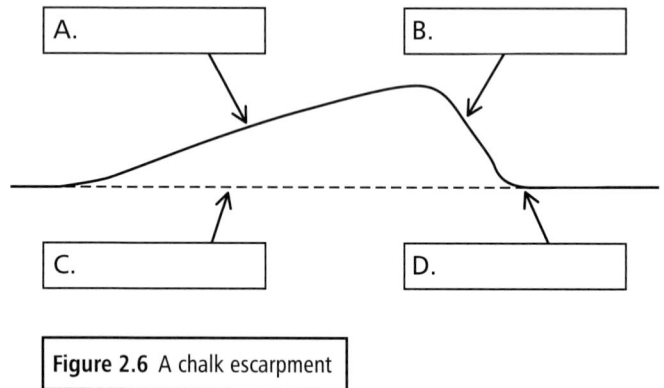

A.

B.

C.

D.

Figure 2.6 A chalk escarpment

Back to ...

The New Wider World website to check your answers to the Exam Practice question.

EXAM TIPS

For question 4 you should consider the economic, social and environmental factors that might affect people's attitudes to a proposed new quarry in their locality.

3 River landscapes and processes

1 The Earth's crust is modified by fluvial processes which result in distinctive landforms

Profiles and processes

Changes in the channel and valley of a river from source to mouth

No two rivers are alike but most show similar changes from source to mouth. Figure 3.1 shows the likely changes in the **long profile** and the **cross profile** of a river.

Erosion

Near the source of a river erosion is mainly **vertical** (downwards into the bed). Towards the mouth of a river erosion is **lateral** (sideways into the banks).

KEY IDEAS

1 The Earth's crust is modified by fluvial processes which result in distinctive landforms.

2 The interaction between people and fluvial environments.

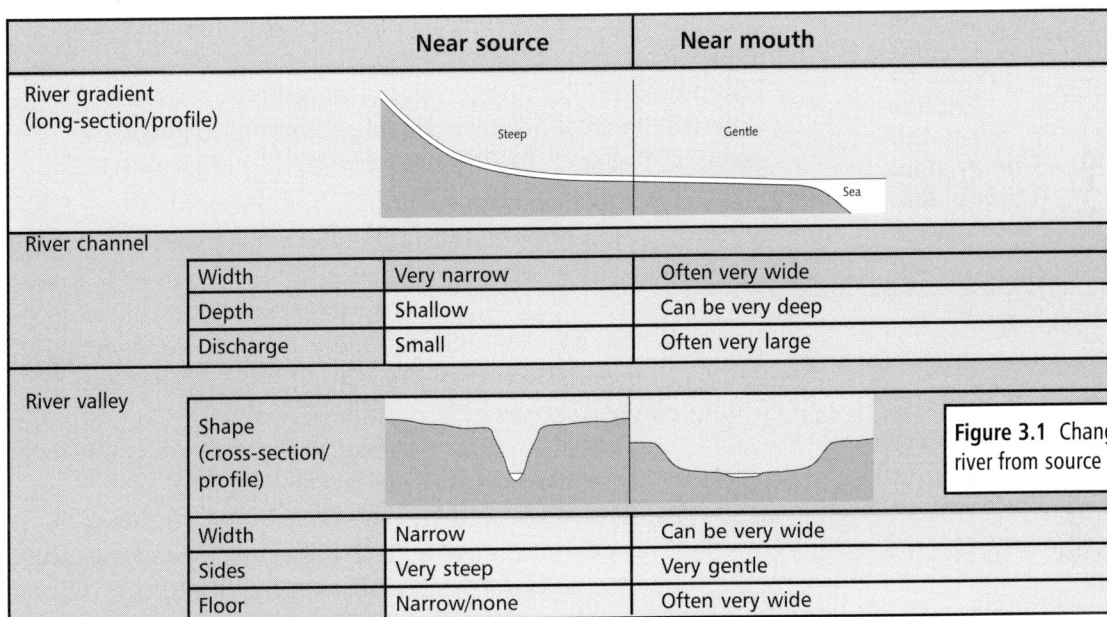

	Near source	Near mouth
River gradient (long-section/profile)	Steep	Gentle / Sea
River channel		
Width	Very narrow	Often very wide
Depth	Shallow	Can be very deep
Discharge	Small	Often very large
River valley		
Shape (cross-section/profile)		
Width	Narrow	Can be very wide
Sides	Very steep	Very gentle
Floor	Narrow/none	Often very wide

Figure 3.1 Changes in a river from source to mouth

The four processes of erosion are:
- **hydraulic action** – when the sheer force of the river dislodges particles from the river's banks and bed.
- **attrition** – when the river's **load** (the material it transports) collides and breaks up into smaller pieces.
- **corrasion** (abrasion) – when the river's load rubs against the banks and bed of the river and wears them away.
- **corrosion** – when acids in the river dissolve rocks, such as limestone, which form the banks and bed.

Transportation

A river can transport its load by one of four processes:
- **Traction**: rolling stones along the bed.
- **Saltation**: sand-sized particles bounce along the bed in a leap-frog movement.
- **Suspension**: silt and clay-sized particles are carried within the water flow.
- **Solution**: some minerals dissolve in the water.

Key words to know

Long profile   *Corrasion*
Cross profile   *Corrosion*
Vertical erosion   *Traction*
Lateral erosion   *Saltation*
Hydraulic action   *Suspension*
Attrition   *Solution*
Load

Back to ...

The New Wider World **p282** Figure 17.12 for a diagram showing the processes of transportation.

Check this!...

1 What is the difference between the long profile and the cross profile of a river?

2 What is the load of a river?

3 Explain two of the processes of river erosion.

4 Draw labelled diagrams to illustrate the processes of transportation in a river.

Key words to know

Waterfall
Plunge pool
Gorge
Meander
Friction
River cliff
Slip-off slope
Ox-bow lake

Deposition

Deposition occurs when a river lacks enough energy to carry its load. Deposition, beginning with the heaviest material first, can occur:

- following a dry spell when the discharge and velocity of the river drop
- where the current slows down (the inside of a meander bend or where the river enters the sea).

River landforms

Waterfalls

Waterfalls form when there is a sudden change in the course of a river. Many waterfalls form when rivers meet a band of softer, less resistant rock after flowing over a relatively hard, resistant rock (Figure 3.2).

- The underlying softer rock is worn away more quickly, and the harder rock is undercut.
- In time the overlying harder rock will become unsupported and will collapse.
- After its collapse, some of the rock will be swirled around by the river, especially during times of high discharge, to form a deep **plunge pool**.
- This process is likely to be repeated many times, causing the waterfall to retreat upstream leaving a steep-sided **gorge**, for example, Niagara Falls (*The New Wider World*, p283 Figure 17.15).

Meanders and ox-bow lakes

- When a river reaches a **meander** most water is directed towards the outside of the bend. This reduces **friction** and increases the velocity of the river at this point.
- The river therefore has more energy to transport material in suspension. This material will erode the outside bank by corrasion.
- The bank will be undercut, collapse and retreat to leave a small **river cliff**.
- Meanwhile, as there is less water on the inside of the bend, there is also an increase in friction and a decrease in velocity. As the river loses energy it begins to deposit some of its load.
- The deposited material builds up to form a gently sloping **slip-off slope**.

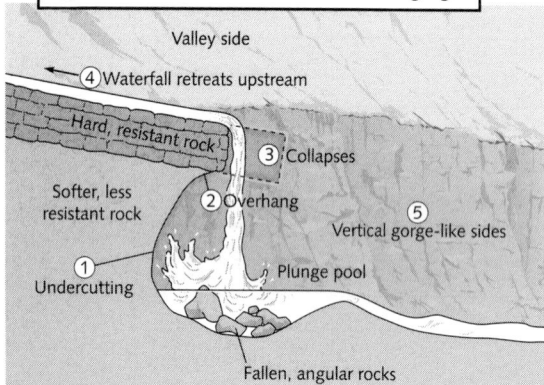

Figure 3.2 Formation of a waterfall and gorge

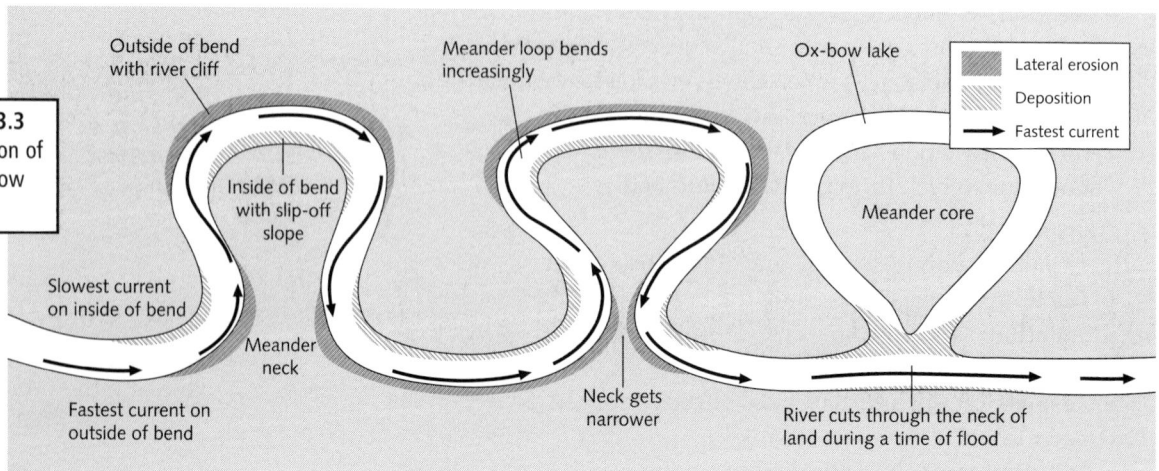

Figure 3.3 Formation of an ox-bow lake

Continual erosion on the outside bends results in the neck of the meander becoming narrower until, usually at a time of flood, the river cuts through the neck and shortens its course. The fastest current will now be flowing in the centre of the channel and deposition is more likely next to the banks. The original meander will be blocked off to leave a crescent-shaped **ox-bow lake**. This lake will slowly dry up, except during periods of heavy rain. The Cuckmere in East Sussex is an example of a meander (*The New Wider World*, p284 Figure 17.16) and the River Arun in West Sussex is an example of an ox-bow lake (*The New Wider World*, p292 Figure 17.39).

Key words to know

Floodplain
Levée
Distributary
Delta

Floodplain and levées

The river widens its valley by lateral erosion. At times of high discharge, the river has considerable amounts of energy which it uses to transport large amounts of material in suspension. When the river overflows its banks it will spread out across any surrounding flat land. The sudden increase in friction will reduce the water's velocity and fine silt will be deposited. Each time the river floods another layer of silt is added and a flat **floodplain** is formed (Figure 3.4). The coarsest material will be dropped first and this can form a natural embankment, called a **levée**, next to the river. Sometimes levées are artificially strengthened to act as flood banks.

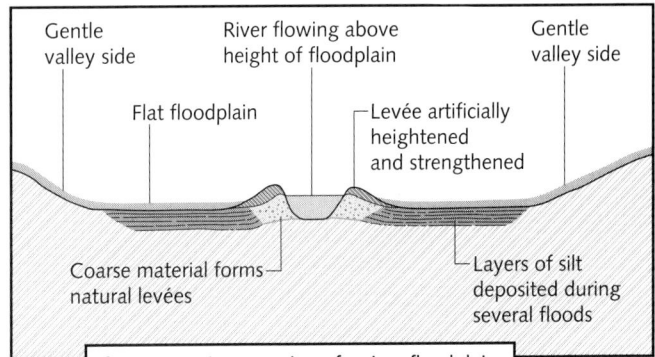

Figure 3.4 Cross-section of a river floodplain

Gentle valley side — River flowing above height of floodplain — Gentle valley side — Flat floodplain — Levée artificially heightened and strengthened — Coarse material forms natural levées — Layers of silt deposited during several floods

Deltas

As large rivers approach the sea, they have the energy to carry huge amounts of fine material in suspension. On reaching the sea, the river current may suddenly be reduced, allowing the material to be deposited. Sometimes deposition occurs in the main channel and blocks it. The river has then to divide into a series of smaller channels, called **distributaries**, in order to reach the sea. Over a period of time the deposited material of sand and silt may build upwards and outwards to form a **delta**, for example, the Mississippi delta (*The New Wider World*, p285 Figure 17.20). Deltas are only likely to form:

- where the amount of material brought down by a river is too great for sea currents to remove it
- in seas that are virtually tideless
- when a river flows into the gentle waters of a lake.

Back to ...

The New Wider World
pp283–292 for more information on river landforms and for examples of: a meander (Figure 17.16 the Cuckmere in East Sussex); a floodplain and an ox-bow lake (Figure 17.39).

Check this!...

1 Draw a fully annotated diagram to explain the formation of a waterfall.

2 How are ox-bow lakes formed?

3 Describe and explain the features of a floodplain.

For further information on river landforms see 'River processes and landforms: River Severn' (GeoActive, April 2001).

Fluvial landforms on OS maps

You need to be able to recognise and describe fluvial features on Ordnance Survey maps.

Back to ...

The New Wider World **p292** for 1:50,000 OS map extracts of the lower Arun valley (East Sussex) (Figure 17.39) and upper Teesdale (Figure 17.38).

Check this!...

Look at Figures 17.38 and 17.39 on p292 of *The New Wider World*.

1 Using Figure 17.38, give six-figure grid references for:
   a) the source of a tributary of the River Tees
   b) a waterfall
   c) the outside bank of a large meander.

2 Using Figure 17.39, describe the characteristics of the river at the following four-figure grid references:
   a) 0308
   b) 0004
   c) 0201.

The flood (storm) hydrograph

Key words to know

Drainage basin
Discharge
Flood (storm) hydrograph
Surface runoff
Throughflow
Lag time

A **drainage basin** is an area of land drained by a main river and its tributaries.

Discharge is the velocity of the river times its volume. It is the amount of water in the river passing a given point at a given time, measured in cumecs (cubic metres per second).

In some drainage basins, discharge and river levels rise very quickly after a storm. In other drainage basins, rivers seem to maintain a more even flow. A **flood** or **storm hydrograph** shows how a river responds to one particular storm (Figure 3.5).

- When a storm begins, discharge does not increase immediately as only a little of the rain will fall directly into the channel.
- The first water to reach the river will come from **surface runoff** (water flowing off the surface of the land).
- This will later be supplemented by water from **throughflow** (water which moves downslope through the sub-soil). The increase in discharge is shown by the rising limb.
- The gap between the time of peak rainfall and peak discharge is called **lag time**.
- A river with a short lag time and a high discharge is more likely to flood than a river with a lengthy lag time and a low discharge.

Factors affecting the shape of the flood hydrograph

It is possible that two drainage basins, located side by side, can receive approximately the same amount of rainfall and yet have very different hydrograph shapes (Figure 3.5). The river in basin A is likely to flood regularly, the river in basin B probably never. The reasons for this difference may be due to one factor, or a combination of factors (Figure 3.6).

Back to ...

The New Wider World **pp280–281** for more information on flood hydrographs.

Extreme weather conditions are often the major cause of a river flooding. A torrential thunderstorm, continuous rainfall for several days, or a heavy snowfall melting while it rains all increase the discharge of a river.

Check this!...

1 Define the following:
   a) drainage basin
   b) discharge
   c) flood hydrograph.

2 Why does discharge react more quickly to a storm in some drainage basins than others?

Figure 3.5
Differences in flood hydrographs between two adjacent drainage basins

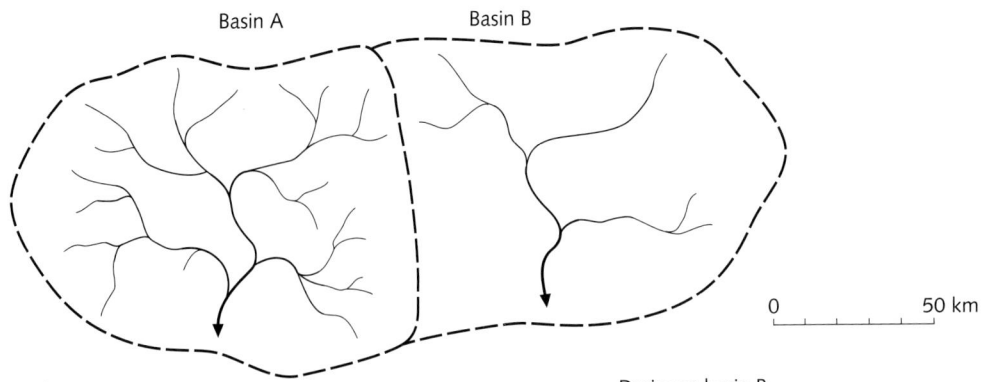

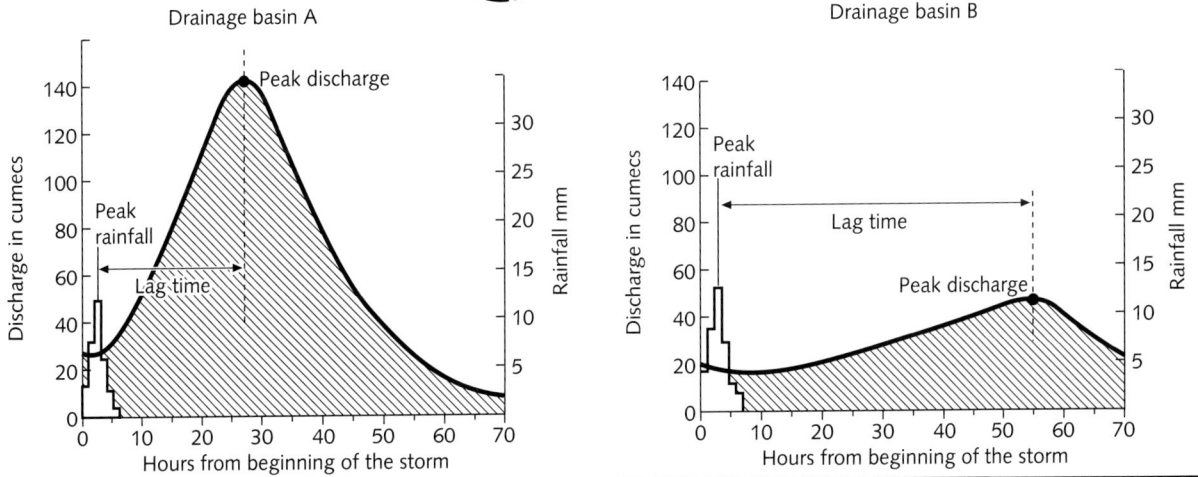

Figure 3.6 Reasons for differences in flood hydrographs for two drainage basins

Factor	Drainage basin A	Drainage basin B
Relief	Faster runoff on steep slopes	Slower runoff on more gentle slopes
Rock type	Surface runoff on impermeable rock	Throughflow and groundwater flow as rainfall infiltrates into permeable (porous) rock
Soil	Very thin soil; less infiltration	Deeper soil; more infiltration
Natural vegetation	Thin grass and moorland; less interception	Forest; more interception. Roots delay throughflow and absorb moisture. Evapotranspiration reduces chances of water reaching river.
Land use	Urbanisation; increased tarmac (impermeable layer) and drains (increased runoff). Arable land exposes more soil.	Rural area with little tarmac, concrete or drains. Tree crops and arable farming increase interception.
Use of river	Limited use	Water extracted for industry, domestic use and irrigation. Dam built to store water.
Drainage density	Higher density means more streams to collect water quickly	Lower density; fewer streams to collect water

2 The interaction between people and fluvial environments

River basin management issues

Should rivers be allowed to flood?

Some rivers, like the Mississippi in the USA, have built up their beds so that they flow above the level of their floodplains. Such rivers can only be prevented from flooding by building dams, diversion channels and artificial embankments. The problem arises when a serious flood risk occurs. If the levées break, or if they have not been built high enough, then large areas of land are flooded and numerous lives are put at risk. Following the Mississippi floods of 1993, scientists and engineers began asking whether the dams, diversion channels and levées had actually aggravated that and other floods. There are two schools of thought. One accepts that as floods are part of a river's natural cycle and the drainage basin's ecosystem, then flooding should be allowed as a natural event (Figure 3.7). The other argues for better flood defences and a more effective control of rivers.

Figure 3.7 Factors for and against controlling floods

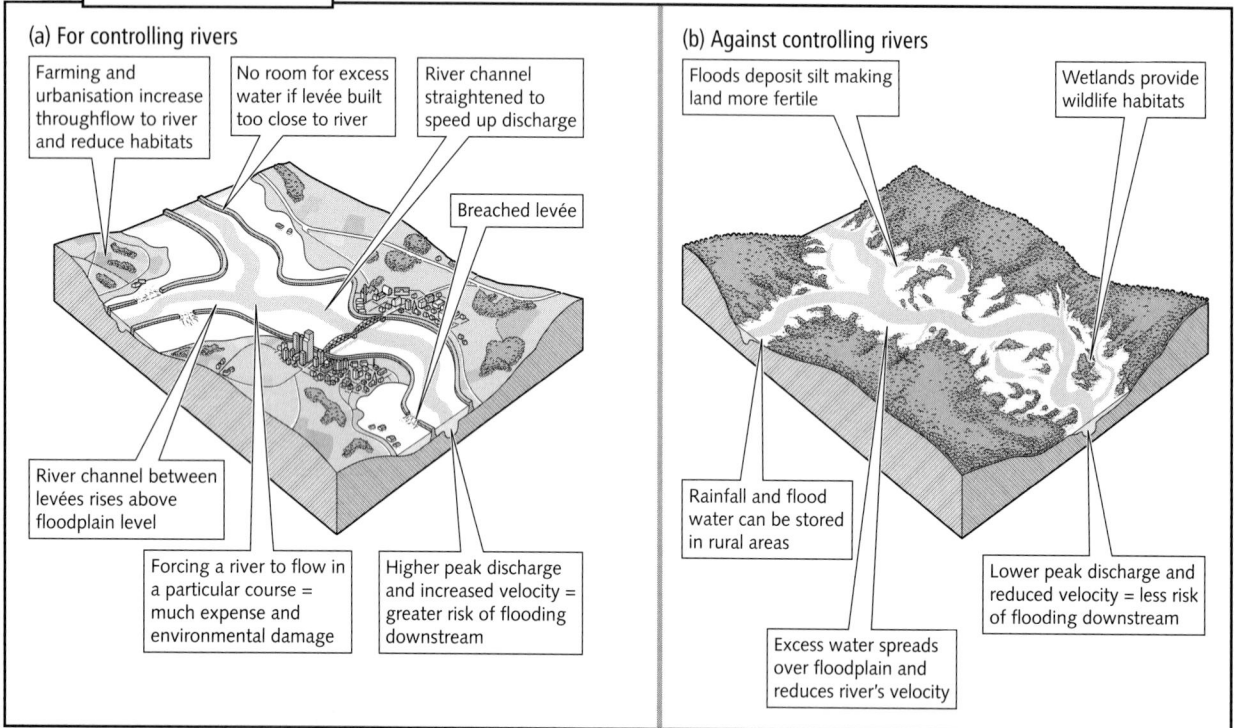

(a) For controlling rivers

Farming and urbanisation increase throughflow to river and reduce habitats

No room for excess water if levée built too close to river

River channel straightened to speed up discharge

Breached levée

River channel between levées rises above floodplain level

Forcing a river to flow in a particular course = much expense and environmental damage

Higher peak discharge and increased velocity = greater risk of flooding downstream

(b) Against controlling rivers

Floods deposit silt making land more fertile

Wetlands provide wildlife habitats

Rainfall and flood water can be stored in rural areas

Lower peak discharge and reduced velocity = less risk of flooding downstream

Excess water spreads over floodplain and reduces river's velocity

Water pollution problems

For many centuries, people across the world have seen rivers as a cheap and convenient way of removing their waste. In England and Wales, the Environment Agency records incidents of water pollution by both source and type. In 2000:

- by source, the sewage and water industry accounted for 30 per cent of incidents (Figure 3.8)
- by type, sewage and oil accounted for over half of the substantiated cases (Figure 3.9).

	Total	%	Major incidents	%
Sewage and water industries	7156	30	48	24
Industry	4763	20	62	31
Agriculture	2720	12	32	16
Transport	1788	8	16	8
Others	7035	30	41	21

Figure 3.8 Water pollution incidents in England and Wales by source, 2000

	Total	%	Major incidents	%
Sewage	6128	26	37	18
Oil	6025	26	45	22
Organic wastes	2699	12	28	14
Chemicals	1725	7	48	24
Others	6886	29	43	22

Figure 3.9 Water pollution incidents in England and Wales by type, 2000

Flood management: 'Hard' v 'soft' strategies

- 'Hard' management schemes, such as dam building, involve costly, large-scale engineering which impacts significantly on the environment.
- 'Soft' management schemes, such as river dredging, are smaller in scale, less expensive and less significant in their impact on the environment. Such strategies are viewed as being more sustainable.

Short, medium and long term flood management strategies

Short term strategies are an immediate response to the flood hazard and may involve:

- the use of sandbags to reinforce embankments and to protect property
- pumping water off streets and out of buildings
- the removal of people and property from flooded or flood-threatened areas.

Medium term strategies include:

- dredging to reduce the build-up of sediment on a river bed
- the introduction or improvement of flood warning systems
- flood-proofing (e.g. sealing walls).

Long term strategies include:

- the construction of dams
- building flood relief channels
- straightening the course of rivers
- land use zonation – restricting construction on floodplains and planting trees in selected areas to increase infiltration and reduce surface runoff.

Issues, values and attitudes

The possibility of flooding in a region raises a range of economic, social, environmental and political issues. When these issues are discussed (on television, in newspapers, on the Internet, in council meeting, in pubs and private houses) it usually becomes clear that opinions, based on different values and attitudes, differ between individuals and different groups of people. For example, some people favour the most formidable 'hard' sea defences to protect the coastline. Others might say the cost is too high and public money could be better spent elsewhere (health, education, roads, etc.) Some of the issues relevant to the flood hazard are:

- economic: the financial costs, direct and indirect, to individuals and organisations (councils, firms, etc.) of a) doing nothing, b) **soft strategies** or c) **hard strategies**.
- social: the impact on the general lives of people of a) flooding and b) the various strategies to control flooding. This would include people displaced from their homes, school closures, flooded playing fields, etc.
- environmental: the impact on the environment of a) flooding and b) alternative ways of controlling flooding.
- political: the views of elected representatives of different political parties, environmental/pressure groups, businesses and local residents.

Check this!...

1 Using examples, explain the difference between hard and soft river basin management strategies.

2 Give one example of each of the following: a) a short term, b) a medium term and c) a long term flood management strategy.

3 Why do people often disagree about what should be done to control flooding?

River flooding in an MEDC

Back to ...

The New Wider World pp286–287 for a case study of the 1952 flood in Lynmouth (Devon).

Using your case study

Use this case study to explain the causes and consequences of a flood in an MEDC. You should be able to:

1 draw a sketch map to show the location of Lynmouth and the drainage basins of the East and West Lyn rivers
2 describe the 24 hour rainfall pattern on 15 August 1952 (see Figure 17.23 on p286 of *The New Wider World*)
3 refer to all the factors that contributed to the flood

4 refer to the various consequences of the flood
5 explain the measures taken to prevent such a flood happening again.

Update

For further information on flooding see 'Flooding in the UK: winter 2000–2001' (GeoActive, September 2002).

Learn it!

a) Describe the pattern of rainfall at the time leading up to the flood.

b) What were the other factors that contributed to flooding?

c) Explain the consequences of the flood.

River flooding in an LEDC

Back to ...

The New Wider World pp288–289 for the case study of the 1998 flood in Bangladesh.

Using your case study

Use this case study to explain the causes and consequences of a flood in an LEDC. You should be able to:

1 draw a sketch map to show the location of Bangladesh and the course of its major rivers
2 discuss the general consequences of different levels of regular flooding (the 'beneficial' level, lower than the beneficial level, higher than the beneficial level)
3 explain the causes of the flood
4 identify the consequences of the flood.

Update

For further information see 'Response to cyclones: the case of Bangladesh' (GeoActive, April 2000).

Learn it!

a) What were the causes of the 1998 flood?

b) What was the impact of the flood on the population and the landscape?

1 On a copy of Figure 3.10, add detailed annotations to show the characteristics and formation of the meander cross-section. (4)

2 With reference to a named example, explain the formation of a delta. (5)

3 Using an example of a flood in an MEDC, describe its effects on the land and people. (6)

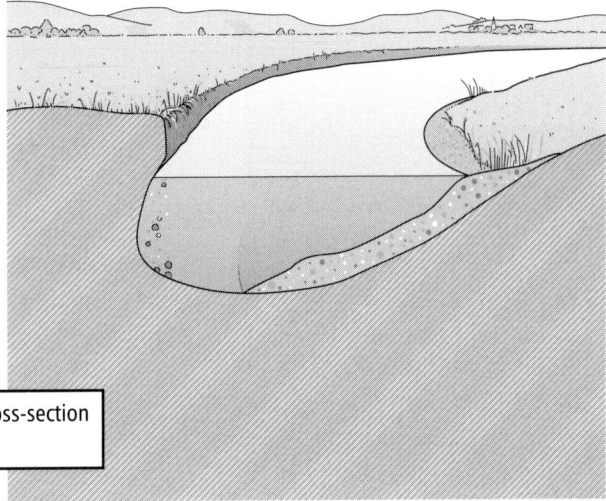

Figure 3.10 Cross-section of a meander

A good answer to question 3 would provide an equal balance between the two demands of the question (environment/local population).

Back to ...

The New Wider World website to check your answers to the Exam Practice question.

4
Glacial landscapes and processes

KEY IDEAS

1 The Earth's crust is modified by glacial processes which result in distinctive landforms.

2 There is interaction between people and glacial environments.

Key words to know

Freeze–thaw
Moraine
Abrasion
Plucking
Corrie
Rock lip
Corrie lake (tarn)
Arête
Pyramidal peak (horn)

Check this!...

1 Explain the processes of freeze–thaw, abrasion and plucking.

2 Draw a fully annotated diagram to show how corries are formed.

3 How is a pyramidal peak formed?

⇨ *The New Wider World*, pp163; 172–175; 246; 316–321

1 The Earth's crust is modified by glacial processes which result in distinctive landforms

Weathering and erosion

A glacier can erode much faster than a river, but, like a river, it can only erode if it has a continuous supply of material. The main source of material for a glacier results from the process of **freeze–thaw** weathering.

- Freeze–thaw occurs in rocks that have many joints and cracks in them, and where temperatures are frequently around freezing point.
- Water, which gets into the cracks during the day, freezes at night. As it freezes it expands and puts pressure on the surrounding rock.
- When the ice melts, pressure is released.
- Repeated freezing and thawing widens the cracks and causes jagged pieces of rock to break off.
- The glacier uses this material, called **moraine**, to widen and deepen its valley.

There are two main processes of glacial erosion:

1 **Abrasion** is when the material carried by a glacier rubs against and, like sandpaper, wears away the sides and floor of the valley. It is similar to corrasion by a river, but on a much larger scale.

2 **Plucking** results from glacial ice freezing on to solid rock. As the glacier moves away it pulls with it large pieces of rock.

Landforms of glacial erosion

Corries

- **Corries** (also known as cwms and cirques) are deep, rounded hollows with a steep back wall and a rock basin.
- They began to form at the beginning of the Ice Age when snow accumulated in hollows on hillsides, especially in hollows with a less sunny north- and east-facing aspect (Figure 4.1a). Snow turned into ice, and the ice moved downhill.
- Freeze–thaw and plucking loosened and removed material from the back of the hollow, creating a steep back wall (Figure 4.1b).
- Moraine, dragged along the base of the glacier, deepened the floor of the hollow by abrasion, and formed a rock basin.
- A **rock lip** was left where the rate of erosion decreased. This lip was often heightened by the deposition of moraine.
- Many rock basins are now occupied by a deep, round **corrie lake** or **tarn** (Figure 4.1c).

Arêtes and pyramidal peaks

When two or more corries develop back to back (or side by side), they erode backwards (or sideways) towards each other. The land between them gets narrower until a knife-edged ridge, called an **arête**, is formed. Where three or more corries cut backwards into the same mountain, a **pyramidal peak**, or **horn**, develops. Arêtes radiate from the central peak.

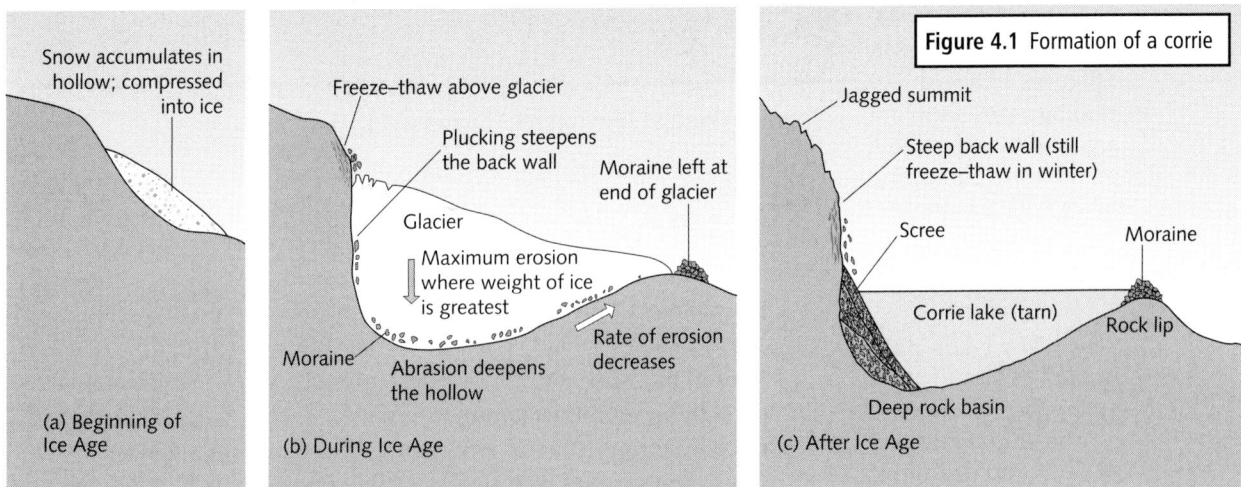

Figure 4.1 Formation of a corrie

(a) Beginning of Ice Age
- Snow accumulates in hollow; compressed into ice

(b) During Ice Age
- Freeze–thaw above glacier
- Plucking steepens the back wall
- Moraine left at end of glacier
- Glacier
- Maximum erosion where weight of ice is greatest
- Moraine
- Abrasion deepens the hollow
- Rate of erosion decreases

(c) After Ice Age
- Jagged summit
- Steep back wall (still freeze–thaw in winter)
- Scree
- Moraine
- Corrie lake (tarn)
- Rock lip
- Deep rock basin

Glacial troughs and truncated spurs

Glaciers, moving downhill from their source in the mountains, follow the easiest possible route which, in most cases, is an existing river valley. The glacier is able, mainly through abrasion, to widen, deepen and straighten its valley (Figure 4.2). The result is that the characteristic V shape of a river valley in a highland area is converted into the equally characteristic U shape of a **glacial trough**. As the glacier moves down valley it removes the ends of interlocking spurs to leave steep, cliff-like, **truncated spurs**.

Hanging valleys

Between adjacent truncated spurs are **hanging valleys**. Before the Ice Age, tributary rivers would have their confluence with the main river at the same height. During the Ice Age, the glacier in the main valley would be much larger than glaciers in the tributary valleys, and so it could erode downwards much more rapidly. When the ice melted, the tributary valleys were left 'hanging' above the main valley. Each tributary river has now to descend to the main river by a waterfall (Figure 4.2).

Ribbon lakes

Many glacial troughs in highland Britain contain long, narrow, **ribbon lakes** (Figure 4.2). Ribbon lakes are partly the result of erosion when a glacier over-deepens part of its valley, perhaps in an area of softer rock

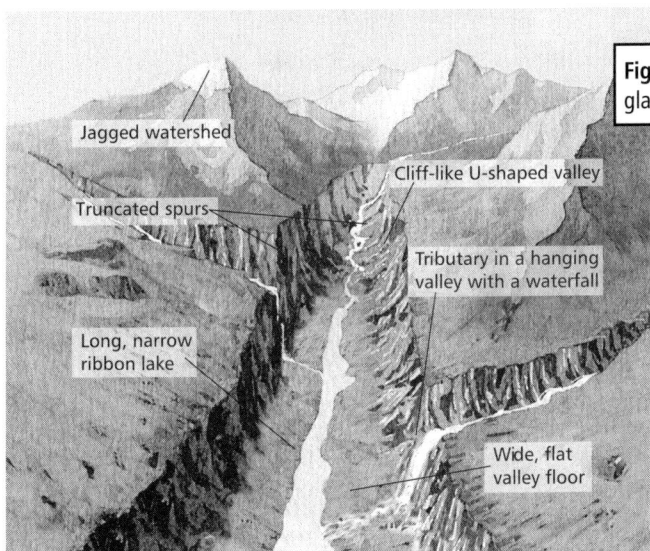

Figure 4.2 A glacial trough

- Jagged watershed
- Cliff-like U-shaped valley
- Truncated spurs
- Tributary in a hanging valley with a waterfall
- Long, narrow ribbon lake
- Wide, flat valley floor

Back to ...

The New Wider World **p317**
Figure 19.6 for a diagram showing the formation of a pyramidal peak.

Key words to know

Glacial trough
Truncated spur
Hanging valley
Ribbon lake

Check this!...

1 List the ways in which a large glacier can change a pre-existing river valley.

2 Draw annotated diagrams to explain the formation of hanging valleys and ribbon lakes.

For further information see 'Features of highland glaciation' (GeoActive, April 1999).

Back to ...

The New Wider World **p318**
Figures 19.8 and 19.9
for photographs showing
a glacial trough with a
ribbon lake and a hanging
valley with a waterfall.

Back to ...

The New Wider World **p319**
Figures 19.11 and 19.13
for photographs showing
terminal moraine
and drumlins.

Key words to know

Lateral moraine
Medial moraine
Ground moraine
Till (boulder clay)
Terminal moraine
Recessional moraine
Drumlins

or due to increased erosion after being joined by a tributary glacier. They may also be partly created by deposition of moraine across the main valley.

Transportation and deposition

Moraine is material, mainly angular rock, which is transported and later deposited by a glacier. It is deposited when there is a rise in temperature. As the glacier begins to melt, it cannot carry as much material. There are several types of moraine (Figure 4.3):

- **Lateral moraine** is material derived from freeze–thaw weathering of valley sides which is carried at the sides of a glacier.
- **Medial moraine** is found in the centre of a glacier and results from two lateral moraines joining together.
- **Ground moraine** is material dragged underneath a glacier which, when deposited, forms the flat valley floor. Ground moraine is also referred to as **till** or **boulder clay**.
- **Terminal moraine** marks the maximum advance of a glacier. It is material deposited at the snout, or end, of a glacier.
- **Recessional moraines** form behind, and parallel to, the terminal moraine. They mark interruptions in the retreat of a glacier when it remained stationary for long enough for further ridges to develop across the valley.

Drumlins are smooth, elongated mounds of material formed parallel to the direction of ice movement. They often consist of stones and clay, and are believed to result from the load, carried by a glacier, becoming too heavy and being deposited. They owe their streamlined shape to later ice movement.

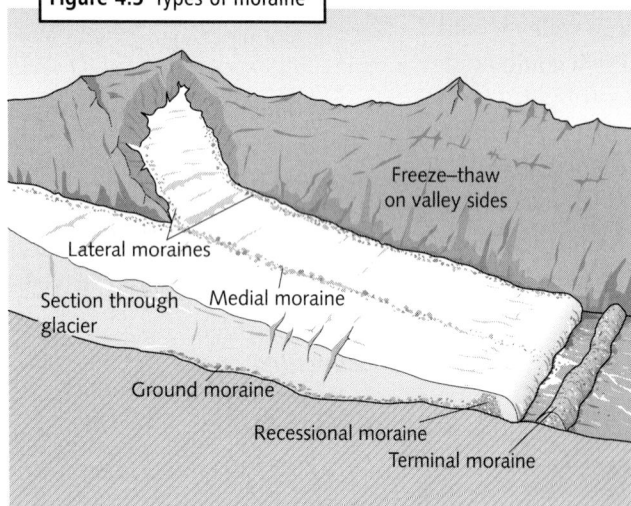

Figure 4.3 Types of moraine

Freeze–thaw
on valley sides

Lateral moraines

Section through
glacier

Medial moraine

Ground moraine

Recessional moraine

Terminal moraine

Check this!...

1 On a copy of Figure 4.3, add labels to explain the formation of each type of moraine.

2 With the help of a diagram, explain the formation of a drumlin.

For further information see 'Landforms of lowland glaciation in the UK' (GeoActive, September 2002).

Back to ...

The New Wider World **p320**
for 1:50,000 map extracts
of Snowdonia (Figure 19.14)
and the Lake District
(Figure 19.15).

Glacial landforms on OS maps

You need to be able to recognise and describe glacial features on Ordnance Survey maps and on photographs.

1 On Figure 19.14 which glacial landforms are located at the following grid references:
    a) 617546
    b) 625541
    c) 653530
    d) 610544.

2 Using Figure 19.15 give six-figure grid references for an example of each of the following:
    a) corrie
    b) hanging valley
    c) truncated spur
    d) arête
    e) glacial trough.

2 The interaction between people and glacial environments

Glacial highlands and human activity

Glaciated highlands such as the Lake District have certain advantages, as well as being nearly always scenically attractive, that encourage human activity. There is, however, the danger that development for economic reasons may spoil the natural beauty of these areas.

Farming
● Sheep farming is the only practical agricultural activity on steep slopes.
● The wide, flat valley floors of glaciated valleys often provide very fertile soils (due to glacial deposition) for arable farming and good quality grass for cattle.

Forestry
● Where the land has some soil, even if it is of poor quality, and the land is not too steep, either natural, or replanted, forests of coniferous trees may be found.
● The trees, when located in more accessible areas, give rise to a logging industry.

Water supply
● Ribbon lakes, especially when located in areas of high rainfall, form natural reservoirs.
● Glacial troughs with their steep sides can provide ideal sites for artificial reservoirs.

Energy resources
● Hanging valleys provide a natural 'head' of water needed to turn turbines in hydro-electric power stations.
● Exposed hillsides provide ideal sites for wind farms.

Tourism
● Areas with winter snow often provide locations for ski-resorts.
● Steep mountainsides are ideal for rock-climbing, the lower slopes for walking.
● Scenic views for the passive tourist who wishes simply to enjoy the natural beauty.
● Ribbon lakes, such as Windermere, can be used for water sports.

The effect of human activities on glaciated highlands

Farming

Farming modifies the natural vegetation, and the use of fertilisers, pesticides, etc. can impact significantly on the ecosystem.

Forestry

- Some people feel that re-afforestation spoils the natural look of hillsides.
- Logging, on a big scale, can leave huge scars and, if not managed carefully, can spoil the environment.

Water supply

The drowning of a glacial trough to provide a reservoir means the loss of homes and jobs for people previously living and working there.

Energy resources

- Hydro-electric power stations may be unsightly, as are the pylons and power lines needed to transfer the electricity to the National Grid.
- Wind farms are considered, by some people, to be inappropriate in areas of scenic beauty.

Tourism

- Winter sports resorts, with their accommodation, après-ski amenities, ski-runs, ski-lifts and approach roads, spoil the natural scenery and erode the fragile natural alpine vegetation.
- Skiing off-piste can also increase the risk of avalanches.
- Walkers can wear away footpaths, while water sports enthusiasts may pollute the ribbon lakes.
- There is an increased demand for amenities such as hotels, B&B facilities, camping and caravan sites, car parks, restaurants and gift shops.

Case Study

The Lake District National Park

Back to ...

The New Wider World pp172–175 for the case study on the Lake District National Park.

Using your case study

Use this case study as an example of an upland glaciated area where:

- many examples of glacial landforms can be found
- social, environmental and political issues can be recognised
- values and attitudes differ between the different interest groups (Figure 4.4 and *The New Wider World* p174)
- management strategies have been put in place in an attempt to solve problems (Figure 4.4 and *The New Wider World* p175).

Case study links

The Lake District National Park can be used as a tourist destination in Managing resources (Chapter 12).

Update

For up-to-date information on the Lake District use the link on *The New Wider World Coursemate* website.

Learn it!

a) Draw a simple sketch map to show the location of the Lake District.

b) Describe the physical landscape.

c) Discuss the human uses of the Lake District.

Figure 4.4 How planning in a National Park can help solve problems such as over-use, congestion and conflicts of use

Problems	Attempted solutions
Footpaths worn away	New routes planned; signposted routes; artificial surfaces laid
Destruction of vegetation, erosion of footpaths	Areas fenced off; education of visitors; landscaping
Litter, vandalism, trespassing	Provision of picnic areas with litter bins; park wardens
Cars parked on grass verges or on narrow lanes	Car parks; one-way systems; park and ride schemes
Congestion on narrow roads	Roads closed to traffic in tourist season/at weekends; park and ride; encouragement to use minibuses, to cycle or walk
Heavy lorries, local traffic and tourist traffic	Scenic routes separating local and tourist traffic
'Honeypots' (views, cafés) cause crowding	Develop alternative honeypots, direct visitors to other attractions
Conflict of users, e.g. a) between local farmers and tourists b) between tourists	Restricting tourist access to footpaths and bridleways, separating activities, e.g. water skiing and angling
Unsightly new cafés, car parks and caravan parks	Screened behind trees, only certain natural colours allowed in paint schemes

EXAM PRACTICE

1 Study Figure 4.5. Which glacial features are found at the following locations? (4)

A _____
B _____
C _____
D _____

2 With the aid of an annotated diagram, describe and explain the formation of a corrie. (5)

3 How can tourism in glaciated areas have an impact on the environment and the local population? (6)

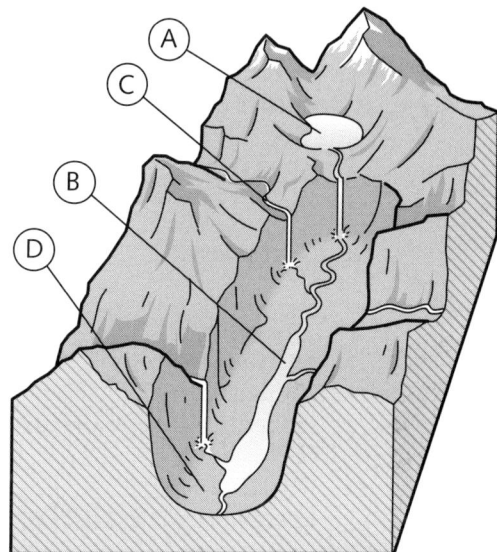

Figure 4.5 A highland landscape after glaciation

Back to ...

The New Wider World website to check your answers to the Exam Practice question.

EXAM TIPS

For question 3 ensure that your answer has a good balance between a) land and people, and b) short term and long term effects.

KEY IDEAS

1 The Earth's crust is modified by coastal processes which result in distinctive landforms.

2 The interaction between people and coastal environments.

Back to ...

The New Wider World **p300**
Figure 18.2 for diagrams showing constructive and destructive waves.

Key words to know

Fetch
Swash
Backwash
Constructive waves
Destructive waves
Corrasion
Attrition
Corrosion
Hydraulic pressure
Headland
Bay
Wave-cut platform

Check this!...

1 What is the fetch of a wave?

2 Draw labelled diagrams to explain the difference between constructive and destructive waves.

3 Explain the four processes of coastal erosion.

⇨ *The New Wider World,* pp164–165; 300–309

1 The Earth's crust is modified by coastal processes which result in distinctive landforms

Coastal processes

The coast is a narrow contact zone between land and sea. It is constantly changing due to the effects of land, air and marine processes. On many coastlines the dominant influence is the action of waves. The larger the wave, the more energy it contains. The largest waves are formed when winds are very strong, blow for long periods and cross large expanses of water. The maximum distance of water over which winds can blow is called the **fetch**.

After a wave breaks the movement of water up a beach is called the **swash**. It is known as the **backwash** when it returns back down the beach.

There are two types of wave.

1 **Constructive waves** have limited energy. Most of this is used by the swash to transport material up the beach.

2 **Destructive waves** have much more energy. Most of this is used by the backwash to transport material back down the beach.

Erosion

Waves, like rivers, can erode the land by one of four processes:

- **Corrasion** (abrasion) – caused by large waves hurling beach material against a cliff.
- **Attrition** – when waves cause rocks and boulders on the beach to collide and to break up into small particles.
- **Corrosion** (solution) – when salts and other acids in seawater slowly dissolve a cliff.
- **Hydraulic pressure** – the force of waves compressing air in cracks in a cliff.

Landforms of coastal erosion

Headlands and bays

Headlands and **bays** form along coastlines where there are alternating outcrops of resistant (harder) and less resistant (softer) rock. Destructive waves erode the areas of softer rock more rapidly to form bays. The waves cannot, however, wear away the resistant rock as quickly and so headlands are left protruding out into the sea. The headlands are now exposed to the full force of the waves.

Cliff recession and wave-cut platforms

Wave erosion is greatest when large waves break against the foot of the cliff. This happens mainly during winter storms. With wave energy at its maximum, the waves undercut the foot of the cliff to form a wave-cut notch. Over a period of time the notch enlarges until the cliff above it, left unsupported, collapses. As this process is repeated, the cliff retreats and, often, increases in height. The gently sloping expanse of rock marking the foot of the retreating cliff is called a wave-cut platform. **Wave-cut platforms** are exposed at low tide but covered at high tide.

Caves, arches and stacks

Cliffs are more likely to form where the coastline consists of resistant rock. However, within resistant rocks there are usually places of weakness, such as a joint or a fault (Figure 5.1).

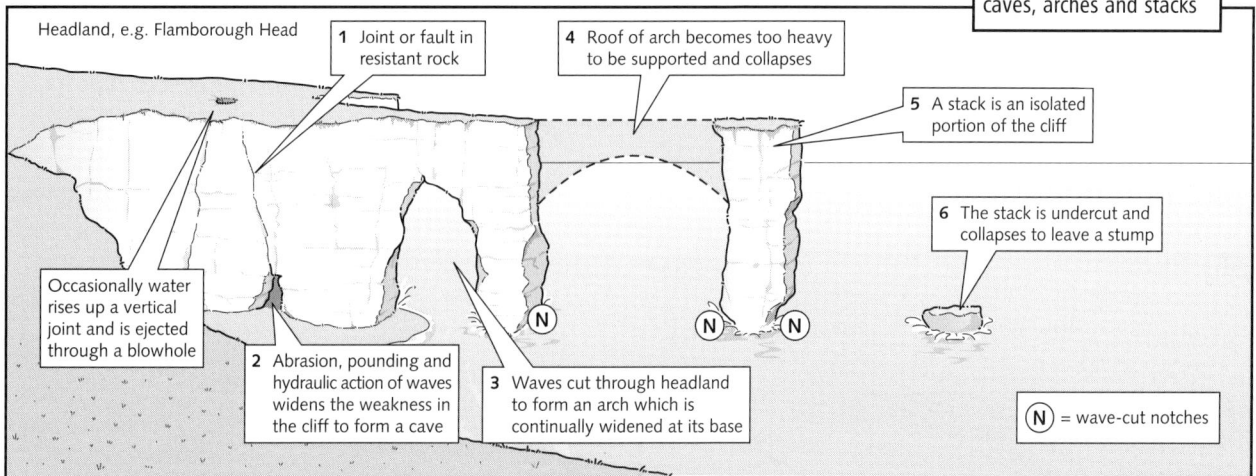

Headland, e.g. Flamborough Head

1 Joint or fault in resistant rock

4 Roof of arch becomes too heavy to be supported and collapses

5 A stack is an isolated portion of the cliff

6 The stack is undercut and collapses to leave a stump

Occasionally water rises up a vertical joint and is ejected through a blowhole

2 Abrasion, pounding and hydraulic action of waves widens the weakness in the cliff to form a cave

3 Waves cut through headland to form an arch which is continually widened at its base

(N) = wave-cut notches

Figure 5.1 Formation of caves, arches and stacks

- Corrasion, corrosion and hydraulic action by the waves will widen any weakness to form, initially, a **cave**.
- If a cave forms at a headland, the cave might be widened and deepened until the sea cuts through to form a natural **arch**. Waves will continue to erode the foot of the arch until its roof becomes too heavy to be supported.
- When the roof collapses it will leave part of the former cliff isolated as a **stack**.
- In time, further wave action will result in the stack collapsing to leave a **stump**.

Transportation

Although waves do carry material up and down a beach, the major movement is along the coast by a process called **longshore drift** (Figure 5.2). Waves rarely approach a beach at right-angles, but rather from a direction similar to that from which the wind is blowing. When a wave breaks, the swash carries material up the beach at the same angle at which the wave approached the shore. As the swash dies away, the backwash returns material straight down the beach, at right-angles to the water, under the influence of gravity. Material is slowly moved along the coast in a zig-zag course. The effect of longshore drift can best be seen when wooden groynes have been built to prevent material from being moved along the beach.

Seawater moves material by the same processes as river-water (p17). These processes are:
- **traction**
- **saltation**
- **suspension**
- **solution**.

Deposition

Beaches

Beaches may form when:
- sediment (sand or shingle) accumulates in a bay
- a constant stream of sediment moves along a straight stretch of coastline due to longshore drift. Here, material moved off the beach is more or less balanced by new material moved on to the beach.

Back to ...

The New Wider World **p301** for diagrams explaining the formation of bays and headlands (Figure 18.3) and cliff recession and wave-cut platforms (Figure 18.4) and a photograph showing a wave-cut notch and platform (Figure 18.5) in the Flamborough Head area of Yorkshire.

Key words to know

Cave
Arch
Stack
Stump
Longshore drift
Traction
Saltation
Suspension
Solution
Beach

Check this!...

1 How are headlands and bays formed?

2 Draw an annotated diagram to explain the formation of a wave-cut platform.

3 Describe and explain the landforms created as headlands are eroded.

The sources of this sediment are material:
- eroded from headlands
- brought on to beaches from offshore
- brought down from inland areas by rivers
- moved from beach to beach by longshore drift.

Beaches are not permanent features as their shape can be altered by waves every time the tide comes in and goes out. Shingle beaches have a steeper gradient than sandy beaches.

Figure 5.2 Longshore drift

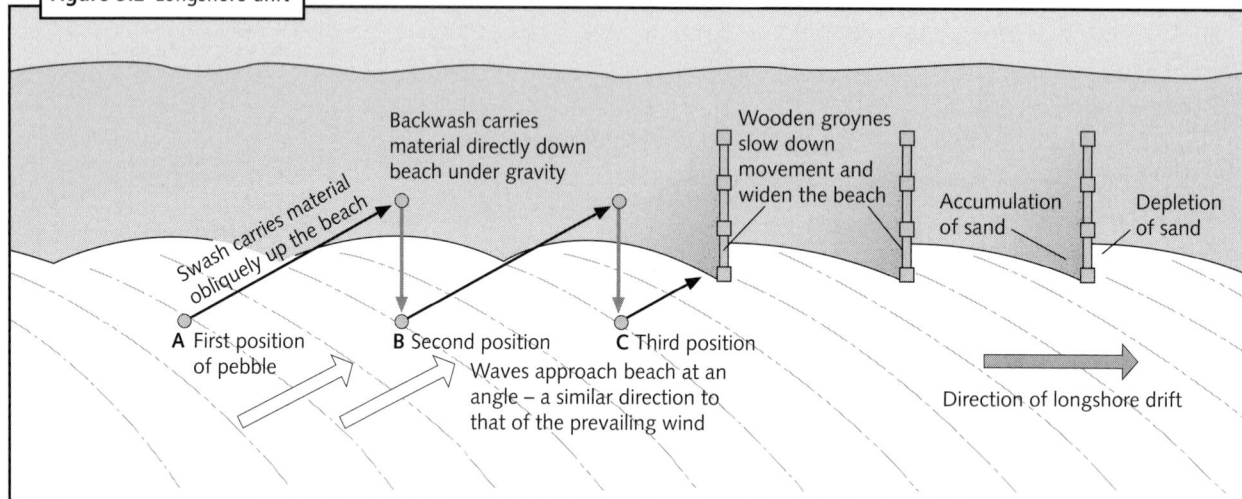

Swash carries material obliquely up the beach

Backwash carries material directly down beach under gravity

Wooden groynes slow down movement and widen the beach

Accumulation of sand

Depletion of sand

A First position of pebble
B Second position
C Third position

Waves approach beach at an angle – a similar direction to that of the prevailing wind

Direction of longshore drift

Back to …

The New Wider World **p303** for further information (based on Figure 18.11) on the formation of a spit and a photograph showing Hurst Spit, Hampshire (Figure 18.10).

Check this!...

1 Where do beaches occur and how are they formed?

2 Draw a fully annotated diagram to explain the formation of a spit.

Spits

A **spit** is a long, narrow accumulation of sand or shingle, with one end attached to the land, and the other projecting at a narrow angle either into the sea or across a river estuary. Many spits have a hooked or curved end, for example Hurst Castle spit in Hampshire. They form where longshore drift moves large amounts of sand and shingle along the coast, and where the coastline suddenly changes direction to leave a shallow, sheltered area of water.

- Spits become permanent when sand is blown up the beach, by the prevailing wind, to form **sand-dunes**.
- **Salt marsh** is likely to develop in the sheltered water behind the spit.
- The spit is unable to grow across the estuary as the river current carries material out to sea. Should there be no river, the spit may grow across the bay to form a **bar**.

Coastal landforms on OS maps

You need to be able to recognise and describe coastal features on Ordnance Survey maps.

Back to …

The New Wider World **p305** for 1:50,000 OS map extracts of the Isle of Purbeck, Dorset (Figure 18.17) and the Hurst Castle area, Hampshire (Figure 18.19).

Check this!...

Look at Figures 18.17 and 18.19 on p305 of *The New Wider World*.

1 Using Figure 18.17, identify the coastal landforms in the following grid squares:
   a) 0385   c) 0379   b) 0582   d) 0376.

2 Using Figure 18.19, describe the coastline in the following grid squares:
   a) 2791   b) 3090.

2 The interaction between people and coastal environments

People and coastal environments

Coastal erosion is of particular concern where settlements are located. In many of these areas tourism is a significant part of the economy. Thus it is important to prevent the loss of land by cliff erosion and to prevent beaches from being depleted. In tourist resorts cliff erosion may threaten hotels, houses, roads, railways and other facilities.

Erosion, however, is not the only problem in coastal areas. The pressures on land use, both natural and human, have steadily increased in recent decades as more and more people visit coastal areas.

Views on how to tackle coastal erosion and the increasing pressure on land use often vary. Sometimes, **decision-making** bodies such as local authorities (councils) have to make very difficult decisions.

Causes of coastal erosion

Parts of Britain's coastline are constantly under threat from coastal erosion. Erosion occurs where:

- cliffs consist of resistant rock – here, waves erode at the cliff base, forming a wave-cut notch, causing the rock above to become unstable and, in time, to collapse
- cliffs consist of less resistant rock – here, heavy rain can cause material to move downslope where it will be removed by waves and coastal currents
- sand and shingle, which forms a natural protection at the foot of a cliff, is removed by human activity enabling erosion by waves to accelerate
- people have built on cliff tops, as this adds weight which can cause **cliff collapse**.

Effects

- A cliff collapse near Scarborough in 1993 destroyed a hotel.
- In Holderness, the coastline is retreating by an average of 2 m a year. Here, it is now 3 km further west than it was in Roman times.
- Cliffs near Barton on Sea have retreated by up to 60 m since 1971.

Responses

Attempts to protect the coastline involve either **'hard'** or **'soft'** **engineering** (Figure 5.3). It is becoming increasingly expensive to provide new defences and maintain existing ones (a £1.3 million scheme at Barton on Sea was destroyed in four years), while the construction of sea defences in one place often seems to increase the rate of erosion elsewhere.

> **Key words to know**
>
> *Decision-making*
> *Cliff collapse*
> *Hard engineering*
> *Soft engineering*

Back to ...

The New Wider World **p304**
Figure 18.16 for examples
of hard engineering.

Figure 5.3 Hard and soft sea-defence engineering

Hard	• Wooden groynes help reduce the force of waves and can trap material being moved along the beach by longshore drift. They help widen beaches and protect cliffs.
	• Concrete sea-walls which may be curved at the top to divert the force of the waves back out to sea
	• Wooden slatted revetments help dissipate the force of the waves
	• Concrete blocks, called riprap, absorb the power of the waves
	• Artificial offshore breakwaters and reefs
Soft	• Beach nourishment, by which the environment agency replaces lost beach material
	• Cliff stabilisation, in which pipes are inserted to remove excess water, and vegetation is planted to stabilise exposed soil

Check this!...

1 Using a number of examples, explain the difference between hard engineering and soft engineering.

2 Why is it often difficult to decide which is the best way to protect a coastline?

The need for coastal management

The coastline in the UK and other parts of the world is dynamic and always changing. The changes may result either from:

- physical processes, or
- human activity.

The problems and pressures created by these changes can vary within short distances along any stretch of coastline. One example is the New Forest coastline in Hampshire.

Case Study

The New Forest coastline

Back to ...

The New Wider World pp306–309 for the case study on the New Forest coastline.

Using your case study

This is a small scale example of a coastal area where management issues occur. You should be aware of the problems caused and their impact on different groups. Sustainable development is now a major objective for local councils in coastal and other areas. To use this case study well you should be aware of the following:

- The characteristics and problems of the three sections of the New Forest coastline – Christchurch Bay, Western Solent, Southampton Water.
- The major management questions along this coastline:
  1) Should the coastline be allowed to retreat naturally or should there be protection for at-risk areas?
  2) Should natural landscapes and wildlife habitats be protected or should they be developed for housing, employment and tourism?
- Coastal protection measures employed to date.

- Attempts to protect wildlife.
- The objectives of the New Forest District Council's coastal management plan.
- Those strategies which constitute sustainable development.

Case study links

The New Forest coastline is a popular tourist destination. Thus, it could be used as the UK case study in Managing resources (Chapter 12).

Update

For up-to-date information on the New Forest use the link on *The New Wider World Coursemate* website.

Learn it!

Learn your case study.

a) Along the New Forest coastline, name an area with cliffs, an area with a shingle spit, and an area with a salt marsh and a river estuary.

b) Describe the pressures on this stretch of coastline.

c) Discuss the objectives of the New Forest District Council's management plan.

d) Which strategies can be classed as sustainable development?

Coastal resorts

Coastal resorts constitute particular points of pressure along coastlines. The social, economic and environmental effects of tourism are evident in all resorts of a reasonable size. Views on how to manage pressures in coastal resorts vary considerably.

The Costa del Sol

Back to ...

The New Wider World pp164–165 for the case study of coastal resorts on the Costa del Sol.

Using your case study

Use this case study to answer questions on the problems caused by tourism. You should be able to divide these problems into those which are:

- social
- economic
- environmental
- political.

Case study links

This popular tourist destination could be used to study the socio-economic and environmental consequences of tourism in an MEDC in Managing resources (Chapter 12).

Update

For up-to-date information on the Costa del Sol use the link on *The New Wider World Coursemate* website.

Learn it!

a) Why did the Costa del Sol become so popular with tourists?

b) What have been the social, economic, and environmental problems associated with rapid tourist development in this area?

c) Discuss the management strategies that have been used to try to tackle these problems.

EXAM PRACTICE

1 a Describe what has happened to the stretch of coastline shown in Figure 5.4. (2)

   b Why do cliffs retreat faster in some areas than others? (2)

2 Draw an annotated diagram to explain the process of longshore drift. (3)

3 a Explain two ways of protecting coastlines against erosion. (4)

   b Why are decisions made not to protect some parts of the coastline from erosion? (4)

Figure 5.4 Sketch of a wave-cut notch and platform: Flamborough Head, Yorkshire

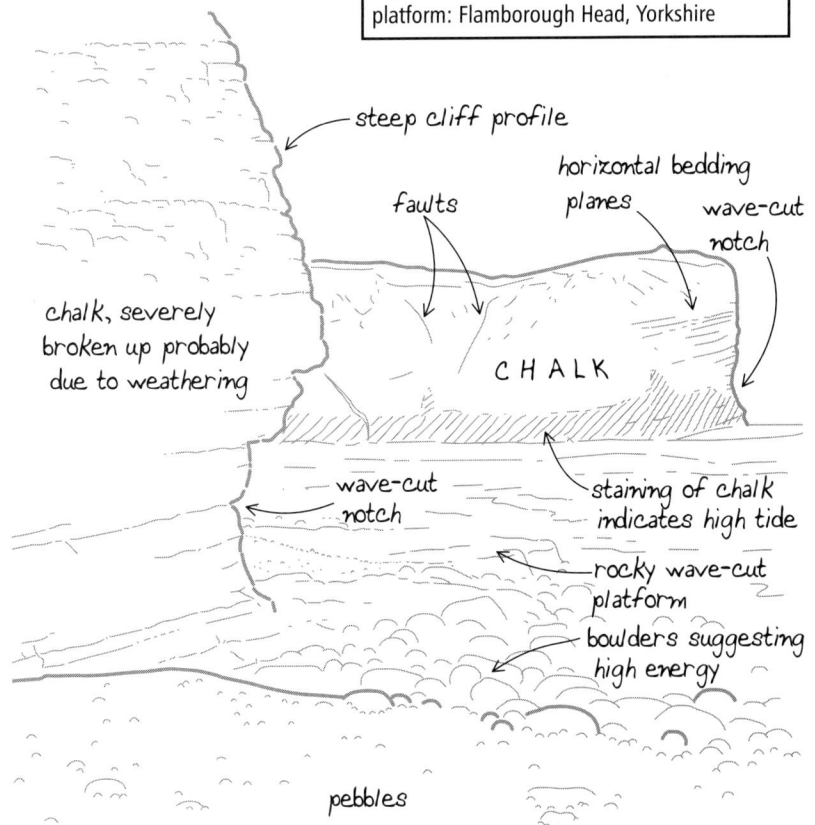

steep cliff profile

faults

horizontal bedding planes

wave-cut notch

chalk, severely broken up probably due to weathering

CHALK

wave-cut notch

staining of chalk indicates high tide

rocky wave-cut platform

boulders suggesting high energy

pebbles

EXAM TIPS

For question 3a pick two measures which are very different to avoid repetition. For each measure describe what it looks like and explain how it is effective in reducing erosion.

Back to ...

The New Wider World website to check your answers to the Exam Practice question.

6
Weather and climate

KEY IDEAS

1 Weather and climate are influenced by location.

2 The interaction between people and the environments and hazards influenced by weather and climate.

1 | Weather and climate are influenced by location

Weather is the hour-to-hour, day-to-day state of the atmosphere. It includes temperature, sunshine, cloud cover, precipitation, atmospheric pressure, wind speed and wind direction. It is short-term and can be localised in relatively small areas.

Climate is the average weather conditions of a place taken over a period of time, often 30 years. It is the expected, rather than the actual, conditions. It is long-term and is often applied to sizeable parts of the globe, e.g. the equatorial and the Mediterranean climates.

World climates

Figure 6.1 shows the location and extent of some of the major world climates. Maps that show the world climates are very simplified as, due to their scale, they cannot show local variations.

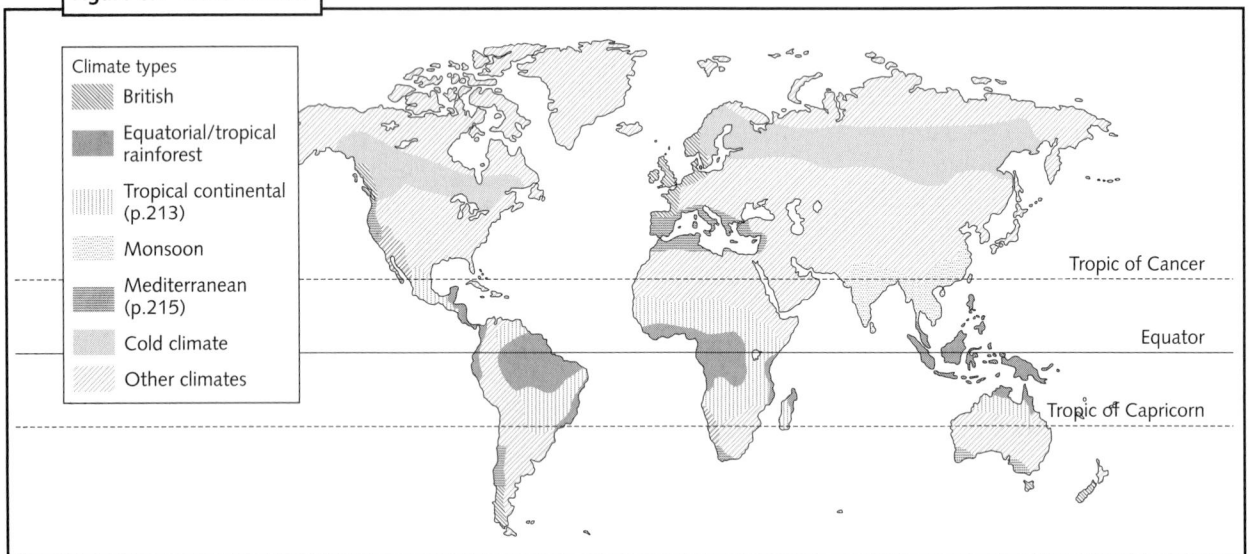

Figure 6.1 World climates

Climate types
- British
- Equatorial/tropical rainforest
- Tropical continental (p.213)
- Monsoon
- Mediterranean (p.215)
- Cold climate
- Other climates

Tropic of Cancer
Equator
Tropic of Capricorn

Key words to know

Weather
Climate
Prevailing winds
Relief rainfall
Frontal rainfall
Convectional rainfall

Factors affecting global temperatures

The main factors that affect temperature on a global scale, include:
- *latitude* Places in the tropics, being nearer the Equator, are much warmer than places towards the Poles. This is due to the curvature of the Earth and the angle of the sun.
- *distance from the sea* As land heats up more quickly during the summer and cools down more rapidly in winter than the sea, places towards the centre of continents will have warmer summers and colder winters than those with a coastal location. As Britain is surrounded by the sea, it tends to get cool summers and mild winters.
- **prevailing winds** The seasonal difference in heating between land and sea also affects the temperature of the prevailing wind. Winds that blow from the warm sea in winter or the warm land in summer will raise temperatures, whereas those that blow from the cold land in winter or the cooler sea in summer will lower temperatures.

38

- *ocean currents* Ocean currents, which are classified as being either warm or cold, affect the climate of coastal areas. Warm currents tend to raise winter temperatures while cold currents usually lower summer temperatures. The North Atlantic Drift is a warm current of water which originates in the Gulf of Mexico. It keeps the west coast of Britain much warmer in winter than other places in similar latitudes.
- *altitude* Temperature decreases, on average, 1°C for every 100 metres. This means that mountains are much colder than lowlands. As many parts of the Scottish Highlands are over 1000 metres, they will be at least 10°C cooler than coastal places.

Figure 6.2 shows climate graphs for four of the world climates illustrated by Figure 6.1.

Global rainfall

The three main types of rainfall that affect world climate are:

- **relief** Rainfall is heavy where prevailing winds blow from the sea and are forced to rise over coastal mountains. Places protected by mountains from the prevailing rain-bearing winds are usually dry.
- **frontal** Rainfall is also heavy where depressions, with their associated fronts, are frequent. At a front, warm air is forced to rise over cold air.
- **convectional** This occurs where temperatures are either continually high, as most afternoons in the equatorial climate, or seasonally, as in southern England in summer. The high temperature causes air molecules to expand and, as a result, the air rises.

In all three cases rainfall results from warm air, which contains water vapour, being forced to rise until it cools sufficiently for condensation to take place. The difference between the three types of rainfall is the condition that forces the warm air to rise in the first place.

The UK climate

Britain's climate has cool summers, mild winters and a steady, reliable rainfall that is spread evenly throughout the year. However, even across an area as small as the British Isles, there are significant differences seasonally and regionally (Figure 6.3).

- Places in the south are warmer and sunnier than places in the north in summer. This is mainly due to latitude.
- Places in the west are milder and cloudier than places to the east in winter. This is due to the prevailing winds from the south-west and the influence of the North Atlantic Drift.
- Places in the west have a lower range of temperature, due to the moderating influence of the sea, than those to the east, which are more likely to be affected by more extremes of weather from the continent.
- Places in the north-west have lower temperatures throughout the year, and more snow in winter, than places in the south and east, due to the influence of altitude.

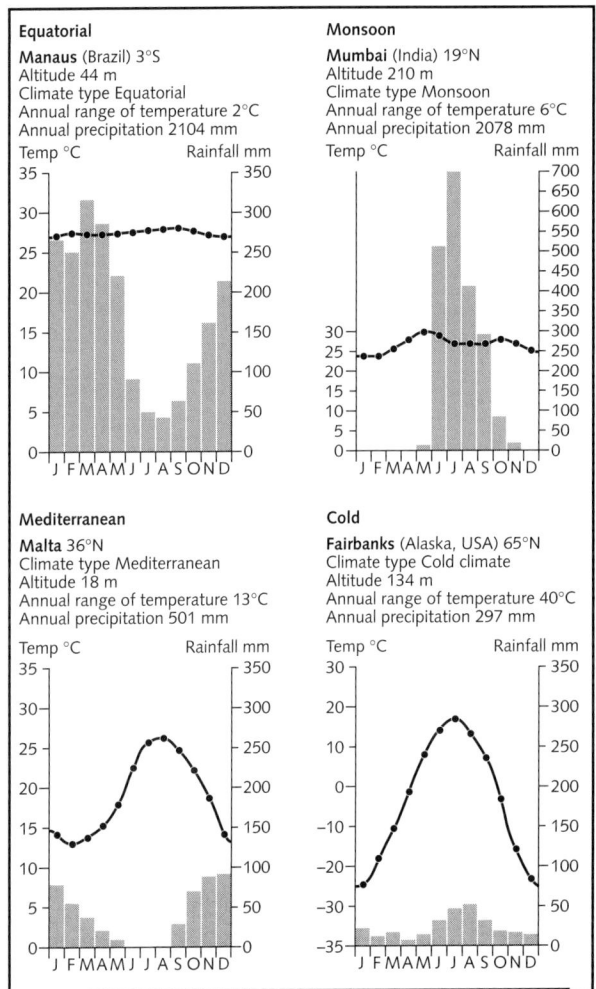

Equatorial
Manaus (Brazil) 3°S
Altitude 44 m
Climate type Equatorial
Annual range of temperature 2°C
Annual precipitation 2104 mm

Monsoon
Mumbai (India) 19°N
Altitude 210 m
Climate type Monsoon
Annual range of temperature 6°C
Annual precipitation 2078 mm

Mediterranean
Malta 36°N
Climate type Mediterranean
Altitude 18 m
Annual range of temperature 13°C
Annual precipitation 501 mm

Cold
Fairbanks (Alaska, USA) 65°N
Climate type Cold climate
Altitude 134 m
Annual range of temperature 40°C
Annual precipitation 297 mm

Figure 6.2 Climate graphs for four world climates

Back to ...

The New Wider World
pp202–203 for more information on types of rainfall, and for diagrams showing the formation of relief, frontal and convectional rainfall.

Check this!...

1 What is the difference between weather and climate?

2 Briefly explain three factors that influence temperature.

3 Describe the main differences between the four climate graphs in Figure 6.2.

- Places in the west are wetter than places in the east due to the prevailing winds bringing frontal rain and giving relief rainfall as they pass over the mountains.
- Places in the west receive most rain in winter, when depressions are most frequent, whereas those in the east have a summer maximum, due to convectional rainfall.

Isotherms

An isotherm is a line which joins places with the same temperature. It is like a contour on an OS map which joins places with the same height above sea-level.

Depressions

Britain's weather changes from day to day. For much of the year our climate is dominated by the passing of **depressions**.

- Depressions are areas of low pressure which bring rain, cloud and wind.
- They form over the Atlantic Ocean when a mass of warm, moist tropical air meets a mass of colder, drier, heavier polar air.
- The boundary between two air masses is called a **front**.
- The lighter, warmer air is forced to rise over the cold air at a **warm front** (Figure 6.4).
- When denser, colder air moves towards warm air, it undercuts the warm air forcing it to rise at a **cold front**.
- The rising warm air is cooled and some of its water vapour content condenses, producing cloud and frontal rain.
- The cold front travels faster than the warm front, catching it up to form an **occluded front**.

As a warm front approaches clouds begin to form. They get lower, and thicken. Winds blow from the south-east, in an anticlockwise direction, and slowly increase in strength. As the air rises, atmospheric pressure drops. The passing of the warm front is usually marked by a lengthy period of steady rainfall, low cloud and strong winds. As the warm front passes there is a sudden rise in temperature and the wind turns to a south-westerly direction. The **warm sector** of a depression is usually a time of low and sometimes broken cloud, decreasing winds, and drizzle or even dry weather. As a cold front passes the weather deteriorates rapidly. Winds often reach gale force and swing round to the north-west. Rainfall is very heavy, though of relatively short duration, and temperatures fall rapidly. After the cold front passes, the weather slowly improves as pressure increases. The heavy rain gives way to heavy showers and eventually to sunny intervals. Winds are cold and slowly moderate, but still come from the north-west. Most depressions take between one and three days to pass over the British Isles.

Depressions can be seen on satellite images as masses of swirling cloud. The state of the weather at any one given time is shown on a **synoptic chart** (a weather map) (Figure 6.5).

Synoptic charts

These show various weather symbols for selected weather stations. They show five weather elements: temperature, wind speed, wind direction, amount of cloud cover, and type of precipitation, while a sixth element, atmospheric pressure, can be obtained by interpreting the isobars.

- The closer the isobars are together the stronger the winds.
- Isobars are always much closer together in a depression compared with an **anticyclone**.

Key words to know

Depression
Front
Warm front
Cold front
Occluded front
Warm sector
Synoptic chart
Anticyclone

Check this!...

1 Study Figure 6.3. Explain the position of:
   a) the 5°C January isotherm
   b) the 15°C July isotherm.

2 What are the reasons for the differences in temperature and rainfall for Fort William and Margate?

Back to ...

The New Wider World
pp204–206 for more information on depressions, anticyclones, satellite photographs (Figures 12.12 and 12.13 show a passing depression, Figure 12.14 shows an anticyclone) and synoptic charts. See also Figure 12.17 for weather map symbols.

- The average atmospheric pressure at sea-level for Britain is 1013 millibars, a useful figure to remember so that you can recognise when pressure is higher or lower than average.

Figure 6.3 Seasonal and regional differences in temperature and rainfall in the British Isles

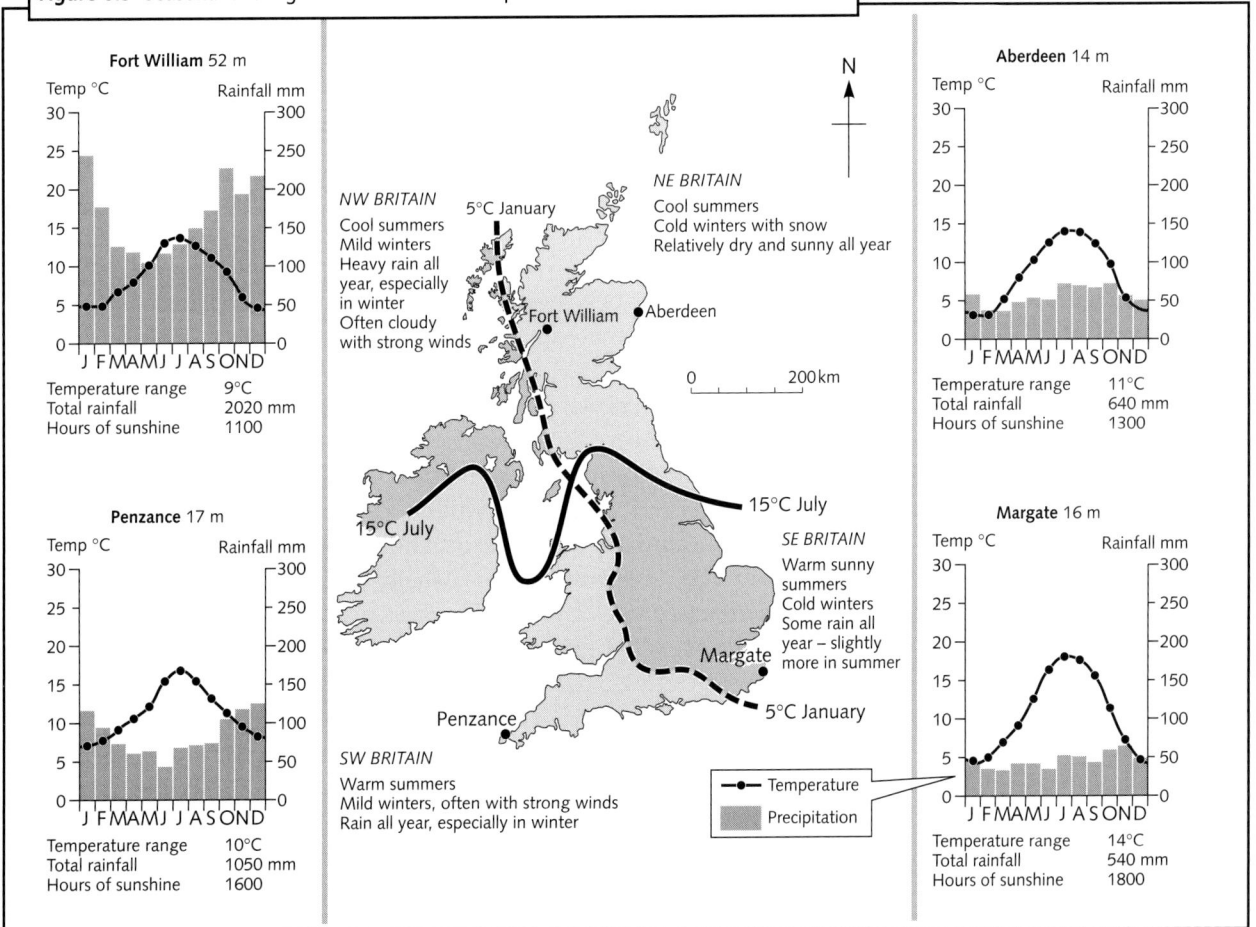

Fort William 52 m

Temperature range 9°C
Total rainfall 2020 mm
Hours of sunshine 1100

Penzance 17 m

Temperature range 10°C
Total rainfall 1050 mm
Hours of sunshine 1600

Aberdeen 14 m

Temperature range 11°C
Total rainfall 640 mm
Hours of sunshine 1300

Margate 16 m

Temperature range 14°C
Total rainfall 540 mm
Hours of sunshine 1800

NW BRITAIN
Cool summers
Mild winters
Heavy rain all year, especially in winter
Often cloudy with strong winds

NE BRITAIN
Cool summers
Cold winters with snow
Relatively dry and sunny all year

SE BRITAIN
Warm sunny summers
Cold winters
Some rain all year – slightly more in summer

SW BRITAIN
Warm summers
Mild winters, often with strong winds
Rain all year, especially in winter

5°C January
15°C July
15°C July
5°C January

0   200km

Temperature
Precipitation

Figure 6.4 Typical weather conditions in a depression

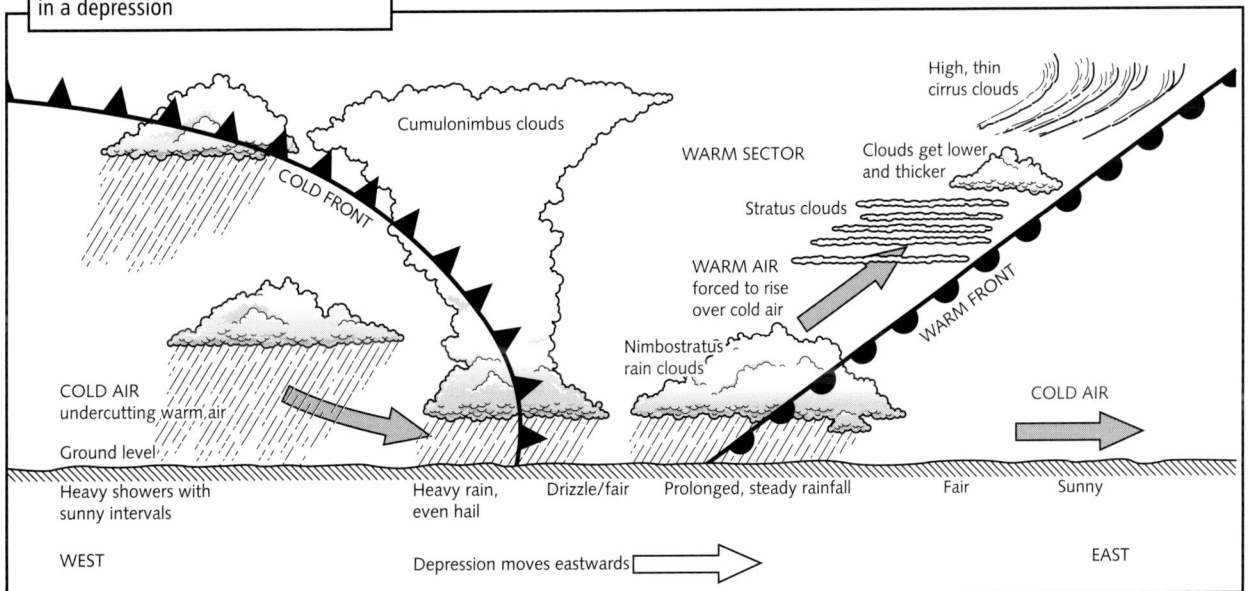

Cumulonimbus clouds

High, thin cirrus clouds

WARM SECTOR

Clouds get lower and thicker

Stratus clouds

WARM AIR forced to rise over cold air

COLD FRONT

WARM FRONT

Nimbostratus rain clouds

COLD AIR undercutting warm air

Ground level

COLD AIR

Heavy showers with sunny intervals

Heavy rain, even hail

Drizzle/fair

Prolonged, steady rainfall

Fair

Sunny

WEST

Depression moves eastwards

EAST

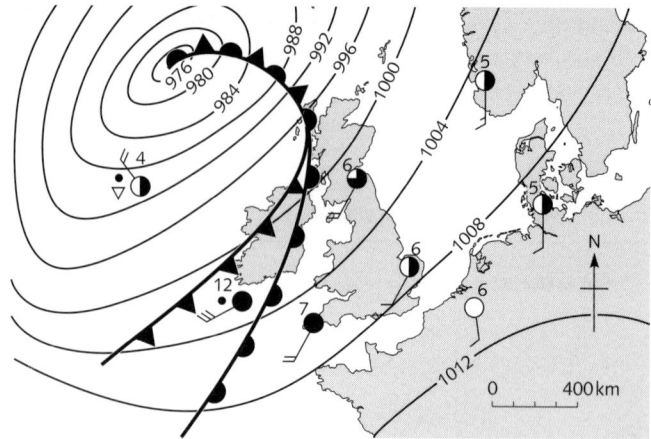

Figure 6.5 Synoptic chart showing a depression

Anticyclones

- In Britain anticyclones are less frequent than depressions but, once established, they can remain stationary for several days and even weeks.
- In an anticyclone, air descends and pressure increases.
- Winds are very light (notice the wide spacing of isobars in Figure 6.6) and blow in a clockwise direction. At times they may even be non-existent and give periods of calm.
- As the air descends it warms and is able to pick up more moisture through evaporation. This usually results in settled conditions with clear skies and a lack of rain.
- However, there are differences between summer and winter anticyclones.

  Summer (Figure 6.6a)   The absence of cloud gives very warm, sunny conditions during the day although at night, when clear skies allow some of this heat to escape, temperatures can fall rapidly. As air next to the ground cools, condensation can occur and dew and mist may form. Thunderstorms are also a risk under 'heat-wave' conditions.

  Winter (Figure 6.6b)   Although temperatures remain low during the day, due to the sun's low angle in the sky, the weather is likely to be dry and bright. The rapid loss of heat under the clear evening skies means that nights can be very cold. Condensation near to the ground can produce frost and fog which may, due to the sun's lack of heat, persist all day.

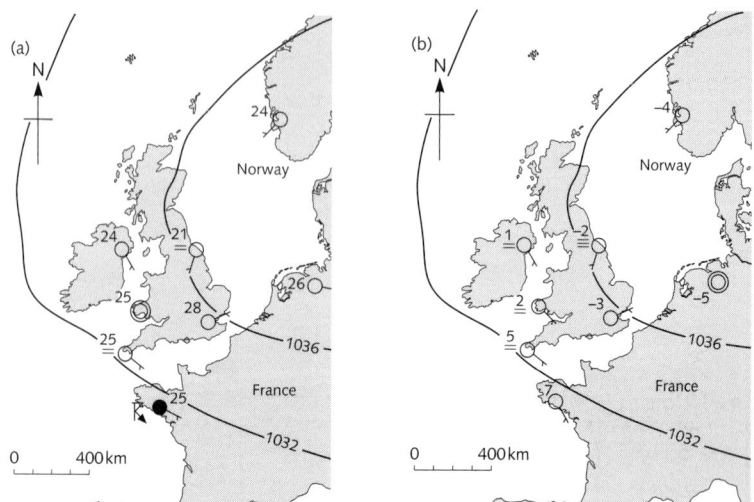

Figure 6.6 (a) Summer and (b) winter anticyclones

1 Look at Figure 6.4. Describe and explain how the weather will change at a place when:
   a) the warm front passes
   b) the cold front passes.

2 Look at Figure 6.6. Account for the typical weather conditions during

   a) a summer anticyclone
   b) a winter anticyclone.

For further information see 'Weather associated with anticyclones' (GeoActive, April 2003).

2 The interaction between people and the environments and hazards influenced by weather and climate

Contrasting environments: The monsoon and cold climates

The monsoon

The word **monsoon** means 'a season'. In much of South-east Asia, as seen in the climate graph for Mumbai (Bombay) (Figure 6.2), there are two seasons. These, the so-called south-west monsoon and the north-east monsoon, result from the reversal in the direction of the prevailing wind.

Key words to know

Monsoon
Tropic of Cancer

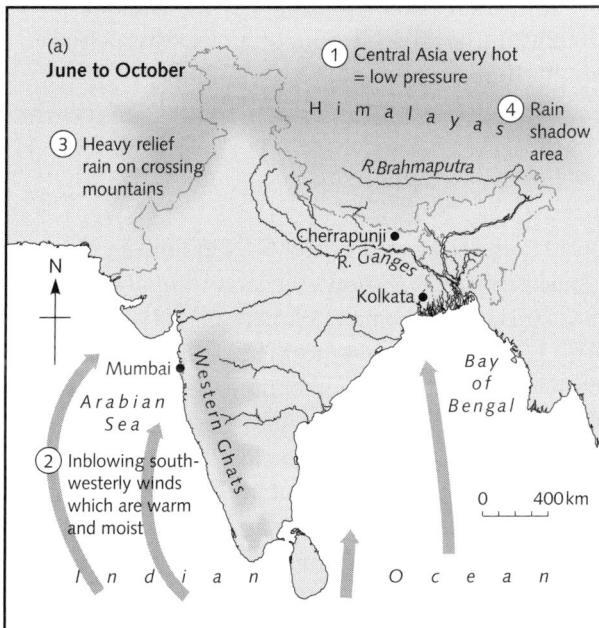

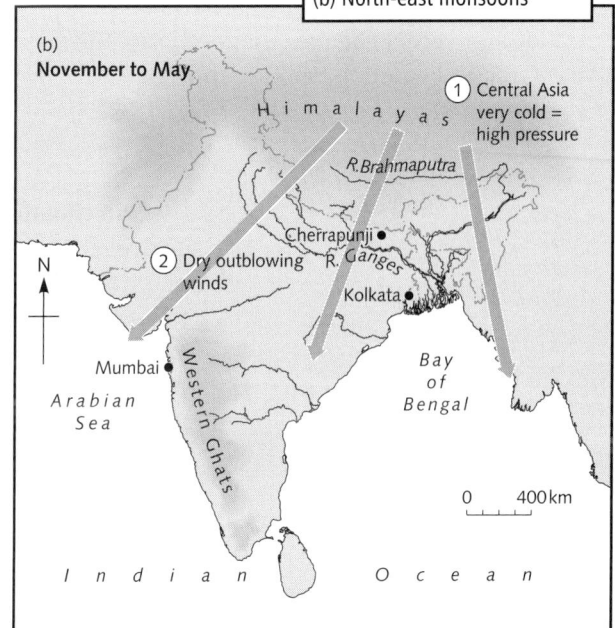

   The south-west monsoon (Figure 6.7a).
   ● The sun appears to be overhead at the **Tropic of Cancer** in June.
   ● Places to the north of the Himalayas, which are a long way from any moderating influence of the sea, become extremely hot.
   ● As the hot air rises, an extensive area of low pressure is formed and warm, moist air is drawn northwards from the Indian Ocean.
   ● Where the air is forced to rise over mountains, it gives large amounts of relief rainfall. Mumbai receives over 2000 mm in five months and Cherrapunji, reputed to be the wettest place on Earth, 14 000 mm.
   ● The rain, ideal for rice, can cause extensive flooding in the Ganges basin.

Figure 6.7 (a) South-west and (b) North-east monsoons

(a) **June to October**
① Central Asia very hot = low pressure
H i m a l a y a s
④ Rain shadow area
③ Heavy relief rain on crossing mountains
R. Brahmaputra
N
Cherrapunji ●
R. Ganges
Kolkata ●
Mumbai ●
Arabian Sea
Western Ghats
Bay of Bengal
② Inblowing south-westerly winds which are warm and moist
0   400km
I n d i a n   *O c e a n*

(b) **November to May**
① Central Asia very cold = high pressure
H i m a l a y a s
R. Brahmaputra
② Dry outblowing winds
Cherrapunji ●
R. Ganges
Kolkata ●
N
Mumbai ●
Arabian Sea
Western Ghats
Bay of Bengal
0   400km
I n d i a n   *O c e a n*

The north-east monsoon (Figure 6.7b).

- During the northern winter, the overhead sun moves southwards.
- Places to the north of the Himalayas now become very cold and an extensive area of high pressure develops.
- Winds blow outwards from the high pressure area but, because they originate in a dry area, they give only small amounts of rain as they cross India – Mumbai, for example, only receives 45 mm in seven months.
- By the end of the 'dry' season, many places are at risk of drought.

Case Study

Subsistence rice farming in the Lower Ganges Valley

Back to ...

The New Wider World pp112–113 for the case study on subsistence rice farming in the Lower Ganges Valley.

Using your case study

Use this case study to show how climate influences the environment and human activity. You should be able to contrast this monsoon region with the example of a cold climate (Alaska) that follows. For the Lower Ganges Valley make sure that you can:

1. draw a simple sketch map of the region
2. explain the deposition of alluvium over the plain and delta, and the **subsistence farming** that characterises the region
3. account for the very high population density
4. describe the annual cycle of rice production and refer to inputs, processes and outputs
5. discuss recent changes – land reform, the **Green Revolution**, and **appropriate technology**.

Case study links

The Lower Ganges Valley can also be used as an example of a farming system in an LEDC in Agriculture (Chapter 10).

Update

For further information see 'Monsoon – case study of the Ganges Plain' (GeoActive 298, September 2003).

Key words to know

Subsistence farming
Green Revolution
Appropriate technology

Learn it!

a) Describe farming in the Lower Ganges Valley under the headings: Physical inputs, Human/economic inputs, Processes, Outputs.

b) Why was the Green Revolution introduced in this region?

c) Why is appropriate technology more suited to the subsistence farmers of the Ganges Basin than the introduction of western-type methods?

Cold climate

The cold climate is found to the poleward side of 60°N in Eurasia. The graph for Fairbanks, Alaska (Figure 6.2) shows the large annual range in temperature that typifies this type of climate. Winters are very long, dark and extremely cold. This is partly due to the northerly latitude which, for places within the Arctic Circle, means a period of time when the sun fails to rise above the horizon, and partly due to the distance from any moderating influence of the sea. Strong winds can lower temperatures, increase the wind-chill factor and bring the risk of frost-bite. Summers are short but relatively warm for the latitude. This is partly due to the long hours of daylight (the sun does not set at all for a short time each year at places within the Arctic Circle, although its angle is always low in the sky) and partly due to its continental location far from the influence of the sea.

Precipitation is light throughout the year partly because the air is too cold to hold much moisture and partly because most places are a long way from any rain-bearing winds from the sea. It falls as snow in winter and may be blown about in blizzards. The summer maximum results from occasional convectional rainstorms occurring when temperatures are at their highest.

Case Study

Energy and the environment – oil in Alaska

Back to ...

The New Wider World pp128–131 for the case study on energy and the environment in Alaska.

Using your case study

Use this case study to show how environment and climate have been overcome in Alaska for oil exploration. Make sure that you can:

1 draw a simple sketch map to show the main physical features and the route of the pipeline
2 describe and explain the climate graph for Fairbanks, Alaska (Figure 6.2)
3 discuss the physical problems and environmental concerns in Alaska
4 explain how these problems and concerns were overcome in the construction of the pipeline
5 discuss how attitudes differ about further development of the oil industry in Alaska.

Case study links

Alaskan oil can be used as an example of developing a non-renewable resource in Managing resources (Chapter 12).

Update

For up-to-date information on Alaska use the link on *The New Wider World Coursemate* website.

Learn it!

a) Describe the physical problems and environmental concerns linked to the development of the Alaska pipeline.

b) How were these issues overcome?

c) What are the arguments for and against further oil development in Alaska?

Climatic hazards: Impact and response

The following section looks at the impact of, and response to, climatic hazards in different parts of the world.

Tropical cyclones (hurricanes)

Formation

Tropical cyclones are areas of intensive low pressure known locally as **hurricanes**, typhoons or cyclones. Hurricanes (Figure 6.8) tend to develop:

- over warm tropical oceans, where sea temperatures exceed 27°C over a vast area, and where there is a considerable depth of warm water
- in late summer and early autumn, when sea temperatures are at their highest
- in the trade wind belt between latitudes 5° and 20° north and south of the Equator.

They appear to originate when a strong vertical movement of air draws with it water vapour from the ocean below. As the air rises, in a

Key word to know

Hurricane

spiral movement, it cools and condenses, releasing enormous amounts of heat energy. It is this heat energy that powers the storm and which must be maintained if the hurricane is to move westwards on a course that is usually erratic and difficult to predict. In time an area of colder air sinks downwards through the centre of the hurricane to form a central **eye**. Once the hurricane reaches land, and its source of heat energy and moisture is removed, it rapidly decreases in strength. Its average lifespan is 7–14 days.

Figure 6.8 The passage of a hurricane

Approach of hurricane	20–30 km	Eye 30–50 km	20–30 km	End of hurricane
Temperatures and pressure begin to fall. Winds are gentle and from the north-west. Clouds begin to form and showers develop. Wind begins to gust.	Pressure falls rapidly. Wind speeds increase – up to 100 km/hr. Cumulonimbus cloud with thunder and torrential rain (250 mm in a day).	Period of calm. Pressure very low. Temperatures rise as sun makes a brief appearance.	Onslaught begins again, with hurricane-force winds (160 km/hr) and torrential rain. Winds now in south-east. Temperatures drop again, but pressure begins to rise.	Pressure and temperatures rise. Rain decreases to showers and some sunny intervals. Winds decrease.

Back to ...

The New Wider World **p216** to see Figure 13.12 – a map showing the location and frequency of tropical cyclones; Figure 13.13 – a photograph of a hurricane near Florida and Figure 13.14 for more information on the formation of a hurricane.

Key words to know

Eye
Storm (tidal) surge

Effects

- Winds often exceed 160 km/hr. In LEDCs, many of which lie in the tropical cyclone belt, whole villages may be destroyed and even in MEDCs, where people have money to reinforce buildings, houses and coastal developments can be severely damaged. High winds uproot trees and disrupt telephone and electricity power supplies. Worst hit are those LEDCs that have their only export crop destroyed.
- Flooding, caused by the torrential rain, is often the major cause of death. It can also pollute water supplies, increasing the risk of cholera.
- **Storm (tidal) surges**, up to 5 m and heightened by storm waves, flood low-lying coastal areas causing loss of life and blocking escape and relief roads.
- Landslides occur where heavy rainfall washes away buildings erected on steep, unstable slopes.

Case Study

The Gulf of Mexico

Back to ...

The New Wider World p217 for the case study on Hurricanes Mitch and Andrew.

Using your case study

Use this case study to compare the impact and responses to tropical storms in MEDCs and LEDCs. Make sure that you can:

1 describe the paths followed by both hurricanes
2 explain the huge contrast in the immediate (short term) impact of Hurricane Andrew on the USA and Hurricane Mitch on Nicaragua, Honduras, Guatemala and El Salvador
3 discuss the contrast in secondary (long term) effects of the two hurricanes.

Learn it!

a) When was Hurricane Andrew and which part of the USA did it affect?

b) When was Hurricane Mitch and which countries in Central America did it affect?

c) Describe and explain the short term and long term effects of both hurricanes.

For further information on hurricanes see 'What are hurricanes?' (GeoActive, April 2001).

Drought in MEDCs and LEDCs

Over the last 300 years, when the world's population has increased sevenfold, the demand for water for domestic, agricultural and industrial use has increased by 35 times. This increased use of water has been accompanied by an increase in its pollution – so much so that the UN estimate that each day 25 000 people die from using contaminated water. This, coupled with the uneven distribution of fresh water, means that some 80 countries (40 per cent of the total) and 1.5 billion people are already experiencing 'severe water stress' either within certain regions or at certain times of the year. By 2050, according to UN estimates, two-thirds of the world's population (up to 5 billion), mainly living in LEDCs in Africa, Asia and Latin America, are likely to be short of reliable, clean water.

Drought is a lack of rainfall over a long period of time. Droughts occur in many places but they are most frequent where the climate is dry and variable. Human activities, such as deforestation and overgrazing, can significantly increase the impact of drought on the landscape and on the population of the region.

Case Study

Drought and water supply in the UK

Back to...

The New Wider World pp222–223 for the case study on drought and water supply in the UK.

Using your case study

This case study focuses on the water shortages of 1995 and 1996. Use it as an example of drought in an MEDC. Make sure that you can:

1 explain the distribution of **water surplus** and **water deficit** areas in the UK
2 describe the sources of water supply
3 suggest why 1995 and 1996 were the two driest consecutive years for over 200 years
4 describe the impact this had on river and reservoir levels

5 comment on which methods of water management are best for **sustainable water management**.

Case study links

Water can be considered as a renewable resource in Managing resources (Chapter 12). The issue of sustainability is important here.

Key words to know

Water surplus
Water deficit
Sustainable water management

Learn it!

a) Where are the areas of water deficit in the UK?

b) What are the reasons for water deficit in these areas?

c) What can be done to improve the water supply situation in areas of water deficit?

Drought and water supply in developing countries
Desertification in the Sahel

Back to...

The New Wider World pp224–225 for the case study on drought and water supply in developing countries, and pp256–258 for the case study on desertification in the Sahel.

Using your case study

Use this case study as an example of the impact of, and response to, drought in the less economically developed world. Make sure that you can:

1 describe the location of the Sahel
2 explain how the impact of drought is affected by the level of development in the region

3 discuss how the response to drought is affected by other social, economic and political issues, including the need for sustainable development.

Case study links
Useful when considering water as a resource in Managing resources (Chapter 12).

Update
For up-to-date information on water use the link on *The New Wider World Coursemate* website.

Learn it!

a) Where is the Sahel?

b) Why is drought such a problem in this region?

c) What has been done to try to improve water supply in the Sahel?

EXAM PRACTICE

Figure 6.9 Synoptic chart showing a depression

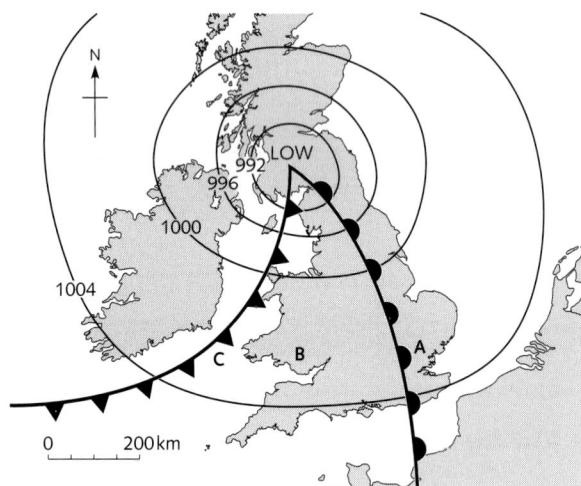

1 a Look at Figure 6.9. Name the stages of the depression found at A, B and C. (3)

 b On a copy of Figure 6.9 insert arrows to indicate the typical pattern of winds in a depression. (2)

2 Describe and explain the weather associated with the passage of a depression across the British Isles. (6)

3 Describe the weather conditions typical of:

 a a summer anticyclone

 b a winter anticyclone. (4)

EXAM TIPS

For question 2 comment on the weather experienced when a) the warm front passes, b) the warm sector passes and c) the cold front passes.

Back to ...

The New Wider World website to check your answers to the Exam Practice question.

1 Globally, different ecosystems can be recognised

An **ecosystem** is a natural system in which the life cycles of plants (flora) and animals (fauna) are closely linked to each other and to the non-living environment. The non-living environment includes:

- water – either in the form of rain or from water stored in the soil
- air – which provides oxygen, essential for all forms of life, and carbon dioxide
- solar energy – the sun being the Earth's primary source of energy as well as providing it with heat and light
- rocks – which provide nutrients and which may be permeable or impermeable
- soils – which vary in depth, acidity (pH), nutrients and fertility.

The living environment includes:

- plants, animals, insects and micro-organisms
- people.

KEY IDEAS

1 Globally, different ecosystems can be recognised.

2 The interaction between people and ecosystems.

Key words to know

Ecosystem
Photosynthesis
Food chain
Open system
Closed system

Figure 7.1 Levels of ecosystems

Level	Examples	
Micro	Water droplet	Under a leaf or stone
Meso (middle)	Freshwater pond	Woodland
	Sand-dunes	Hedgerows
	Salt marsh	Wetland
Global (biome)	Tropical rainforest	Tropical grassland
	Coniferous forest	Tundra

Ecosystems vary in size (Figure 7.1). Figure 6.1 on page 38 shows the location of global scale ecosystems. Any ecosystem depends upon two basic processes: the flow of energy and the recycling of nutrients.

1 Energy flows

- Each ecosystem is sustained by the flow of energy through it. The main source of energy is sunlight which is absorbed by green plants and converted by the process of **photosynthesis**.
- Energy is then able to pass through the ecosystem in the **food chain** (Figure 7.2).
- As energy only passes one way, the ecosystem is an **open system**, with inputs, flows, stores and outputs.

2 Recycling of nutrients

- Certain nutrients are continually circulated within the ecosystem and, therefore, are part of a **closed system**.
- Each cycle consists of plants taking up nutrients from the soil. The nutrients are then used by plants, or by animals which consume the plants.
- When the plants or animals die, they decompose and the nutrients are released and returned to the soil ready for future use (Figure 7.3).

Figure 7.2 Transfers of energy in an ecosystem

NON-LIVING ENVIRONMENT	PRODUCERS	CONSUMERS	CONSUMERS	DECOMPOSERS
– obtaining solar energy	– green plants which convert this energy by photosynthesis	– herbivores which eat green plants	– carnivores which consume herbivores	– e.g. bacteria which break down dead matter

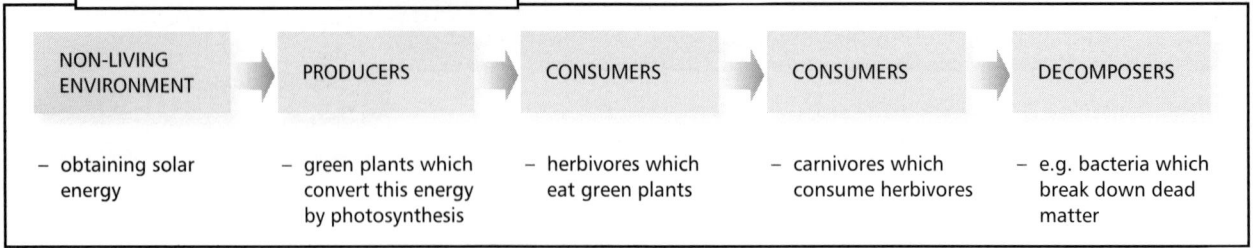

Figure 7.3 The nutrient cycle

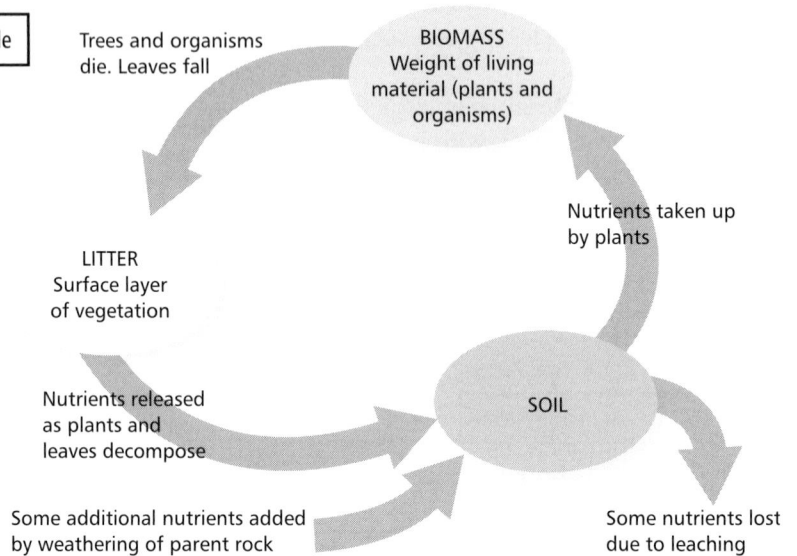

Trees and organisms die. Leaves fall

BIOMASS
Weight of living material (plants and organisms)

Nutrients taken up by plants

LITTER
Surface layer of vegetation

Nutrients released as plants and leaves decompose

SOIL

Some additional nutrients added by weathering of parent rock

Some nutrients lost due to leaching

Check this!...

1 Look at Figure 7.1. Provide other examples of a micro, meso, and global ecosystem.

2 Explain the terms:
   a) photosynthesis
   b) food chain
   c) nutrient cycle.

3 What is the difference between an open system and a closed system?

Key words to know

Buttress roots
Lianas
Canopy

Tropical rainforest

- Tropical rainforests grow in places that have an equatorial climate. Its trees have had to adapt to the constant high temperatures, the heavy rainfall and the continuous growing season.
- Vegetation grows in distinct layers (Figure 7.4). Trees have to grow rapidly in order to reach the life-giving sunlight.
- Tree trunks are straight and, in their lower parts, branchless in their efforts to grow tall.
- Large **buttress roots** stand above the ground to give support to the trees.
- **Lianas**, which are vine-like plants, use the large trees as a support in their efforts to reach the **canopy** and sunlight.
- As only about 1 per cent of the incoming sunlight reaches the forest floor, there is little undergrowth. Shrubs and other plants which grow here have had to adapt to the lack of light.
- Leaves have drip-tips to shed the heavy rainfall.
- Fallen leaves soon decay in the hot, wet climate.
- There is dense undergrowth near rivers and in forest clearings where sunlight is able to penetrate the canopy.

Despite its luxuriant appearance, the rainforest is a fragile environment whose existence relies upon the rapid and unbroken recycling of nutrients. Once the forest is cleared, then the nutrient cycle is broken. Humus is not replaced and the underlying soils soon become infertile and eroded. Not only is the rainforest unable to re-establish itself, but the land becomes too poor to be used for farming. Figure 7.5 shows the relationship between climate, vegetation and soil type, while Figure 7.6b shows the characteristics of **tropical red earth** soils.

Key words to know

Tropical red earth
Emergents
Main canopy
Under canopy

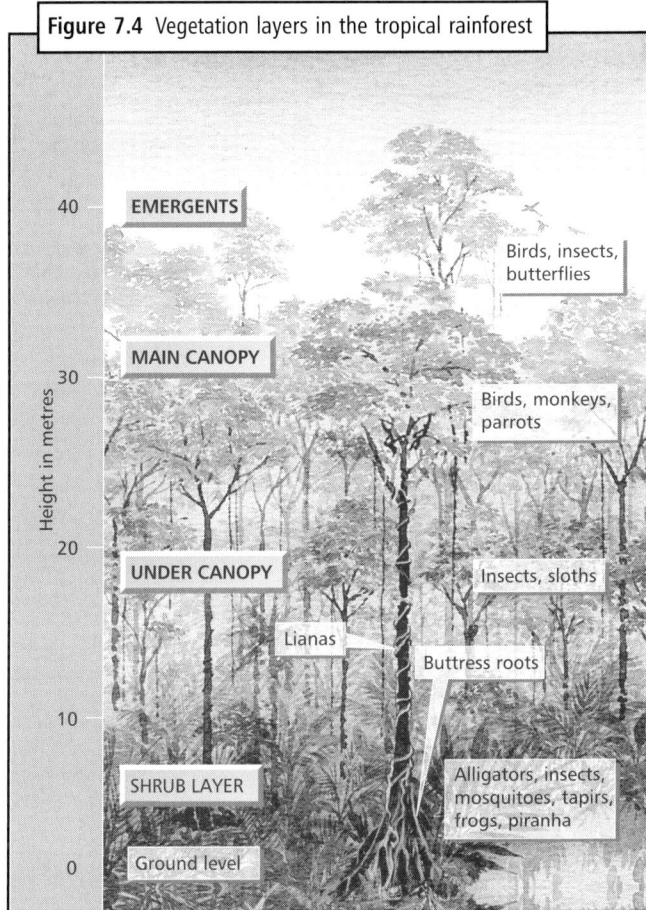

Figure 7.4 Vegetation layers in the tropical rainforest

Figure 7.5 Relationship between the world's climate, vegetation and soil types

Climate (biome)	Vegetation	Soil type
Arctic	Tundra	Tundra
Cold	Coniferous forest	Podsol
British type	Deciduous forest	Brown earth
Temperate continental	Temperate grassland	Chernozem
Mediterranean	Mediterranean	Mediterranean
Desert	Desert	Red-yellow desert
Tropical continental	Tropical grassland	Ferruginous
Equatorial	Tropical rainforest (ferralitic)	Tropical red earth

(a) Coniferous forest

Podsols tend to occur in higher, wetter areas of northern and western Britain, especially where the vegetation is coniferous forest. Pine needles form a thin, acid layer and, due to lower temperatures, take a long time to decay. The cold climate also discourages earthworms and other living organisms. This creates a marked boundary between the A and B horizons and slows down the rate at which nutrients are recycled. Although precipitation is fairly light, the low temperatures limit evapotranspiration. This results in minerals, especially iron, being leached downwards to leave the A horizon an ash-grey colour. Where the iron is deposited, it forms a rust-coloured hard pan which impedes drainage. The slow rate of weathering of the parent rock gives a shallow soil which, due to its acidity and lack of humus, is usually infertile.

(b) Tropical rainforest

Tropical red earths are associated with tropical rainforests. The heavy, continuous leaf fall gives a thick litter layer. This layer is rapidly broken down, partly due to the hot, wet climate and partly due to the presence of large numbers of soil organisms. As precipitation exceeds evapotranspiration, there is a steady leaching of minerals which include recycled nutrients and iron. Whereas leaching often transports nutrients to rivers (where they are lost to the system), iron is deposited in the lower layers to give the soil its characteristic red colour. Leaching and mixing agents (living organisms) also prevent the formation of well-defined horizon boundaries. The climatic conditions are ideal for chemical weathering, and the resultant rapid decomposition of the bedrock gives a deep soil.

Under normal conditions, the tropical red earths are relatively fertile soil, but once the nutrient cycle is broken (by farming or deforestation), leaching increases and the soil rapidly loses its fertility.

(c) Tropical savanna grassland

The high temperatures encourage high evaporation rates. As a result there is an upward movement of water through the soil. The water carries with it dissolved minerals such as calcium. The calcium is deposited in the upper layers of the soil, making the soil calcium rich. However, the heavy rains in the wet season may also cause some leaching of the soils. The litter layer is large, especially at the start of the dry season when the grasses die off. Decomposition is quite rapid in the wet season but much slower in the dry season.

Figure 7.6 Profiles of soils found in (a) coniferous forests, (b) tropical rainforests and (c) savanna grasslands

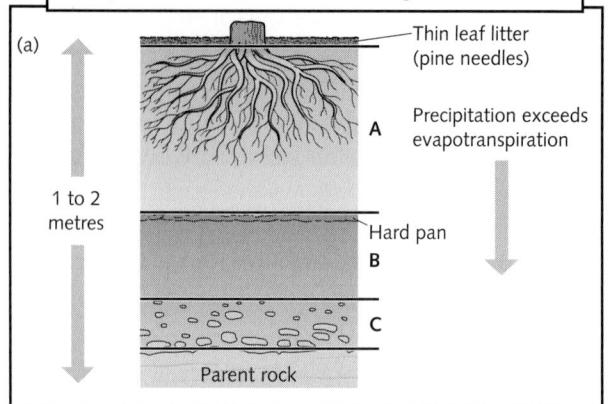

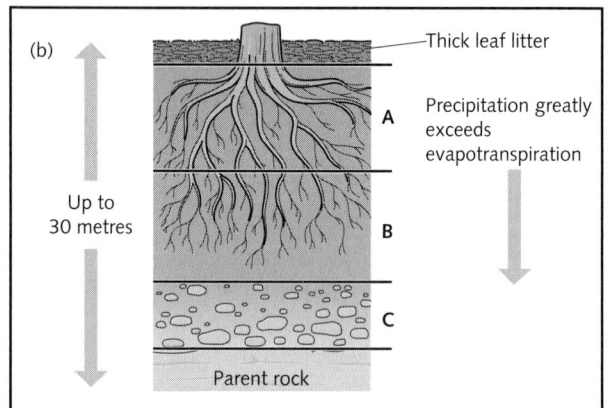

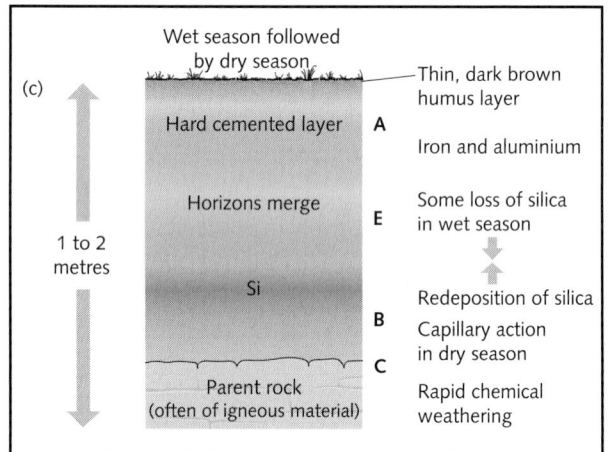

(a) 1 to 2 metres — Thin leaf litter (pine needles); A — Precipitation exceeds evapotranspiration; Hard pan; B; C; Parent rock

(b) Up to 30 metres — Thick leaf litter; A — Precipitation greatly exceeds evapotranspiration; B; C; Parent rock

(c) 1 to 2 metres — Wet season followed by dry season; Hard cemented layer — A — Thin, dark brown humus layer; Iron and aluminium; Horizons merge — E — Some loss of silica in wet season; Si — B — Redeposition of silica; Capillary action in dry season; C — Parent rock (often of igneous material); Rapid chemical weathering

Check this!...

1 Explain the vegetation layers found in tropical rainforests.

2 Describe the characteristics of tropical red earth soils.

Key word to know

Xerophytic

Tropical savanna grassland

A transect (section) across the savanna grasslands shows how the natural vegetation changes in response to the climate (Figure 7.7). Figure 7.6c shows a profile of Savanna grassland soil.

The dry season

The scattered deciduous trees lose their leaves, grasses turn yellow and dry up, and the ground assumes a dusty, reddish-brown colour. Some trees shed their leaves while others produce thin, waxy and even thornlike leaves to try to keep transpiration to a minimum. Most plants are **xerophytic** (drought-resistant) with very long roots to tap underground water supplies or with thick bark to store water in the trunk, like the baobab tree. Grasses grow in tufts, separated by patches of bare soil. As the dry season progresses, their stalks become stiff, yellow and straw-like and, in time, the plants wither.

The wet season

After the first rains, the grass seeds germinate and trees produce new leaves. Under the hot, wet conditions the grasses grow quickly and can reach a height of 3–4 metres before flowering and producing new seeds. The seemingly endless plains of the Serengeti (Tanzania) and Maasai Mara (Kenya) resemble a vast green sea occasionally interrupted by acacia trees. The acacias, with their crowns flattened by the trade winds, provide welcome shelter for wildlife.

The vegetation of these areas has been altered over a period of time by fire, either started deliberately or as a result of electrical storms. More recently, areas nearer the desert margins have experienced desertification mainly from pressures resulting from rapid population growth. Trees and shrubs have been removed for fuelwood. As settlements and cultivated areas increase, many nomadic herders, like the Fulani in West Africa and the Maasai in East Africa, find their traditional grazing grounds reduced in size. This leads to overgrazing and soil erosion in the areas to which they are restricted.

Check this!...

1 Explain the changes in vegetation shown in Figure 7.7.

2 How do savanna grasslands change between their wet and dry seasons?

Key words to know

Taiga
Softwoods
Podsol

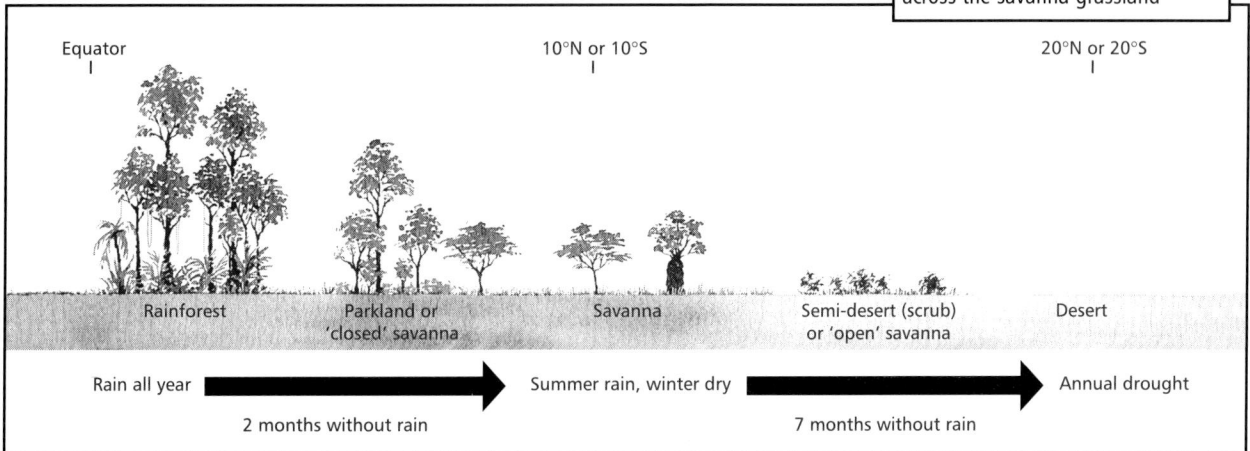

Figure 7.7 Changes in vegetation across the savanna grassland

Coniferous forest

The natural vegetation of the coniferous forest, or **taiga**, consists of vast uninterrupted stands of spruce, pine and fir. The most common trees are the Norwegian spruce and Scots pine in upland Britain and Scandinavia, and the Sitka spruce and Douglas fir in North America. Often, only one or two species of tree grow across a wide area. The trees have had to adapt to the harsh physical environment (Figure 7.8) where:

- winters are long and extremely cold, often with strong winds; precipitation falls as snow and, as groundwater is frozen, moisture is unavailable for plants
- summers are cool and the growing season is short, but there is some rain for plant growth
- soils are often thin and poor.

Coniferous trees are **softwoods**. They are valuable for timber, as well as for pulp and paper. The coniferous forest, covering vast tracts of mainly inhospitable land, has been less affected by human activity than most other biomes.

Figure 7.6a shows a profile of a **podsol** – the soil typical of coniferous forest.

Figure 7.8 Adaptation of conifers to cold climates

- Evergreen – no need to renew leaves for the short growing season
- Compact conical shape helps stability in the wind
- Needles to reduce moisture loss
- Trunk is usually straight and tall in attempt to reach the sunlight
- Thick resinous bark acts as a protection against cold winds
- Cones protect the seeds during very cold winters
- Downward-sloping and springy branches allow snow to slide off
- Very little undergrowth as trees are closely spaced and branches cut out sunlight
- Long roots for anchorage against strong winds

Check this!...

1 Which species are commonly found in coniferous forest?

2 Discuss the ways in which conifers have adapted to the cold climate.

2 The interaction between people and ecosystems

The human uses of tropical rainforests

Case Study

Deforestation – the destruction of an ecosystem

Back to ...

The New Wider World pp236–237 for the case study of deforestation in the Amazon Basin.

Using your case study

Use this case study to show that you are aware of the conflicts of interest that exist in the development of the rainforests. Make sure that you can:

1 draw a simple sketch map of the Amazon Basin

2 discuss the reasons why the rainforest is being cleared (farming, transport, resources, settlement)

3 comment on the rate of forest clearance

4 explain the effects of clearance on the soil, hydrology, vegetation and local people

5 identify the different attitudes of the interested groups.

Update

For further information on the rainforest see 'Brazilian rainforest destruction: An update' (GeoActive 291, April 2003).

Learn it!

a) Describe the location of the Amazon Basin.

b) Make a list of the factors that have contributed to deforestation.

c) What effect does deforestation have on:
   i   soils
   ii hydrology?

The human uses of savanna grasslands

Case Study

Tourism and the environment Desertification in the Sahel

Back to ...

The New Wider World pp170–171 (tourism and the environment in Kenya), p233 (population pressure, overcultivation, overgrazing, soil erosion), pp254–258 (soil erosion, desertification).

Using your case study

Use these pages and case studies to show that you are aware of all the pressures on the savanna grassland environment leading to desertification and the strategies employed to reverse the process. Make sure that you can:

1 identify the main areas of savanna grassland

2 describe the range of human uses of savanna grasslands

3 discuss the reasons for population pressure, overcultivation and overgrazing

4 explain the process of soil erosion

5 define desertification and identify where it is occurring

6 discuss the need for sustainable development

7 discuss the advantages and disadvantages of solutions to sustainable development.

Case study links

The tourism in the Kenya case study is useful for the tourism in LEDCs section of Managing resources (Chapter 12 p115). The case study of desertification in the Sahel can be used as an example of water supply in developing countries in Weather and climate (Chapter 6).

Update

For up-to-date information on desertification use the link on *The New Wider World Coursemate* website.

Learn it!

a) List the human uses of savanna grassland.

b) Define:
   i   overgrazing
   ii overcultivation.

c) Why is sustainable development so important in the effort to maintain this ecosystem?

The need for the global management of forests

Case Study

Sustainable forestry in Malaysia

Back to …

The New Wider World pp238–240 for the case study on sustainable forestry in Malaysia.

Using your case study

Use this case study to explain why there is a need for sustainable forestry and how it can be achieved. Make sure that you can:

1 draw a simple sketch map of Malaysia

2 discuss the conversion of natural forest to tree crops

3 describe the process of deforestation

4 explain the different methods of logging

5 comment on the move towards more sustainable forestry.

Update

For up-to-date information on sustainable forestry use the link on *The New Wider World Coursemate* website.

Learn it!

a) Why have considerable areas of natural forest been converted to tree crops?

b) List the different methods of logging.

c) What is being done to make forestry in Malaysia more sustainable?

1 Place the following labels in the correct boxes on a copy of Figure 7.9. (4)
Shrub layer
Main canopy
Emergents
Lianas

2 Carefully describe the location of one area of rainforest. (2)

3 Why is the rainforest considered to be a fragile environment? (4)

4 Why do people have different attitudes about the economic development of the rainforest? (5)

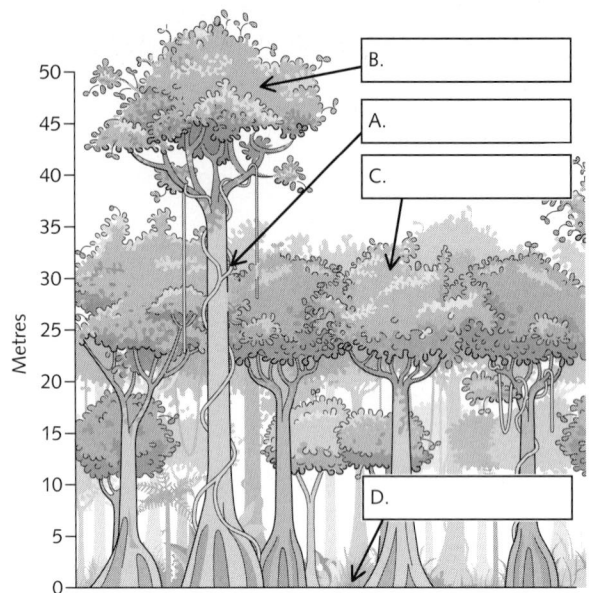

Figure 7.9 Vegetation layers in the tropical rainforest

Back to ...

The New Wider World website to check your answers to the Exam Practice question.

EXAM TIPS

For question 2 be as accurate about the location as possible. Which country (countries) is it in? What are its latitudinal limits?

8

Population

1 The global distribution of population is uneven

Distribution and density

Distribution describes the way in which people are spread out across the Earth's surface. This distribution is uneven and changes over time. It is usual to show population distribution by means of a dot map (Figure 8.1). Notice how people are concentrated into certain parts of the world making those places **densely populated**. Other areas have relatively few people living there. These are said to be **sparsely populated**.

Figure 8.1 Dot map showing world population distribution

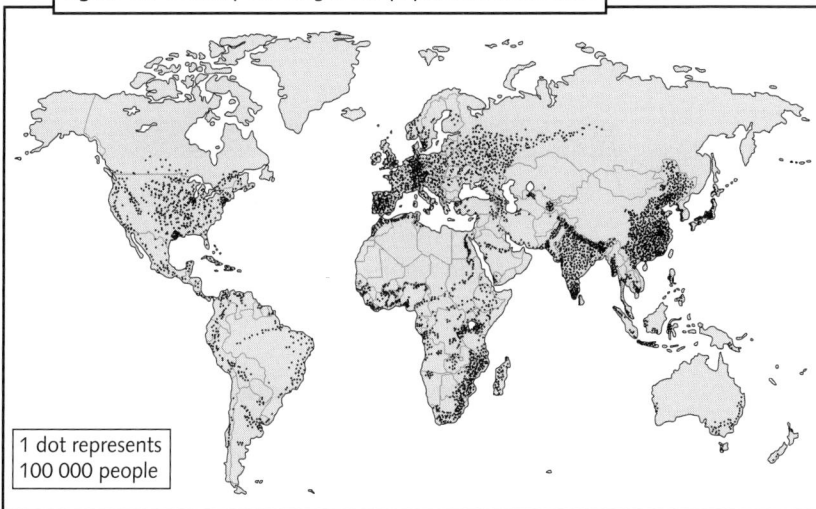

1 dot represents
100 000 people

KEY IDEAS

1 The global distribution of population is uneven.

2 Population change depends upon birth rate, death rate and migration and presents challenges to human populations.

Back to ...

The New Wider World **pp4–5**
Figure 1.3 to see the factors which affect distribution and density of population.

Key words to know

Distribution
Densely populated
Sparsely populated
Density
Physical factors
Human factors

Density describes the number of people living in a given area, usually a square kilometre (km^2). Density is found by dividing the total population of a place by its area.

On global and continental scales, patterns of distribution and density are mainly affected by **physical factors** such as relief, climate, vegetation, soils, natural resources and water supply. At regional and more local scales, patterns are more likely to be influenced by **human factors** which may be economic, political or social. Figure 1.3 pp4–5 of *The New Wider World* gives reasons, with examples, why some parts of the world are densely populated while others are sparsely populated.

Check this!...

1 What is the difference between population distribution and population density?

2 What do you understand by the terms 'sparsely populated' and 'densely populated'?

3 List the physical factors that can affect population density.

4 List the human factors that can affect population density.

Population distribution and density in Brazil

Back to...

The New Wider World pp16–17 for the case study of population in Brazil.

Using your case study

Use this case study to explain population distribution in a less economically developed country (LEDC) you have studied.

- You should know the average population density in Brazil (20.3 per km²) and be able to describe how density varies. For example, from under 1 per km² in much of the North and West Central to an average of over 50 per km² in the most densely populated coastal areas. Show that you know there are variations in these areas.
- Use as many of the headings in Figure 1.3 of *The New Wider World* as you can to explain the low population density of the North. Refer to the very hot and wet climate throughout the year which hinders settlement and economic activity, fragile soils and soil erosion problems, inaccessibility, the lack of known natural resources in much of the region, poor provision of services and a relatively low quality of life. Explain the relatively high population density of the South East. Refer to the attractive climate, fertile soils, natural resources, high density road and rail networks, major sea and air ports, good energy supplies, the best educational and skill levels in Brazil, the location of major cities and the focus of TNC (transnational corporation) activity in the country.

Case study links

You can link this case study with the information in Chapter 11 on Industry. The high population density of the South East and the infrastructure that has developed in the region has made it an attractive location for TNCs.

Update

For a summary of the main finding of the latest census in Brazil see 'Brazil: Census 2000 Update' (Geofile Online No. 429, September 2002).

Learn it!

a) How does population density vary in Brazil?

b) What are the reasons for low population density in the North?

c) What are the reasons for high population density in the South East?

2 Population change depends upon birth rate, death rate and migration and presents challenges to human populations

Back to ...

The New Wider World **p6** for examples of natural decreases of population.

Key words to know

Birth rate
Death rate
Natural increase
Natural decrease

Population growth

Population change depends mainly upon the balance between the birth rate and the death rate. It is also affected by migration.

The **birth rate** is the average number of live births in a year for every 1000 people in the total population. The **death rate** is the average number of deaths in a year per 1000 people in the population. The difference between the two is either the **natural increase** (where the birth rate is the higher) or the **natural decrease** (where the death rate is the higher).

Throughout history the world's population, and that of individual countries, has usually shown a natural increase. However, exceptions have occurred.

The demographic transition model

This shows the relationship between birth rates and death rates. It describes how, over a period of time, a sequence of change in population growth rates takes place (Figure 8.2). The **demographic transition model** suggests that there are four stages through which all countries will eventually pass. The UK, being one of the world's first industrialised countries, has passed through all four stages.

Back to ...

The New Wider World **p7**
Figure 1.5 for further information on demographic transition in the UK.

Figure 8.2 Demographic transition model

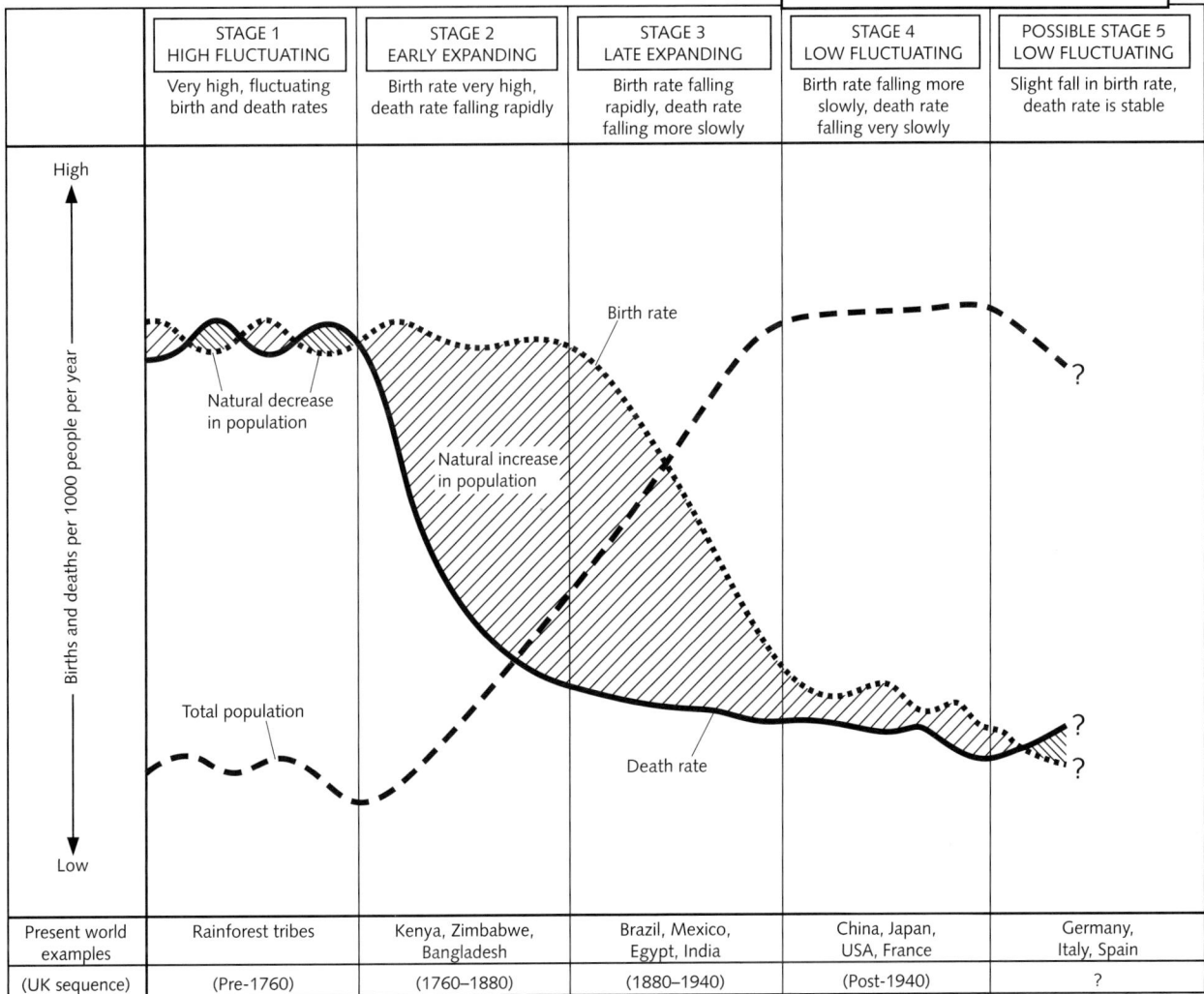

	STAGE 1 HIGH FLUCTUATING	STAGE 2 EARLY EXPANDING	STAGE 3 LATE EXPANDING	STAGE 4 LOW FLUCTUATING	POSSIBLE STAGE 5 LOW FLUCTUATING
	Very high, fluctuating birth and death rates	Birth rate very high, death rate falling rapidly	Birth rate falling rapidly, death rate falling more slowly	Birth rate falling more slowly, death rate falling very slowly	Slight fall in birth rate, death rate is stable
Present world examples	Rainforest tribes	Kenya, Zimbabwe, Bangladesh	Brazil, Mexico, Egypt, India	China, Japan, USA, France	Germany, Italy, Spain
(UK sequence)	(Pre-1760)	(1760–1880)	(1880–1940)	(Post-1940)	?

Since the 1990s several more economically developed countries (MEDCs) appear to be entering a new and fifth stage. This stage (indicated on Figure 8.2) is where the birth rate is beginning to fall below the death rate. It is predicted that countries entering this stage will eventually see a decrease in their total population.

Key words to know

Demographic transition model

Check this!...

1 Define:
   a) birth rate
   b) death rate
   c) the rate of natural increase/decrease.

2 How does the birth rate, the death rate and the rate of population growth change through the five stages of demographic transition?

3 Explain the reasons for the rapid fall in the death rate in stage 2.

4 Explain the reasons for changes in the birth rate over the five stages of the model.

Back to ...

The New Wider World
pp10–11 for graphs showing
the contrasting rates of
population growth of LEDCs
and MEDCs.

Population trends

The annual growth rate of the world's population rose slowly but steadily until the beginning of the nineteenth century. For the next century and a half it grew at an increasingly faster rate, a process referred to as a **population explosion**. During the 1960s and 1970s the world's population grew, on average, by a record 2 per cent per year. This growth rate, which was even higher in the less economically developed countries, caused increasing concern.

The growth rate fell to 1.6 per cent per year in 1999 and is likely to drop to 1.0 per cent by 2015 and 0.5 per cent by 2050. October 1999 saw the world's population reaching the 6000 million (6 billion) mark, growing by 140 persons per minute, which is 78 million each year.

So, although people across most of the world are living longer, why is the annual growth rate slowing down? This is due to:
- a faster than predicted decline in the birth rate across the world
- improvements in family planning, basic education and female literacy that have all led to a reduction in family size
- the one-child policy in China, a country with over 20 per cent of the world's population
- diseases such as AIDS and malaria which reduce life expectancies, especially in sub-Saharan countries in Africa that have, at present, the world's highest birth rates.

Population change in developed and developing countries

Most of the LEDCs still fit into either stage 2 or stage 3 of the demographic transition model, whereas most of the MEDCs have long since reached stage 4. This is because the LEDCs have a higher birth rate and a greater increase in their total population.
- Continents with the fastest population growth are Africa, Asia and Latin America. Africa has the greatest growth despite its high death rate caused by AIDS, crop failure and civil war.
- Continents with the slowest growth rate are Europe, North America and Australasia (Oceania). Europe is likely to show a population decrease by the middle of the twenty-first century.
- Most of the world's population live in Asia (approximately 40 per cent live in China and India). In 1950, 76 per cent of the total lived in the three developing continents. This had risen to 82 per cent by 2000 and is estimated to reach 88 per cent by 2050.

Check this!...

1 What is meant by the term 'population explosion'?

2 Why is the world's population growth rate slowing down?

3 At what stage of demographic transition are:
 a) the LEDCs
 b) the MEDCs?

Key words to know

Population explosion
Life expectancy
Population structure
Population pyramid
Dependency ratio

Population structures

The rate of natural increase, the birth rate, the death rate and **life expectancy** (the number of years that the average person born in a country can expect to live) all affect the **population structure** of a country. The population structure can be shown by a **population pyramid**.

A population pyramid shows:
- the total population divided into five-year age groups, e.g. 5 to 9 years
- the percentage of the total population, subdivided into males and females, in each of those groups.

The population pyramid for the United Kingdom is taken from the 2001 census (Figure 8.3). An important term is the **dependency ratio**, i.e.

$$\frac{\text{Non-economically active}}{\text{Economically active}} \qquad \frac{\text{i.e. Children (0–14) and elderly (65+)}}{\text{Those of working age (15–64)}}$$

e.g. UK 2001 (figures in millions):
$$\frac{11.105 + 9.341}{38.342} \times 100 = \text{dependency ratio of } 53.33$$

This means that for every 100 people of working age, there were 53.33 people dependent upon them.

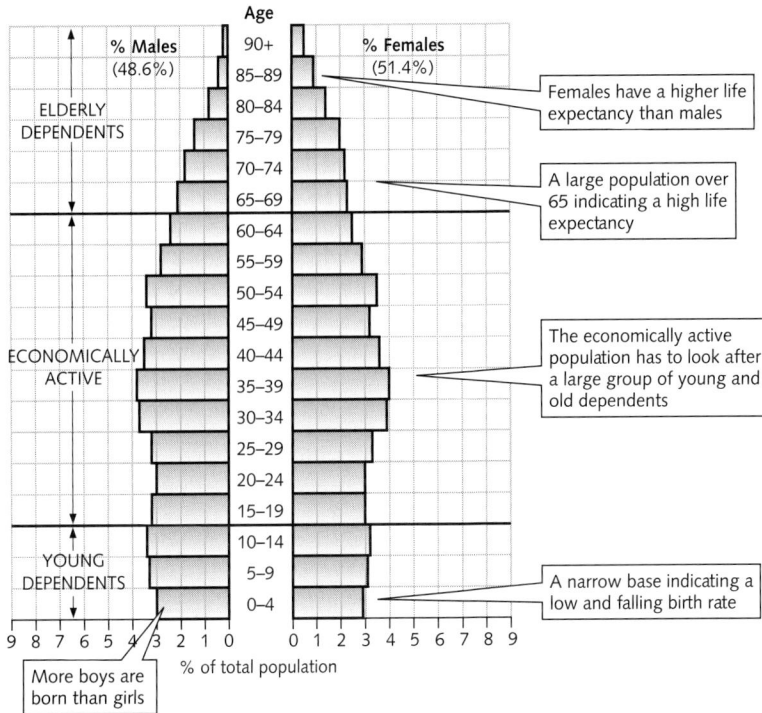

Figure 8.3
Population pyramid for the United Kingdom, 2001

Annotations on Figure 8.3:
- Females have a higher life expectancy than males
- A large population over 65 indicating a high life expectancy
- The economically active population has to look after a large group of young and old dependents
- A narrow base indicating a low and falling birth rate
- More boys are born than girls

Labels: ELDERLY DEPENDENTS, ECONOMICALLY ACTIVE, YOUNG DEPENDENTS
% Males (48.6%), % Females (51.4%)
% of total population

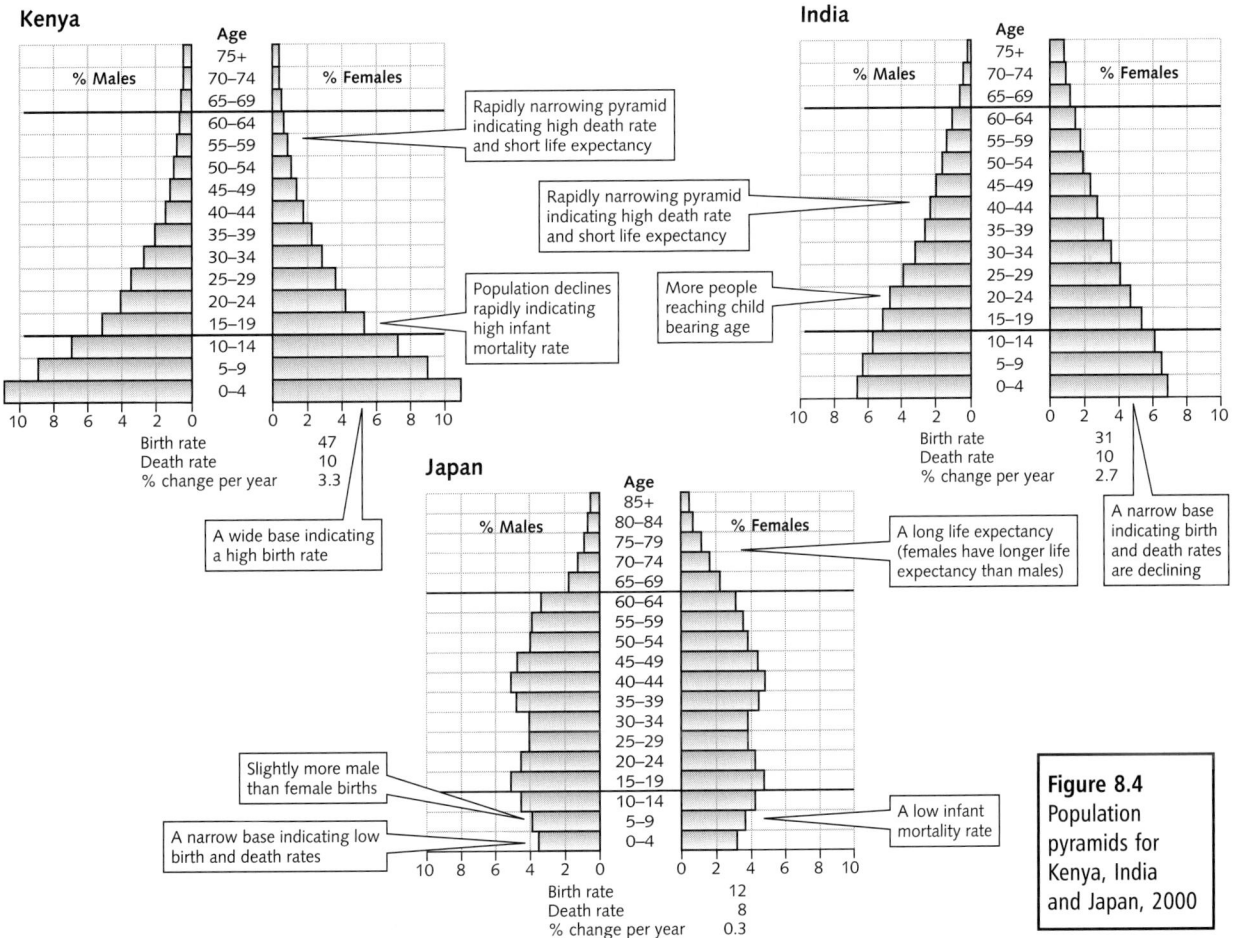

Kenya

Birth rate	47
Death rate	10
% change per year	3.3

Annotations:
- Rapidly narrowing pyramid indicating high death rate and short life expectancy
- Population declines rapidly indicating high infant mortality rate
- A wide base indicating a high birth rate

India

Birth rate	31
Death rate	10
% change per year	2.7

Annotations:
- Rapidly narrowing pyramid indicating high death rate and short life expectancy
- More people reaching child bearing age
- A narrow base indicating birth and death rates are declining

Japan

Birth rate	12
Death rate	8
% change per year	0.3

Annotations:
- A long life expectancy (females have longer life expectancy than males)
- A low infant mortality rate
- Slightly more male than female births
- A narrow base indicating low birth and death rates

Figure 8.4
Population pyramids for Kenya, India and Japan, 2000

Check this!...

1   What is meant by the terms:
    a) life expectancy
    b) population structure
    c) dependency ratio?

2   What is a population pyramid?

3   Describe and explain the population structure
    of the UK (Figure 8.3).

4   Describe and explain the differences between
    the population structures of Kenya, India and
    Japan (Figure 8.4).

Key words to know

Migration
Emigrants
Immigrants
Migration balance
Voluntary migration
Forced migration

What is migration?

Migration includes temporary, seasonal and daily movements as well as permanent changes both between countries and within a country (Figure 8.5).

- International migration is the movement of people between countries.
- **Emigrants** are people who leave a country.
- **Immigrants** are those who arrive in a country.
- The **migration balance** is the difference between the numbers of emigrants and immigrants.
- Countries with a net migration loss lose more people through emigration than they gain by immigration.
- Countries with a net migration gain receive more people by immigration than they lose through emigration.

Figure 8.5 Types of migration

	External (International)	**Between countries**
Permanent	i) Voluntary	West Indians to Britain
	ii) Forced (refugees)	Negro slaves to America, Kurds, Rwandans
	Internal	**Within a country**
	i) Rural depopulation	Most developing countries
	ii) Urban depopulation	British conurbations
	iii) Regional	North-west to south-east of Britain
Semi-permanent	For several years	Migrant workers (Turks in Germany)
Seasonal	For several months or several weeks	Mexican harvesters in California, holiday-makers, university students
Daily	Commuters	South-east England

International migration can be divided into two types – **voluntary** and **forced** (Figure 8.6).

Figure 8.6 Voluntary and forced migration

Voluntary migration is the free movement of migrants looking for an improved quality of life and personal freedom. For example:
- Employment – either to find a job, to earn a higher salary or to avoid paying tax
- Pioneers developing new areas
- Trade and economic expansion
- Territorial expansion
- Better climate, especially on retirement
- Social amenities such as hospitals, schools and entertainment
- To be with friends and relatives

Forced migration is when the migrant has no personal choice but has to move due to natural disaster or economic or social imposition. For example:
- Religious and/or political persecution
- Wars, creating large numbers of refugees
- Forced labour as slaves or prisoners of war
- Racial discrimination
- Lack of food due to famine
- Natural disasters caused by floods, drought, earthquakes, volcanic eruptions or hurricanes
- Overpopulation, when the number of people living in an area exceeds the resources available to them

Economic migrants

These are people who move voluntarily from one country to another hoping to find jobs and, consequently, a higher standard of living and a better quality of life.

Figure 8.7 Advantages and disadvantages of migrant workers

Advantages	Disadvantages
Losing country (e.g. Turkey)	
• Reduces pressure on jobs and resources, e.g. food	• Loses people in working-age group
• Loses people of child-bearing age, causing decline in birth rate	• Loses people most likely to have some education and skills
• Migrants develop new skills which they may take back to turkey	• Mainly males leave, causing a division of families
• Money earned in Germany sent back to turkey	• Left with an elderly population and so a high death rate
Receiving country (e.g. Germany)	
• Overcomes labour shortage	• Pressure on jobs but most likely to be the first unemployed in a recession
• Prepared to do dirty, unskilled jobs	• Low-quality, overcrowded housing lacking in basic amenities (inner city slums – bidonvilles in France, favelas in South America)
• Prepared to work long hours for a low salary (London underground)	• Ethnic groups tend not to integrate
• Cultural advantages and links (e.g. Notting Hill carnival)	• Racial tension
• Some highly skilled migrants (e.g. Pakistani doctors)	• Limited skilled/educated group
• In a developing country these migrants could increase the number of skilled workers	• Lack of opportunities to practise their own religion, culture, etc.
	• Language difficulties
	• Often less healthy

Check this!...

1 What is migration?

2 Explain the meaning of the term 'migration balance'.

3 Using examples, explain the difference between voluntary migration and forced migration.

Case Study

Turks into Germany

Back to ...

The New Wider World pp28–29 for the case study of Turkish migrants in Germany.

Using your case study

Use this case study as an example of either voluntary or economic migration.

- You should be able to discuss the causes of this migration with reference to the origin (Turkey) and the destination (Germany). Explain why Turks would consider working abroad and why Germany needed extra workers.
- Figure 8.7 provides a useful summary of the consequences of migration for both the

country of origin and the country of destination. You can use all of these points in your discussion of economic migration between Turkey and Germany.

Case study links

This case study links with Chapter 11 Industry as labour supply is an important factor in industrial location.

Learn it!

a) Why was Turkey the origin of this migration and Germany the destination?

b) What were the consequences of this migration for both countries?

Refugees

- **Refugees** are people who have been forced to leave their home country for fear of persecution, civil war or due to environmental disaster.
- Refugees do not include **displaced persons**, who are people who have been forced to move within their own country.
- The United Nations (UN) suggested that, at the beginning of 2000, there were almost 15 million refugees in the world.
- More than half of the world's refugees are children and most of the adults are women.
- Over 80 per cent of refugees are in developing countries.
- Refugees live in extreme poverty, lacking food, shelter, clothing, education and medical care. They have no citizenship, few rights, virtually no prospects, and are unlikely to return to their homeland.

The present refugee situation began over 50 years ago in war-torn Europe. However, it was the Palestinian Arab refugee camps, set up after the creation of the state of Israel in 1948, which first showed that the problem had become permanent, and 1.75 million people still live in camps in this part of the Middle East.

Check this!...

1 What is the difference between a refugee and a displaced person?

2 Why do most refugees live in developing countries?

Case Study Extra

Palestinian refugees

When Jewish settlers declared an Israeli state in 1948, starting the first Arab-Israeli war, 85 per cent of Palestinians who lived in what became Israel were driven out of their homes. One-third fled to the West Bank, another third to the Gaza Strip, and the remainder to Jordan, Syria and Lebanon. Subsequent Arab-Israel hostilities have caused further displacement.

- Between 4 and 5 million Palestinians are refugees today.
- Population density and unemployment rates within the refugee camps are among the highest in the world.
- Local employment opportunities are extremely limited.
- The result is chronic poverty, overcrowding and a very low standard of living.
- Infant mortality is high and life expectancy relatively low.
- Some camps are in urban areas, in or close to towns such as Jenin. Others are in sparsely populated rural areas.
- The intense pressure on the environment at refugee camp locations has led to environmental degradation – clearance of vegetation, soil erosion, pollution of rivers, problems of refuse disposal, etc.

- The very poor conditions in the camps are a significant factor fuelling continued resentment towards Israel.

Using your case study

Palestinian refugee camps can be used as an example of international refugees. You should understand the cause of this major refugee problem and the consequences of it (the harsh social and economic conditions under which the refugees live and the environmental degradation in the areas where the camps are located).

Update

For up-to-date information on refugees use the links on *The New Wider World Coursemate* website.

Learn it!

a) Where are Israel and its neighbouring countries located?

b) What was the cause of the Palestinian refugee problem?

c) What are the consequences of this problem?

The problems of population growth in LEDCs

Population (total numbers, growth rates, population structures) is a major influence on sustainable development (Figure 8.8). **Sustainable development** means meeting the needs of the present without compromising the ability of future generations to meet their own needs.

Sustainable development	Non-sustainable development
• Family planning, steady replacement rate	• High birth rate, rapid natural increase, ageing population

Figure 8.8 Population and sustainability

Too many under 15s

A high birth rate results in a high proportion of the total population being aged 15 or under. In Africa and much of southern Asia this proportion is likely to be over 40 per cent and in Latin America over 30 per cent (in the MEDCs it is often under 20 per cent). This means that:

- at present, the large youthful population will need child health care and education which these countries can ill-afford
- in the future, there will be more people reaching child-bearing age.

Figure 8.9 suggests reasons for the high birth and fertility rates, and the large family size, of many LEDCs.

- Many children are needed to help work on the land, to carry wood and water, and to care for parents when they are old

- A high **infant mortality rate** means that many children die before their first birthday

- Religious beliefs may forbid birth control

- A lack of education, especially for women, has an effect on **family planning**

- There is a lack of access to and insufficient money for the supply of contraceptives

- A large family can enhance a family's reputation in the local community, especially for the husband

Figure 8.9 Why birth and fertility rates are high in LEDCs

The three key factors leading to a decline in birth rate and fertility are improvements in the following areas: family planning, health care, women's education and status.

Back to ...

The New Wider World **p12** for further information on these key factors.

Check this!...

1 What is sustainable development?

2 How does population affect sustainable development?

3 Why do many countries have high birth rates? What problems does this cause?

4 Explain the key factors leading to a decline in birth rate.

Key words to know

Sustainable development
Infant mortality rate
Family planning

China's one-child policy

Back to ...

The New Wider World p13 for the case study on China's one-child policy.

Using your case study

This is an example of a national family planning programme which was set up because of China's very large population and its fast rate of increase. People were left with very little choice but to follow government policy. A good answer to an exam question on the ways in which one country has reduced its rate of population growth could be structured around the following points:

- conditions before the policy began in 1979 – government encouragement for large families with population growth of 55 million every three years. Although the birth rate had fallen from 44 per 1000 in 1950 to 31 per 1000 in 1975 the annual increase was still very large.
- In 1979 – a) the one-child policy was introduced, b) the age of marriage was raised to 22 years for men and 20 years for women, c) couples had to apply to be married and to have a child and d) those who followed the policy gained a range of benefits while whose who did not were deprived of benefits and fined heavily.
- By 1999 the state had begun to relax the policy as the birth rate had fallen to 19 per 1000 and there were growing concerns about the ageing of China's population.

Case study links

This case study provides a link with Chapter 12 (Managing resources) since population growth has a major impact on the use of resources.

Update

For up-to-date information on population use the links on *The New Wider World Coursemate* website.

Learn it!

a) What were the demographic conditions in China prior to the one-child policy?

b) What did this new family planning policy mean to the people of China?

c) Although population growth is much lower in China now, what other problems has the one-child policy caused?

The problem of ageing populations in MEDCs

Too few under 15s

Several of the most economically developed countries are approaching stage 5 in the demographic transition model. Here the problem is becoming 'too few' children. In countries like Germany, Italy and Spain birth rates are at, or below, death rates. The **replacement rate**, when there are just sufficient children born to balance the number of people that die, is not being met. These countries face a decrease in their total population, e.g. Italy from 56 million in 2000 to a predicted 41 million by 2050. The fear is that, in time, they will:

- have too few consumers and skilled workers to keep their economy going
- see a reduction in their competitive advantage in science and technology
- have closures of schools and shops, especially in smaller towns and villages
- experience problems in providing pensions and social care for an ageing population.

People aged over 65 – an ageing population

Life expectancy has increased due to:
- improved standards of hygiene and health education

Key words to know

Replacement rate

- improvements in primary health care
- the development of new drugs and vaccines
- a better diet, both in quantity and quality
- advances in medical knowledge and techniques.

The increase in life expectancy, together with a falling birth rate, means that an increasingly higher proportion of a country's population live beyond 65, and even beyond 80 years. This process is referred to as ageing. By 2000, several of the most economically developed countries (mainly Japan and several in western Europe) had over 16 per cent of their population aged over 65. They now had more people aged over 65 than children aged under 15. The proportion of over 65s is predicted to rise to over 20 per cent by 2020 and, in some countries such as Japan and Italy, to reach 35 per cent by 2050. Figure 8.10 gives some of the problems created by an increasingly ageing population.

Check this!...

1 What is the replacement rate of a population?

2 Why is a fall in the birth rate one of the causes of an ageing population?

3 List the potential consequences for a country of a decline in population.

4 Why has life expectancy increased in so many countries?

Problems created in a country...	Problems facing the elderly...
An increasing amount of money is needed for residential homes and sheltered accommodation; health care (e.g. home visits and free prescriptions); social services (e.g. home help and providing meals); and subsides (e.g. free TV licences and bus passes).	Many have to live alone, especially women, when their married partner dies.
	Most cannot afford the cost of a residential home which may be over £2000 a month, especially in the south of England. Others may only be able to afford such accommodation by selling their home or using their life savings.
An increasing amount of the family doctor's financial budget and time is taken up by the elderly.	
	There are lengthy waits for hospital operations such as hip replacements.
There is an increase in long-term illnesses and those that make people house-bound, such as Parkinson's and Alzheimer's.	
	Those who are still fit enough and willing to work often face bias and prejudice due to their age.
There is an increasing dependence upon a smaller group of economically active people to provide consumer goods and services as well as money through taxation.	
	Those living in urban areas have a fear of crime and traffic; those in rural areas who cannot drive and where there is no public transport have difficulty getting to the doctor, hospital and shops.
Less money is available for younger age groups, e.g. for education, improvements in transport or the provision of leisure and social amenities.	

Figure 8.10 Problems of an ageing population

Case Study

Ageing populations in Italy and China

Back to ...

The New Wider World p15 for a case study of ageing populations in Italy and China.

Using your case study

Use the information provided on Italy and China to answer questions which ask you:

1 to describe the population structure of an aging population – use Figure 1.20, p15 of *The New Wider World* to describe the population structure of an ageing population. Note a) the low populations of the age groups under 20, indicating a very low birth rate in recent decades, b) the higher populations in the 20–65 age groups, indicating that the birth rate was considerably higher when these population groups were born and c) the significant proportions of the total population over 65 and over 80 (the oldest old).

2 to explain why the populations of many countries are ageing – here, quote figures on a) increasing life expectancy and b) the decline in the birth rate

3 to discuss the consequences of population ageing – refer to a) the falling ratio of workers to pensioners (the increasing dependency ratio), b) the increasing number of people dependent on state pensions and c) the health and other demands of a large number of elderly people in a population.

> **Case study links**

As a population ages more resources have to be allocated to the elderly. Resource management is crucial to sustainable development (Chapter 12).

Update

For up-to-date information on population use the link on *The New Wider World Coursemate* website.

Learn it!

a) Why are the populations of Italy and China ageing?

b) Why is this considered to be a problem?

c) Discuss possible solutions to this problem.

EXAM PRACTICE

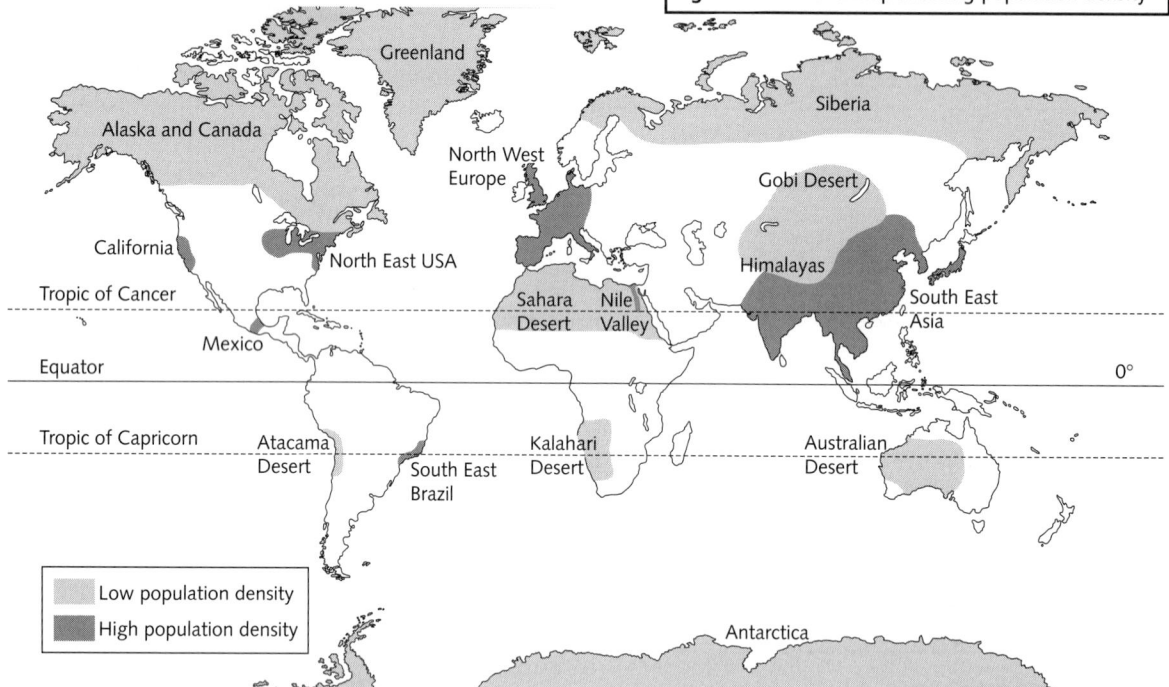

Figure 8.11 World map showing population density

1 Study the following list of areas:

| mountain range | hot desert |
| river valley | industrial area |

a Which two areas are most likely to have a high density of population? (2)

b For an area you have studied, explain why it has a high population density. (5)

Country	Birth rate	Death rate	Population change
A	High	High	Little change
B	Low	High	
C	High	Low	

Figure 8.12

2 a Describe the pattern of population density shown on Figure 8.11. (4)

 b Complete the empty boxes on a copy of Figure 8.12. (2)

3 Using examples, explain why some countries have high birth rates and others have low birth rates. (6)

4 LEDCs often have youthful populations, whereas MEDCs' populations are often ageing. Describe the problems which may result from this. (6)

Back to ...

The New Wider World website to check your answers to the Exam Practice question.

EXAM TIPS

With 6 marks available for question 3 it is important to refer to a number of reasons for differences in birth rate. A very good answer would quote birth rate figures for the countries used as examples.

1 Settlements vary in site, size, function and structure

Site and situation

Site describes the point at which a settlement is located. Factors such as local relief, soil, water supply and resources were important in choosing the initial site of a settlement.

Situation describes where the settlement is located in relation to surrounding features such as other settlements, mountains, rivers and communications. It is the situation of a settlement that determines whether or not it will continue to grow or whether it remains as a small hamlet or village.

Early settlements developed within a rural economy which aimed to be self-sufficient. Their sites were determined by a series of mainly physical factors. An ideal site was likely to have the benefit of several of these factors.

- A **wet-point site** was essential as water is needed virtually every day and is heavy to carry any distance. In early times, rivers were still sufficiently clean to give a safe, permanent supply. In lowland Britain, many early settlements were located at springs at the foot of chalk or limestone escarpments.
- A **dry-point site** was needed to avoid flooding or to be above unhealthy marshland.
- Building materials, which ideally included stone, wood and clay, had to be obtained locally as these were heavy and bulky to move at a time when transport was poorly developed.
- Defence against surrounding tribes was sometimes necessary. Good defensive sites may have been within a river meander, or on a hill with steep sides and commanding views.
- A fuel supply was needed for heating and cooking – usually wood.
- Food supplies were needed from land nearby, some of which was suitable for rearing animals and some for growing crops.
- **Nodal points** were where several valleys (natural routes) met to create a route centre, or where two rivers joined.
- Bridging points may originally have been at a ford in the river, or where the river was shallow and narrow enough to enable a bridge to be built.
- Shelter and **aspect**. In Britain it is an advantage to be sheltered from the strong prevailing south-westerly and cold northerly winds, and to have a south-facing aspect, as this gives most sunshine, heat and light.

Functions

The **function** of a settlement relates to its economic and social development and refers to its main activities (Figure 9.1). Normally, larger settlements will have more functions than smaller settlements. Large settlements tend to be **multi-functional** (i.e. they have several

KEY IDEAS

1 Settlements vary in site, size, function and structure.

2 Urbanisation is a global phenomenon and presents challenges to human populations.

Key words to know

Site
Situation
Wet-point site
Dry-point site
Nodal point
Aspect
Function
Multi-functional

Back to …

The New Wider World **pp34–35** for more information and examples of different sites and situations and photographs of different settlements.

functions) although one, or possibly two or three, is likely to be predominant, e.g. London is a capital city, Cambridge is a university town and Dover is a port.

In some cases, the original function may no longer be applicable, e.g. British towns no longer have a defensive function. In other cases, functions have changed over a period of time, e.g. a former South Wales mining town may now be a location for high-tech industry.

Figure 9.1 Types of function

		UK example	World example
Market towns	Originally collecting and distribution centres for surrounding farming area. Today they may service and process agricultural machinery and produce.	York	Winnipeg
Mining towns	Developed to exploit local mineral or fuels	Corby	Prudhoe Bay
Industrial-manufacturing	Where raw materials are processed into manufactured goods	Birmingham	Pittsburgh
Ports	Located on coasts, rivers and lakes for the movement of goods and people from land to sea, or vice versa	Southampton	Thunder Bay
Route centres	At the convergence of several natural routes or at nodal points resulting from economical development	Carlisle	Paris
Commercial	Providing the needs of industry and business	London	Hong Kong
Cultural/religious	Attracting people, perhaps for a short period, for educational and religious purposes	Cambridge	Rome
Administrative	Developed to control areas which may vary from a small region (county town) to a country (capital city)	Exeter	Brasilia
Residential	Where the majority of residents live but do not work	Telford	Marne-La-Vallee
Tourist resorts	Include spa towns, coastal and mountain resorts	Bath	Orlando

Back to ...

The New Wider World **p37** Figure 3.11 for information on the changing functions of Chester.

Check this!...

1 Define the terms 'site' and 'situation'.

2 What is the difference between a wet-point site and a dry-point site?

3 What is:
   a) a nodal point
   b) a bridging point?

4 Using an example, explain why the functions of a settlement may change over time.

For more information see 'Changes in settlement functions: Bristol' (GeoActive, April 2003).

Hierarchies

The term **hierarchy** refers to the arrangement of settlements within a given area in an 'order of importance' (Figure 9.2). Three different methods have been used to determine the 'order of importance' in the hierarchy:

1 Population size

Early attempts to determine a settlement hierarchy were based on size. Figure 9.2 lists the conventional hierarchy, as applied to Britain, in terms of types of settlement. Notice that the larger the settlement the fewer there are in number and the greater the distance between them.

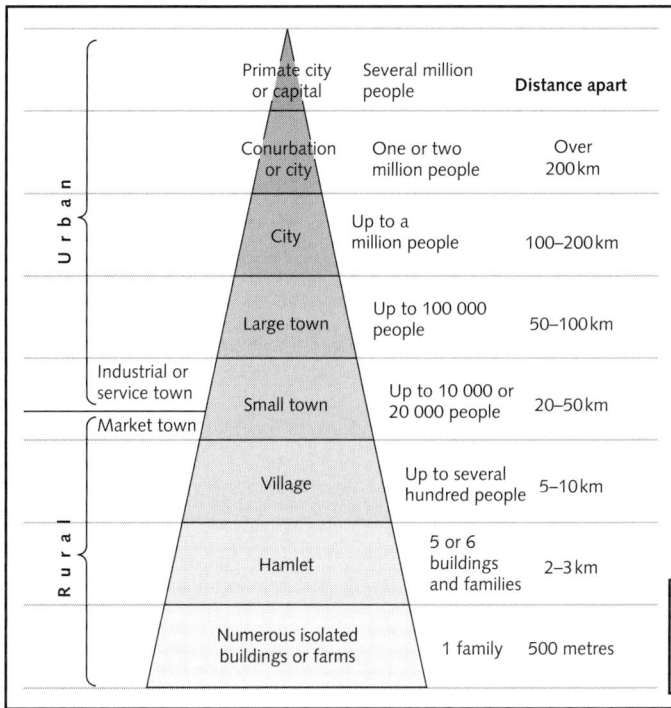

Figure 9.2 Hierarchy of settlements according to population size

2 Range and number of services

Villages provide a limited range and number of services. Services that do exist are those likely to be used daily (the village shop) or which reduce the need to travel to other places (a primary school). In Figure 9.3, where the hierarchy is based on services, each place in the hierarchy is likely to have all the services of settlements below them.

Figure 9.3 Hierarchy of settlements according to services

Capital	Cathedrals, government buildings, banking HQ, railway termini, museums and art galleries, large theatre, shopping centre, several universities, international airport
City	Large railway station, large shopping complex, cathedral, opticians and jewellers, large hospital, large football team, university, theatre, county hall, airport
Large town	Several shopping areas/arcades, hypermarket, railway station, bus station, hotels, banks, small hospital, small football team
Small town	Town hall, doctor, several churches/chapels, cafés and restaurants, small secondary school, railway station, several shops
Village	Church, post office, public house, shop for daily goods, small junior school, village hall
Hamlet	Perhaps none, or public telephone

3 Sphere of influence

The **sphere of influence**, or **market area**, is the area served by a particular settlement. The area of the sphere of influence depends upon the size and services of a town and its surrounding settlements, the transport facilities available and the level of competition from rival settlements.

Two main ideas should be noted:

- A **threshold population** is the minimum number of people needed to ensure that demand is great enough for a special service to be offered to the people living in that area.
- **Range** is the maximum distance that people are prepared to travel to obtain a service.

Back to ...

The New Wider World **pp38–39** for more information on settlement hierarchies.

Key words to know

Hierarchy
Sphere of influence (market area)
Threshold population
Range

Check this!...

1 Define the terms:
   a) hierarchy of settlement
   b) sphere of influence
   c) threshold population
   d) range.

2 Why does a village have fewer services than a town?

3 What is a 'central place'?

Each settlement which provides a service is known as a **central place**. A central place provides goods and services for its own inhabitants and to people living in the surrounding area. The larger the settlement the more services it will provide and the more people it will serve. Large towns and cities will therefore have larger spheres of influence than smaller villages.

Changes in time

Few settlements remain constant in size. Villages near to large cities tend to increase in size as they become more suburbanised. Villages in more isolated areas tend to lose population. So villages increasing in size are likely to gain additional or improved services while villages declining in size will lose services.

Urban land use models

Urban land use models in MEDCs

A model is a theoretical framework which helps to explain reality. Two of the earliest land use models to be put forward are shown in Figure 9.4a and b.

- Burgess claimed that in the centre of all towns and cities there was a **central business district (CBD)**. He suggested, initially using Chicago as his example, that towns grew outwards from this CBD in a **concentric** pattern. The resultant circles were based on the age of houses and the wealth of their occupants, with buildings becoming newer and the occupants more wealthy with increasing distance from the CBD.

- Hoyt proposed his model after the development of public transport. He suggested that urban areas developed in **sectors**, or wedges, alongside main transport routes into and out of a city. He also claimed that if, for example, industry and low-cost housing developed in one part of a town in the nineteenth century, then newer industry and modern low-cost housing would also locate in the same sector.

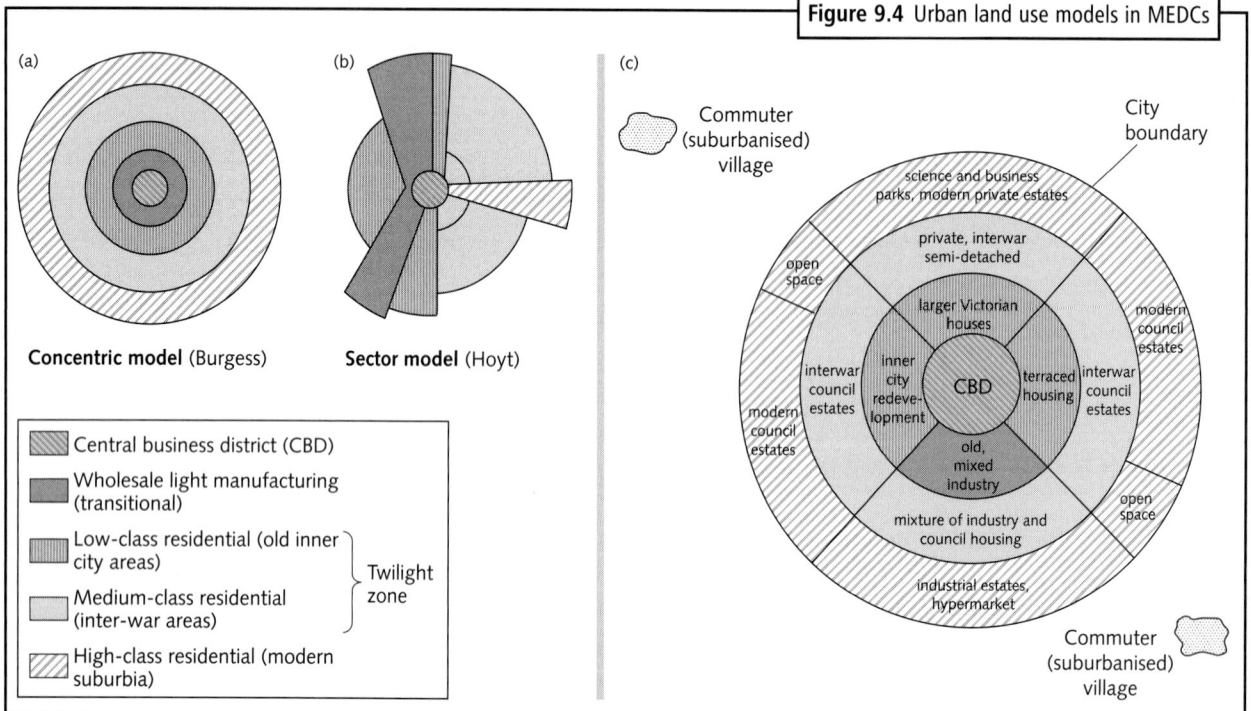

Figure 9.4 Urban land use models in MEDCs

(a) Concentric model (Burgess)

(b) Sector model (Hoyt)

Key:
- Central business district (CBD)
- Wholesale light manufacturing (transitional)
- Low-class residential (old inner city areas) ⎫
- Medium-class residential (inter-war areas) ⎬ Twilight zone
- High-class residential (modern suburbia)

(c) Commuter (suburbanised) village; City boundary; science and business parks, modern private estates; private, interwar semi-detached; larger Victorian houses; open space; modern council estates; interwar council estates; inner city redevelopment; CBD; terraced housing; interwar council estates; modern council estates; old, mixed industry; open space; mixture of industry and council housing; industrial estates, hypermarket; Commuter (suburbanised) village

Figure 9.4c is a more up-to-date model showing land use patterns and **functional zones** in a British city. You can see that it has both the concentric rings of the Burgess model and the sectors of the Hoyt model.

Key words to know

Functional zone
Accessibility

Urban land use and functional zones
Each of the zones shown in Figure 9.4 has a function.

The four main types of function are shops and offices, industry, housing, and open space. The location of each zone and the distribution of each functional zone are related to several factors.

- *Land values and space*   Land values are highest and available sites more limited in the CBD where competition for land is greatest. As land values decrease rapidly towards the urban boundary then both the amount of space and the number of available sites increase.
- *Age*   As towns developed outwards, the oldest buildings were near to the city centre and the newest ones in the outskirts.
- *Accessibility*   The CBD, where the main routes from the suburbs and surrounding towns meet, has been the easiest place to reach from all parts of the city although this ease is now often reduced due to increased congestion.
- *Wealth of the inhabitants*   The poorer members of the community tend to live in cheaper housing near to the CBD (with its shops) and the inner city (where most jobs used to be found). These people are less likely to be able to afford the higher transport (private or public) and housing costs of places nearer the city boundary.
- *Changes in demand*   Land use and function change with time. For example:
  a) Nineteenth-century industry was located next to the CBD whereas modern industry prefers edge-of-city sites.
  b) The main land use demand in the nineteenth century was for industry and low-cost housing. Today it is for industry, shops and better-quality housing, all in a more pleasant environment, and open space.

Back to ...

The New Wider World
pp42–43 for more
information on
urban land use models
in MEDCs.

Urban land use models in LEDCs
Cities in developing countries develop their own distinctive pattern in the same way that those in developed countries do (Figure 9.5) although this differs from the model for developed cities in several ways:

- Most of the better-off housing is located near to the city centre.
- The quality of housing decreases rapidly towards the city boundary where many people are forced to live as squatters in shanty settlements.
- Industry tends to locate along main roads leading into the city centre.

Figure 9.5 can be applied to São Paulo and other Brazilian cities.

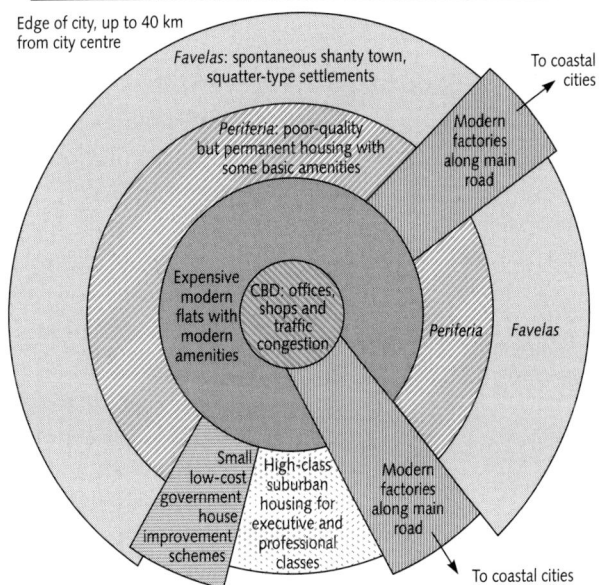

Figure 9.5 Model of land use structures and residential areas in a developing city

Edge of city, up to 40 km from city centre

Favelas: spontaneous shanty town, squatter-type settlements

Periferia: poor-quality but permanent housing with some basic amenities

Modern factories along main road

To coastal cities

Expensive modern flats with modern amenities

CBD: offices, shops and traffic congestion

Periferia   *Favelas*

Small low-cost government house improvement schemes

High-class suburban housing for executive and professional classes

Modern factories along main road

To coastal cities

Check this!...

1 What is an urban land use model?

2 List four functions that you would expect to find in a central business district.

3 Why would you expect to find the CBD at the centre of a town or city?

4 Explain the arrangement of land use in Figure 9.4c.

Key words to know

Slum clearance
Urban redevelopment
Urban renewal
Brownfield site
Urban sprawl

Back to ...

The New Wider World **pp44, 45 and 48** for more information on traditional land use in the CBD and inner city areas.

The characteristics of urban zones in MEDCs

The CBD

The CBD became the most accessible part of a town or city because most road and rail routes met there. Its accessibility made it a prime site for several types of land use which increasingly competed with each other to locate here. This competition, together with the limited amount of space that was available, pushed up land values.

- The major land users in the CBD became shops, banks and offices.
- They located here mainly because they needed to be as accessible to the largest number of people possible and only they could afford the high cost of land.
- Even so, many shops and offices have located in high-rise buildings to offset high rates and rent.
- Shops tended to be large department stores and specialist shops which had a high turnover, a high profit margin or a large threshold population.
- In time, CBDs became increasingly congested which reduced their accessibility.

Old inner city areas

- Most inner city areas developed along with industry in the nineteenth century.
- Nineteenth-century houses were built as close together as possible creating a high density.
- Most houses were built in long straight rows and in terraces.
- Few amenities were provided either in the house (no indoor toilet, bathroom, running water, sewerage or electricity) or around it (no gardens or open space).
- Dampness, the lack of sanitation, the closeness of the people and smoke from the nearby factories all combined to reduce life expectancy.

Over the years, attempts have been made to improve living conditions by:

1 bulldozing large areas (**slum clearance**) and building high-rise flats (**urban redevelopment**)

2 improving existing properties (**urban renewal**).

Industry

Inner cities were characterised by large factories built during the Industrial Revolution. Since then many factories have been forced to close either due to:

- a lack of space for expansion and modernisation, or
- narrow, congested roads.

Some factories have been left empty while others have been pulled down to leave large areas of derelict land (**brownfield sites**).

Suburbia

Suburbia was the name given to areas that developed during the inter-war period (1920s and 1930s). Urban areas grew rapidly at this time due mainly to the introduction of public transport, the increase in popularity of the private car and, in London, the extension of the Underground. This outward growth, known as **urban sprawl**, led to the growth of numerous private, car-dependent suburbs.

- Many inter-war houses were semi-detached and now correspond to Burgess's zone of medium-cost housing.
- As each new housing estate was built, its distance from the CBD and its shops increased. This led to the growth of small shopping parades within the estate.
- Apart from individual houses having their own gardens, many inter-war estates had their own small park or play area.
- The inter-war estates rarely had industry nearby and so residents, especially in London, had to travel long distances to their place of work – a process known as **commuting**.

The rural–urban fringe

After the 1960s, urban sprawl continued with land on the rural–urban fringe being used mainly for:
- one of two types of housing – private estates or outer-city council housing
- new industrial and/or trading estates.

Most of the new private estates had low-density, high-quality housing, many of which were large and detached. They were built either in a cul-de-sac or along winding roads that were usually tree-lined and relatively free of traffic. The estates also contained areas of open space.

Outer city council estates were created mainly during the 1950s and 1960s when local councils cleared the worst of the slums from the inner city-areas. Many of the evicted residents were re-housed on what were then **greenfield** edge-of-city **sites**. Accommodation usually consisted of a mixture of high-rise tower blocks, low-rise flats and single-storey terraces.

By the end of the twentieth century, an increasing number of land users saw the rural–urban fringe as the ideal location for future development.

There is, however, an increase in conflict between those who wish to see the economic development and extension of the urban area and those who wish to protect the rural environment that surrounds it (Figure 9.6).

The characteristics of urban zones in LEDCs

In most cities in developing countries there is an extreme contrast between the living conditions of the well-off, who usually live near to the city centre, and those of the poor, who are forced to live towards the city boundary. This contrast can be seen in São Paulo.

São Paulo is the largest, richest and most industrialised city in Brazil. Its rapid growth has been accompanied by increased social and economic segregation, with the poor being relegated to the city's periphery with its shanty settlements (**favelas**) and tenement slums (**corticos**). With the city's population having grown from 7 million in 1970 to 16.6 million by 2000, the authorities have had an almost impossible task in providing sufficient housing and services.

Housing for the well-off

These people live in expensive housing ranging from elegant apartment complexes to Californian-style detached houses. These properties, protected by security guards, are located near to the CBD where most of the residents work and shop.

Check this!...

1 What is the difference between urban redevelopment and urban renewal?

2 Explain why housing in inner city areas is at a higher density than housing in the suburbs.

3 a) What is a brownfield site?
   b) why are many brownfield sites located in inner cities?

For further information see 'Inner-city regeneration: Hulme, Manchester' (GeoActive, September 2001).

Key words to know

Commuting
Greenfield site
Favelas
Corticos

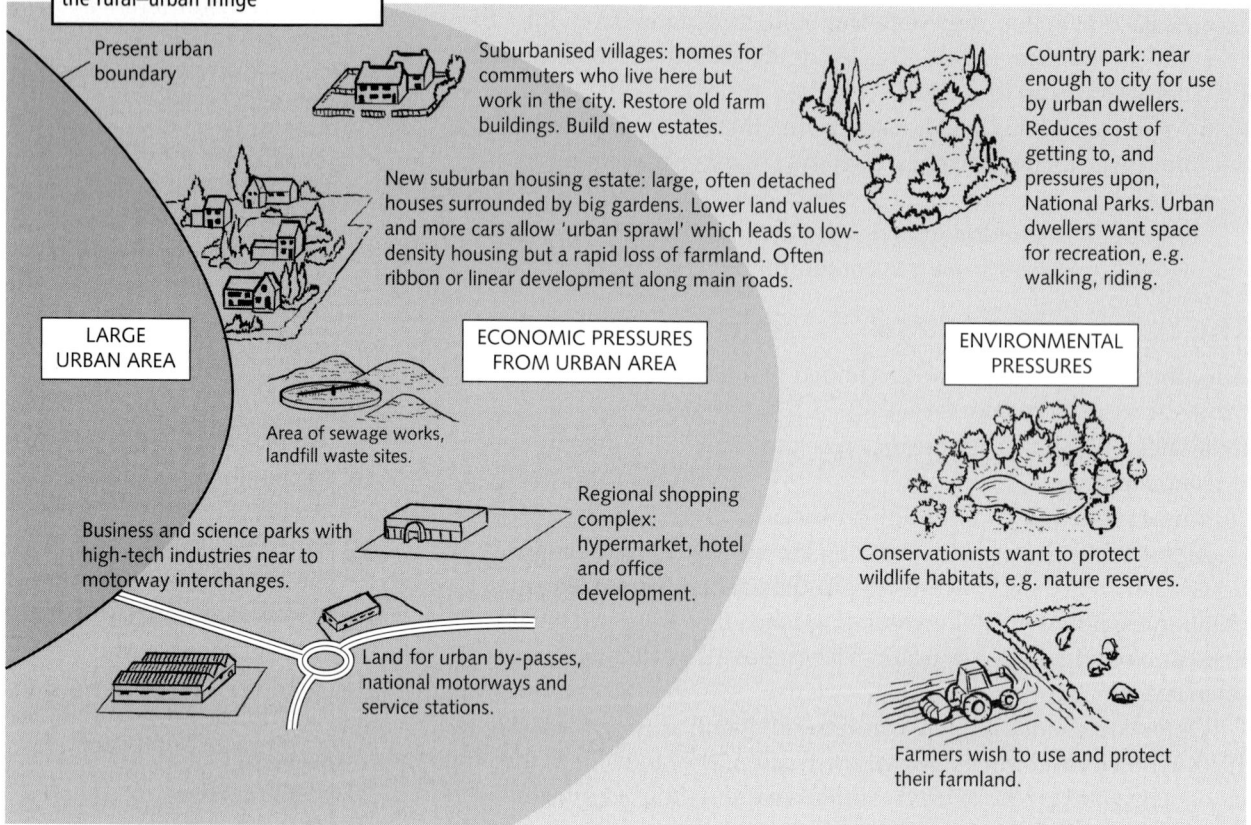

Figure 9.6 Competition for land at the rural–urban fringe

Present urban boundary

Suburbanised villages: homes for commuters who live here but work in the city. Restore old farm buildings. Build new estates.

Country park: near enough to city for use by urban dwellers. Reduces cost of getting to, and pressures upon, National Parks. Urban dwellers want space for recreation, e.g. walking, riding.

New suburban housing estate: large, often detached houses surrounded by big gardens. Lower land values and more cars allow 'urban sprawl' which leads to low-density housing but a rapid loss of farmland. Often ribbon or linear development along main roads.

LARGE URBAN AREA

ECONOMIC PRESSURES FROM URBAN AREA

ENVIRONMENTAL PRESSURES

Area of sewage works, landfill waste sites.

Business and science parks with high-tech industries near to motorway interchanges.

Regional shopping complex: hypermarket, hotel and office development.

Conservationists want to protect wildlife habitats, e.g. nature reserves.

Land for urban by-passes, national motorways and service stations.

Farmers wish to use and protect their farmland.

Check this!...

1 List three ways in which suburbs differ from inner cities.

2 Define:
   a) urban sprawl
   b) commuting.

3 What is a greenfield site?

4 Explain why attitudes about the use of land in the rural–urban fringe differ between various groups of people.

For further information see 'Urban sprawl, green belt policies and brownfield sites' (GeoActive, September 2000), and 'Land use pressures in Manchester's urban fringe' (GeoActive, January 2000).

Back to ...

The New Wider World **pp46, 47 and 49** for more information on the characteristics of suburbia and the rural–urban fringe.

Housing for the poor (favelas)

Many of São Paulo's poor live in shanty settlements. This is sometimes on vacant space next to modern factories or alongside main roads leading to the city, but is usually on the outskirts of the city. These people are 'squatters' and have no legal right to the land they occupy. Favelas often develop on steep hillsides which are liable to landslides, or on badly drained, unhealthy valley floors.

- The housing is often a collection of primitive shacks made from any material available – wood, corrugated iron, cardboard or sacking.
- Most houses lack such basic amenities as electricity, clean running water, toilets and main sewerage.
- Any empty space between houses will soon be occupied either by later migrants or, as there is no refuse collection, with rubbish.
- Favelas are overcrowded and have a high housing density.

Housing improvements in São Paulo

Two local government-assisted schemes in São Paulo aimed at improving the quality of life in a favela are:

Community housing projects

Low-cost improvements

- Existing homes may be improved by rebuilding the houses with cheap and quick and easy-to-use breeze-blocks.
- A water tank on the roof collects rainwater and is connected to the water supply and, in turn, to an outside wash basin and an indoor bathroom/toilet.
- Electricity and mains sewerage are added.

Self-help schemes

- Groups of people are encouraged to help build their own homes.
- The local authority will then provide breeze-blocks and roofing tiles, and the group provides the labour.
- The money which this saves the authorities can be used to provide amenities such as electricity, a clean water supply, tarred roads and a community centre.

São Paulo, like most other large cities, sees sustainable urban development as the best hope for the future. Self-help schemes along with recycling of refuse and increasing investment in public transport are important aspects of sustainable development.

2 Urbanisation is a global phenomenon and presents challenges to human populations

Growth of world cities

Urbanisation is the proportion of people living in towns and cities. Although most developed countries have experienced urbanisation since the early 1800s, the process has only gathered pace in developing countries since the 1950s (Figure 9.7). Today:

- the developed countries of North America, Western Europe and Oceania are usually those with the highest level of urbanisation
- the developing countries in Africa and South-east Asia often have the lowest level of urbanisation
- South America, the most economically advanced of the developing continents, is an exception (an anomaly), as several of its countries have an urban population exceeding 75 per cent.

There are two additional factors to consider:

1 The growth of very large cities with a population exceeding 1 million. In 1850 there were only two 'million' cities – London and Paris. This number increased to 70 by 1950 and, according to an international website, to an estimated 405 in 2002. A new term, **megacity**, refers to places with a population in excess of 10 million.

2 Prior to 1950, most of the 'million' cities were in developed countries and in temperate latitudes north of the Equator (i.e. 40° to 55°N in Europe and North America). Since then there has been a dramatic increase in 'million' cities in developing countries, the majority of which lie within the tropics.

Back to ...

The New Wider World
pp82–83
for more information on differences in residential areas in São Paulo.

Check this!...

1 Describe the differences in housing between the well-off and the poor in São Paulo.

2 What has been done to try to improve housing conditions for the poor in São Paulo?

Key words to know

Urbanisation
Megacity

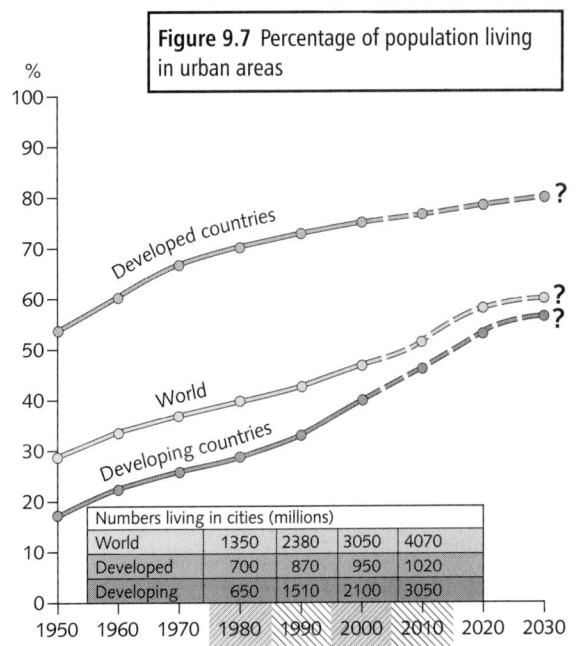

Figure 9.7 Percentage of population living in urban areas

Numbers living in cities (millions)				
World	1350	2380	3050	4070
Developed	700	870	950	1020
Developing	650	1510	2100	3050

Key words to know

Rural–urban migration
Rural push factors
Urban pull factors

Back to …

The New Wider World **pp78–79** for more information on the growth of world cities.

Back to …

The New Wider World **pp80–81** for more information on the causes of urbanisation and Figure 5.6, the extract from the Brandt Report.

Figure 9.8 gives the rank order of the world's largest cities over a period of years. In 1970 half of these cities were located in the industrialised, developed countries in North America and Europe. By 2000, however, 15 of the 19 largest cities were in developing countries in Asia, Latin America and Africa.

Since the 1970s the growth rate of most cities in developed countries has slowed down, with some having even declined. At present the fastest-growing cities are in southern Asia. The population of Dhaka (Bangladesh) doubled between 1985 and 1995 and that of Karachi, Delhi and Bangkok between 1985 and 2000.

Figure 9.8 The world's largest cities (population in millions)

Rank order	1970	1985	2000
1	New York 16.5	Tokyo 23.0	Tokyo 27.0
2	Tokyo 13.4	Mexico City 18.7	São Paulo 16.6
3	London 10.5	New York 18.2	New York 16.4
4	Shanghai 10.0	São Paulo 16.8	Mexico City 15.9
5	Mexico City 8.6	Shanghai 13.3	Mumbai (Bombay) 15.4
6	Los Angeles 8.4	Los Angeles 12.8	Shanghai 15.3
7	Buenos Aires 8.4	Buenos Aires 11.6	Beijing 12.7
8	Paris 8.4	Rio de Janeiro 11.1	Los Angeles 12.5
9	São Paulo 7.1	Kolkata (Calcutta) 9.2	Kolkata 11.8
10	Moscow 7.1	Mumbai 8.2	Seoul 11.7 Jakarta 11.7

Check this!…

1 Define:
   a) urbanisation
   b) megacity.

2 Make a list of the world's megacities and the countries in which they are located.

3 Describe and explain the global pattern of urbanisation.

Urban growth

The movement from country areas to towns and cities is called **rural–urban migration**. In developing countries, movement to the city is partly due to **rural push** and partly due to **urban pull** (Figure 9.9). (Also see the Migration section in Chapter 8 of this book.)

In most developing countries the 'pull' factors are often greater than the 'push' factors. Figure 9.9 presents the perceptions of the city held by many rural families, i.e. what they think, expect or were led to believe the city is like. The reality is often very different. As many of the new arrivals are unlikely to have much, if any, money they will be unable to buy or rent a house – even if one was available – and will probably have to make a temporary shelter using cheap or waste materials.

Rural 'push' factors	Urban 'pull' factors
Drought	Better paid jobs in industry
Overgrazing by animals: soil erosion	Higher salaries
Lack of job opportunities	Better housing / schools / hospitals / shops and entertainment
Large families: • not enough land for each heir • many do not own any land • high birth rate	More reliable sources of food
Poor seed / poor tools / little fertiliser / low output / insufficient food / malnutrition	
Remoteness: • lack of services • lack of investment	
Pests eat crops and cause ill-health	
Floods	
Crops for export not local use	
Farm machinery replaces workers: unemployment	

Figure 9.9 Rural 'push' factors and urban 'pull' factors

The problems of urbanisation and possible solutions

Cities in both MEDCs and LEDCs exhibit a range of problems due to the ways in which they have grown.

Case Study

Osaka–Kobe

Back to ...

The New Wider World pp70–73 for the case study of Osaka–Kobe, twin cities which are located in the Kansai region of the island of Honshu.

Using your case study

Use this case study to discuss a) the problems faced by a large urban area in Japan, an MEDC, and b) some of the planning measures undertaken to try to solve these problems. Make sure that you can:

1 draw a simple sketch map to show the location of Osaka–Kobe
2 discuss the physical problems of a) a restricted area of low land, and b) a location on a plate boundary
3 comment on population growth and density
4 explain problems relating to housing, high land values and transportation
5 discuss the problems relating to the twin cities' status as a major industrial region
6 outline the attempts to improve urban organisation in Osaka–Kobe under the headings a) housing, b) port development, c) industry, d) transport, e) pollution and f) environment.

Update

For up-to-date information use the link on *The New Wider World Coursemate* website.

Learn it!

a) What are the physical geography problems that Osaka–Kobe has faced?

b) Outline the human problems that have developed as the urban area has grown.

c) How have the urban planners tried to solve these problems?

Case Study

Rio de Janeiro

Back to ...

The New Wider World pp86–88 for the case study of problems in Rio de Janeiro, a city in the developing world.

Using your case study

Use this case study to discuss the problems faced by a large urban area in Brazil, an LEDC. Make sure that you can:

1 draw a simple sketch map to show the location of Rio de Janeiro
2 discuss the physical constraints on urban growth
3 comment on population growth and density
4 explain problems relating to housing, crime, traffic and pollution
5 discuss the attempts to solve some of Rio's problems.

Update

Google News can be a good source for recent developments in Rio.

Learn it!

a) Describe the location of Rio de Janeiro.

b) What are the main problems affecting people in the city?

c) What has been done to try to solve these problems?

Back to ...

The New Wider World **pp58–59** for more information on changes in the CBD.

Check this!...

1 Give four rural push factors to explain why large numbers of people have left the countryside in LEDCs.

2 What are the urban pull factors that have attracted people to urban areas in LEDCs?

Urban change

Changes in the CBD

By the 1970s most CBDs were suffering from the following problems:

- many of the older properties were in need of improvement and modernisation
- the narrow streets were often congested
- the large volume of traffic caused air pollution
- there was insufficient space for car parks, and buses found it difficult to keep to time
- increasingly taller buildings were constructed to try to offset the high rates and rents
- larger shops moved out and re-located on less congested sites
- smaller shops were forced to close as the area became increasingly expensive
- there was a need for modern, carefully planned city centres that considered social, economic and environmental needs.

Recent changes

The first major change to occur in most city centres was the creation of **pedestrianised zones**. Later came the development of **shopping malls**.

More recently has come an increased demand for a more relaxing atmosphere within the city centre and an increase in leisure amenities, especially in the evenings.

Changes in old inner city areas

During the 1980s, the government set up **Urban Development Corporations (UDCs)** in an attempt to regenerate those inner city areas that had large amounts of derelict and unused land and buildings. UDCs had the power to acquire, reclaim and use land and to convert buildings. By encouraging private-sector investment, UDCs were able to promote industrial, housing and community developments.

The first two UDCs, the London Docklands Development Corporation (LDDC) and the Merseyside Development Corporation (MDC), came into existence in 1981. They were followed, between 1986 and 1993, by 10 more in England and one in Wales. The English UDCs were wound up in 1998 and the Welsh UDC in 2000.

Changes at the rural–urban fringe

In an attempt to control urban growth, **green belts** were created by Act of Parliament in 1947.

- A green belt was defined as an area of land around an urban area where development was to be severely restricted and where the open character of the countryside was to be preserved for farming and recreation.
- Planning permission was normally not meant to be granted for development proposals but in reality planners often came under

Key words to know

Pedestrianised zones
Shopping malls
Urban Development Corporation (UDC)
Green belt

Check this!...

1 Discuss three problems found in most CBDs in recent decades.

2 Explain the planning decisions that have been taken to improve the efficiency and environment of CBDs.

London Docklands

Back to ...

The New Wider World pp60–61 for the case study on London Docklands.

Using your case study

Use this case study as an example of the comprehensive redevelopment of an inner city area. Make sure that you can:

1 draw a simple sketch map of London Docklands

2 briefly describe the decline of the docks

3 discuss the environmental, economic and social regeneration of the area

4 show awareness of conflicting opinions about redevelopment

5 suggest how sustainable development has been an important aspect of the regeneration of the Docklands.

Update

For more information use the link on *The New Wider World Coursemate* website.

Learn it!

a) Why did the docks in east London decline?

b) Why was the LDDC set up?

c) Comment on redevelopment in terms of:
i   housing
ii business
iii transport
iv leisure
v   the environment
vi health and education.

---

considerable pressure to release land for more housing, jobs and roads.

● Most large British cities are surrounded by a green belt.

By the end of the twentieth century, there was increasing competition for land at the rural–urban fringe. The main reasons are that at the fringe there is:

● cheaper land
● less traffic congestion and pollution
● a better road infrastructure that gives easier access to surrounding settlements and other urban areas
● a more pleasant environment with more open space.

Places at the rural–urban fringe that have not yet been built upon are known as **greenfield sites**. These sites, still used for farming or recreation, are under constant threat for:

● housing development as urban sprawl continues and nearby villages become suburbanised
● science and business parks, and office development
● retail parks and regional shopping centres
● hotels and conference centres
● road development schemes, including motorways and urban by-passes
● sewage works and landfill sites for urban waste
● recreational areas such as country parks, playing fields and new sports stadiums.

Suburbanised villages

In parts of the developed world there has been a reversal of the movement to large urban areas, with groups of people moving out into surrounding villages. This is known as **counterurbanisation** and has

Key words to know

Greenfield site
Counterurbanisation

Check this!...

1 What is a green belt?

2 Make a list of the land uses that are commonly found in the rural–urban fringe.

3 Why has competition for land in the rural–urban fringe increased?

Settlement 81

led to changes in the characteristics of these settlements and to them being called **suburbanised** (Figure 9.10). Some are also known as **commuter** or dormitory **settlements** as many of their residents have to travel to nearby towns and cities for work.

Characteristic	Original village	Suburbanised village
Population structure	An ageing population; mostly born in village; labouring/manual groups	Young/middle-aged married couples with children; very few born in village; wealthy professional/executive groups; some wealthy retired people
Community/social	Close-knit community (many people were related) have lived here for several generations	Local community swamped by newcomers; division between local people and newcomers; may be deserted during the day (commuters absent)
Housing	Detached, stone-built houses/cottages with slate/thatch roofs; some farms, many over 200 years old; old barns	Many new detached houses, semi-detached houses and bungalows; renovated barns and cottages; expensive estates
Services	Village shop; small junior school; public house; village hall; church	More shops; enlarged school; modern public houses; restaurants; garage
Transport	Bus service (limited); some cars; narrow, winding roads	Good bus service (unless reduced by private car); most families have one or two cars; improved roads
Employment	Farming and other primary activities (forestry, mining); low-paid local jobs	New light industry (high-tech and food processing); good salaries; local shops and transport
Environment	Quiet, relatively pollution-free	Increase in noise and pollution, especially from traffic; loss of farmland/open space

Figure 9.10 Changes in a suburbanised village

Back to …

The New Wider World **pp64–66**
for more information on
suburbanised villages and
urban sprawl.

Brownfield and greenfield sites

Britain is short of houses. Estimates suggest that 4.1 million new homes could be needed by 2016. The question then is, 'Where will all these new houses be built?' In 1998 the government announced that:

- 50 per cent would be on brownfield sites
- 50 per cent would be on greenfield sites.

After a major public outcry to 'save the countryside', the government revised the figures to 60 per cent brownfield and 40 per cent greenfield.

Why build on brownfield sites?

Groups such as the Council for the Protection of Rural England (CPRE) and Friends of the Earth argue that:

- there are already three-quarters of a million unoccupied houses in cities that could be upgraded

- a further 1.3 million could be created by either subdividing large houses or using empty space above shops and offices

- according to the database, 1.3 million homes could be built on vacant and derelict land and another 0.3 million by re-using old industrial and commercial premises

- urban living reduces the need to use the car and maintains services, especially retailing, in city centres.

The government assumes that 80 per cent of the demand for new houses will come from single-parent families who prefer, or need, to live in cities.

Why build on greenfield sites?

Developers claim that:

- most British people want to own their own home, complete with garden, set in a rural, or semi-rural location

- people are healthier and generally have a better quality of life in rural areas

- at present, for every three people moving into cities (almost 160 000 a year), five move out into the countryside (250 000 a year)

- greenfield sites are cheaper to build on than brownfield sites.

Figure 9.11 Brownfield and greenfield sites

Figure 9.11 gives some of the arguments as to why some groups of people would prefer most of the new developments to be on brownfield sites and why other groups favour greenfield sites.

Transport in urban areas

It is the widespread use of the car that is bringing traffic in many large cities to a standstill and which is a major cause of urban environmental, economic and social problems (Figure 9.12).

Commuting

Urban traffic problems are often at their worst during the early morning and late afternoons when commuters are travelling to and from work. The increase in car ownership and the improvements in the road network mean that commuters can live further from their place of work. This has led to large **commuter hinterlands** (the areas around large cities) where commuters live.

A more recent trend is a 'reversed' flow of commuters. This group includes:

- the less skilled and poorly paid, together with members of ethnic minorities, who live in low-cost inner city housing and who travel long distances to their place of work on edge-of-city industrial and retail parks
- some well-paid people who have moved into regenerated areas near to the city centre but who work on science and business parks on the rural–urban fringe.

Check this!...

1 How has counterurbanisation changed the character of villages within commuting distance of major urban areas?

2 Discuss the arguments for and against building on brownfield sites and greenfield sites.

For further information see 'Wilmington: The development of a commuter village' (GeoActive, April 2000).

Key words to know

Commuter hinterland

Figure 9.12 The impact of traffic on urban areas

Why has traffic in urban areas increased?	• Greater affluence and increased car ownership. Many families even have two cars. • People commuting to work and travelling to city centres or edge of cities for shopping and entertainment • Reduction in public transport at expense of private cars • Increased volume of road freight, e.g. delivery lorries
What are the damaging effects of increased traffic in urban areas?	**Environmental** • Air pollution from vehicle exhausts – especially in large cities like Los Angeles, Athens and Tokyo. Some cities, e.g. London, issue daily air quality forecasts/reports. • Noise pollution from cars, lorries and buses • Visual pollution of motorways • Loss of land for road widening and car parks
	Economic • Congestion, especially at peak times (rush hour), in central London, even though many people travel by public transport, the average speed of traffic in 2000 was the same as it was in 1900, i.e. 18 km/hr • Time wasted sitting in traffic jams and in gridlock conditions, looking for parking spaces and avoiding unloading lorries • Cost of building and maintaining roads; delays due to repairs of roads and underground utilities (electricity, gas and water) • Cost of petrol/diesel and the use of a non-renewable resource (oil)
	Social • Danger of accidents • Health problems: increase in stress both to drivers and pedestrians; respiratory illnesses (e.g. asthma) caused by fumes and low-level ozone • Destruction of property for new or wider roads and car parks • Damage to foundations caused by traffic vibration • Overcrowding on commuter trains and buses
How can transport systems in urban areas be managed to reduce the damaging effects of increased traffic?	• Exclude, reduce or accommodate traffic by schemes such as traffic-free zones, park and ride schemes and urban motorways • Try to reduce pollution, especially from vehicle exhausts • Improve public transport, e.g. supertrams in Sheffield, Metrolink in Manchester, metros in Tyne and Wear, Singapore and Hong Kong. These rapid transport systems have resulted from improved technology. • Smaller, more affordable and sustainable schemes, e.g. park and ride, cycle tracks, traffic calming, speed cameras • Future schemes? Road tolls, charges to drive into large cities.

Everybody agrees that traffic problems in urban areas need drastic solutions, but people are less likely to agree on what those solutions might be. Future plans must be sustainable, i.e. they should improve people's mobility without damaging the environment in which they live.

Case Study

Out-of-town shopping centres

Back to ...

The New Wider World p63 for the case study of the MetroCentre in Gateshead, an out-of-town shopping centre.

Using your case study

Use this case study as an example of urban sprawl and change at the rural–urban fringe. Make sure that you can:

1 draw a simple sketch map to show the location of the MetroCentre

2 explain why out-of-town sites became popular for retailing
3 discuss the advantages of this particular site
4 describe the facilities of the MetroCentre.

Update

For up-to-date information on the MetroCentre use the link on *The New Wider World Coursemate* website.

Learn it!

a) Describe the location of the MetroCentre.

b) List the advantages of the MetroCentre site.

Case Study

Lille – an integrated traffic system

Back to ...

The New Wider World pp68–69 for the case study on Lille – an integrated traffic system.

Using your case study

Use this case study to show how a new, planned traffic system has helped to solve many of the transport problems of this French city. Make sure that you can:

1 describe the location of Lille
2 comment briefly on its history as a major industrial area
3 explain the different aspects of Lille's integrated transport system.

Learn it!

a) Why was the TGV station built in the centre of the city rather than on the outskirts as first planned?

b) How does the TGV station link with other transport routes in Lille?

1 Look at Figure 9.13.

   a Give three functions you would expect
      to find in a CBD.   (3)

   b Why do these functions locate in
      CBDs?   (3)

   c Explain why land values decrease with
      distance from the CBD.   (3)

   d What are the main differences in
      housing between inner cities and
      suburbs?   (4)

   e Describe and explain the land uses
      usually found in the rural–urban fringe.
                                                     (4)

2 With reference to one or more examples,
   describe and explain the housing
   problems in LEDC cities.   (8)

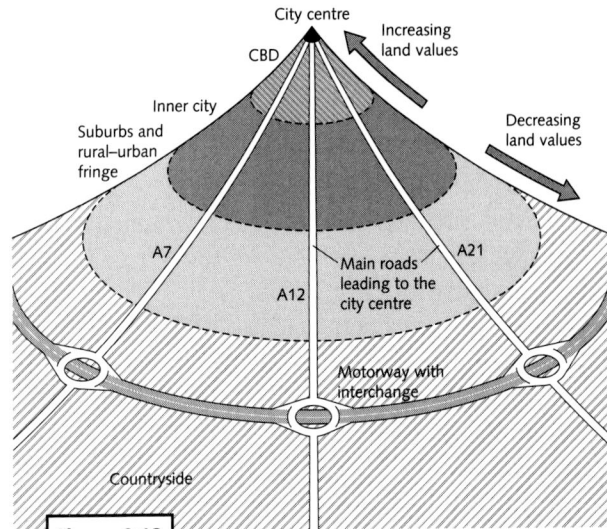

Figure 9.13

City centre
Increasing land values
CBD
Inner city
Suburbs and rural–urban fringe
A7
A12
A21
Main roads leading to the city centre
Decreasing land values
Motorway with interchange
Countryside

Back to ...

The New Wider World website
to check your answers to the
Exam Practice question.

EXAM TIPS

A good answer to question 2 will include detailed references to
the city (cities) selected (population figures, names of favelas,
etc.) rather than vague generalisations which could apply to any
LEDC city.

KEY IDEAS

1 Farming as a system.

2 Agricultural activity varies from place to place.

3 Agricultural activity is influenced by many factors.

4 Agricultural change can have both advantages and disadvantages.

Key words to know

System
Inputs
Processes
Outputs

1 Farming as a system

Farming systems

Farming is an industry and operates like other industries. It is a **system** with **inputs** into the farm, **processes** which take place on the farm and **outputs** from the farm (Figure 10.1).

The farmer as a decision maker

Each individual farmer's decision on what crops to grow or animals to rear, and which methods to use to maximise outputs, depends on an understanding of the most favourable physical and economic conditions for the farm (Figure 10.2). Sometimes the farmer may have several choices. On other occasions the choice may be limited by extreme physical conditions or economic and political pressures.

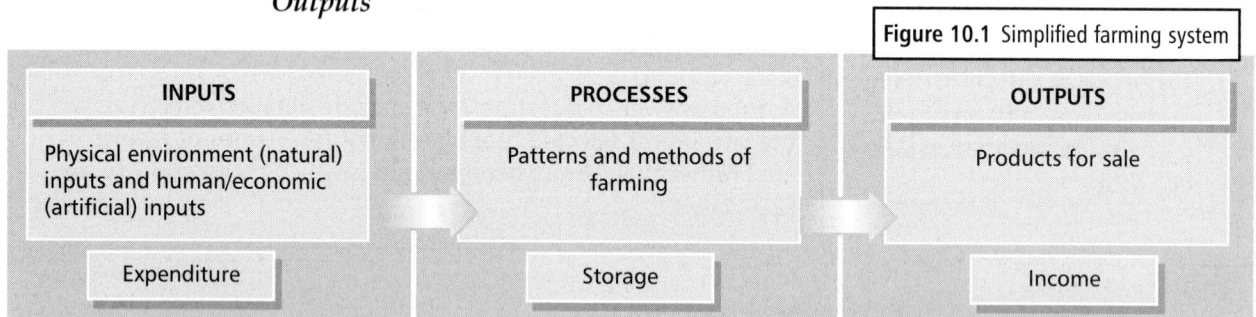

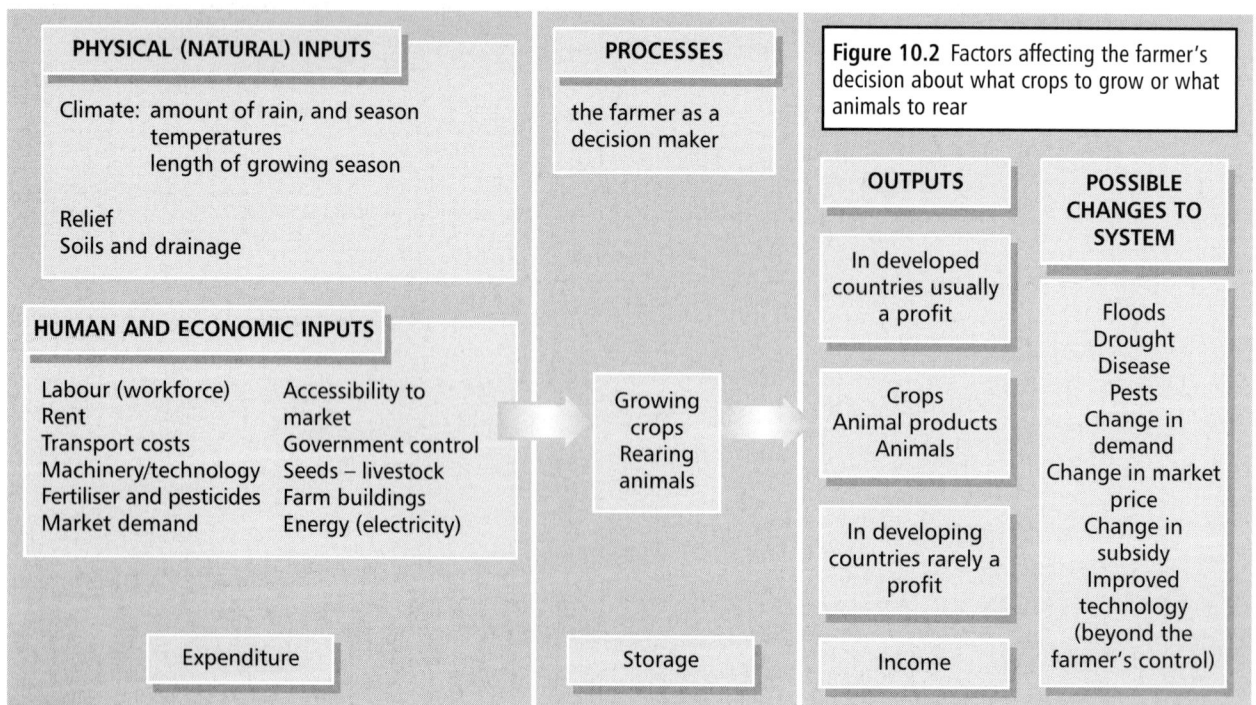

Figure 10.1 Simplified farming system

INPUTS	PROCESSES	OUTPUTS
Physical environment (natural) inputs and human/economic (artificial) inputs	Patterns and methods of farming	Products for sale
Expenditure	Storage	Income

Figure 10.2 Factors affecting the farmer's decision about what crops to grow or what animals to rear

PHYSICAL (NATURAL) INPUTS

Climate: amount of rain, and season
temperatures
length of growing season

Relief
Soils and drainage

PROCESSES

the farmer as a decision maker

HUMAN AND ECONOMIC INPUTS

Labour (workforce)	Accessibility to market
Rent	
Transport costs	Government control
Machinery/technology	Seeds – livestock
Fertiliser and pesticides	Farm buildings
Market demand	Energy (electricity)

Growing crops
Rearing animals

OUTPUTS

In developed countries usually a profit

Crops
Animal products
Animals

In developing countries rarely a profit

POSSIBLE CHANGES TO SYSTEM

Floods
Drought
Disease
Pests
Change in demand
Change in market price
Change in subsidy
Improved technology (beyond the farmer's control)

Expenditure	Storage	Income

2 Agricultural activity varies from place to place

Farming in the UK

Factors affecting farming

The location of different types of farming at all scales depends upon the interaction of three factors: physical (environmental); human (social) and economic; and political (Figure 10.3).

Check this!...

1 List three physical and three human inputs to farming.

2 Name two processes that occur on farms.

3 Give three outputs produced by farms.

Back to …

The New Wider World **pp96–97** for more information on farming systems.

Figure 10.3 Factors affecting the location and distribution of farming types in the UK

Physical (environmental factors)	
Relief and altitude	Usually the flatter and the more low-lying the land, the more efficient and commercial is the farm (arable in East Anglia). Output tends to decrease as the land gets steeper and higher and farming becomes less commercial and more extensive (pastoral in the Lake District).
Soils	The deeper and richer the soil, the more intensive and commercial the farming (alluvium of the Fens). Ideally soils should be well drained yet capable of retaining water.
Temperature/sunshine	In Scotland, summers are cool and the growing season is too short for most cereals. Moving south, temperatures, the amount of sunshine and the length of the growing season all increase. Aspect is an important local factor (maximum sunlight, protection against frost and wind).
Rainfall/water supply	Areas with adequate and reliable rainfall throughout the year tend to produce good grass for rearing animals (western Britain). Drier areas to the east grow cereals (East Anglia) and fruit (Kent).
Human (social) and economic inputs	
Land ownership/tenure	Many British farmers own their own farms but some are tenant farmers (the former are usually more commercial). A small, but increasing, number are run by processing companies (frozen foods in East Anglia).
Size of farms/fields	Farms increase in size as larger, more efficient farmers buy up smaller, less successful farms. Field size has also increased, especially where hedgerows have been removed (eastern England). The EU encourages larger farms and larger fields.
Competition for land	Many traditional farming areas, especially near the rural–urban fringe, are under threat from urban sprawl and the demand for new roads, industry, housing and recreation.
Transport and markets	Perishable goods need to be produced near to markets for freshness, and bulky goods near to markets due to their weight. Fruit and vegetables (market gardening) are grown near most large urban areas.
Capital (money)	By world standards the UK is well-off, so farmers can find money to improve their farm buildings and machinery and to buy fertiliser and good-quality seed and animals
Mechanisation/ technology	The increased use of labour-saving machinery and computers increase outputs but reduces the need for farm workers. Farms in the south and east tend to be more mechanised than those in the north and west.
Political factors	
Government/ EU policies	Governments have provided grants for new stock and machinery and subsidies to guarantee a fixed income. This now comes from the EU's Common Agricultural Policy (CAP).
Variable inputs	Farmers are vulnerable to changes in Government/EU policies, market prices and market demand. They are also affected by changes in weather (floods, drought and frost) and by disease (foot and mouth, potato blight).

Distribution of the main farming types in the UK

Figure 10.4 shows that there are five main types of farming in the UK.

- **Arable farms** are found in the east where summers are sunny and warm, there is less rain, the land is low-lying and flatter, soils are deep and fertile, transport systems are good, and where there are large urban markets nearby.

Key words to know

Arable farming

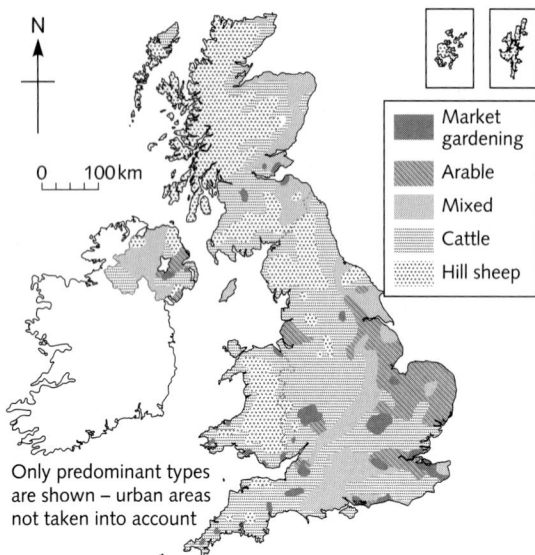

Figure 10.4 Farming types in the UK

Map legend:
- Market gardening
- Arable
- Mixed
- Cattle
- Hill sheep

N

0   100 km

Only predominant types are shown – urban areas not taken into account

- Cattle farms are important where summers are cool and winters are mild, there is plenty of rain throughout the year, the land is low-lying and relatively flat, transport is good and urban markets are within easy reach.
- Hill sheep farms predominate in those parts of Scotland, Wales and northern England where the land is high and steep, soils are poor, temperatures are cool, rainfall is heavy, transport systems are poorly developed and urban markets are not within easy reach.
- **Mixed farming** tends to be found in a transition zone between the crop-growing areas in the east and the animal-rearing areas in the west.
- **Market gardening** is important near large urban areas and where transport links are good. As some market garden produce can be grown undercover in artificial conditions (flowers, tomatoes), human factors tend to be more important than physical factors.

Key words to know

Mixed farming
Market gardening

Back to ...

The New Wider World **pp98–99** for more information and photographs on farming in the UK.

Check this!...

1 What do you understand by the following terms:
   a) arable farming
   b) mixed farming
   c) market gardening?

2 Look at Figure 10.4. Describe the distribution of farming types in the UK.

3 State three ways in which physical factors have affected farming in the UK.

3 Agricultural activity is influenced by many factors

Case Study

Arable farming in East Anglia

Back to ...

The New Wider World p101 for the case study on arable farming in East Anglia.

Using your case study

Use this case study as an example of a) commercial farming and b) the extensive farming of cereals. East Anglia contains the largest cereal farms in the UK, hence the extensive nature of farming in this region. A very high level of investment means that farming in this region is very highly mechanised and capital intensive. Make sure that you can:

1 locate East Anglia
2 show understanding of the inputs, processes and outputs of East Anglian farms

3 explain why average farm size is so large compared to most other parts of the UK
4 explain the very high level of mechanisation of farming
5 discuss the reasons for recent changes in farming in the region.

Update

See 'UK farm case study: An ICT investigation' (GeoActive, April 2001).

Learn it!

a) Why can farming in East Anglia be described as both extensive and commercial?

b) Describe the relief, climate and soils of the region.

c) List the main crops produced in East Anglia.

Farming in Denmark

Back to ...

The New Wider World pp102–103 for the case study on farming in Denmark.

Using your case study

Use this case study as an example of farming systems in an EU country. The least intensive farms in Denmark are in the west with the most intensive farms to the east due mainly to differences in soil type. EU membership has had a significant impact on Danish farming. Make sure that you can:

1 draw a simple sketch map of Denmark to show the three main farming zones
2 describe the physical factors which affect farming
3 explain the co-operative system
4 discuss recent changes to Danish farming, including the impact of EU membership
5 describe a typical Danish farm.

Update

For up-to-date information on Danish farming use the link on *The New Wider World Coursemate* website.

Learn it!

a) Describe the influence of relief, climate and soils on farming in Denmark.

b) Explain how the co-operative system of farming operates.

c) Discuss the impact of EU membership on farming in Denmark.

Subsistence rice farming in the Lower Ganges Valley

Back to ...

The New Wider World pp112–113 for the case study on subsistence rice farming in the Lower Ganges Valley.

Using your case study

Use this case study as an example of subsistence farming in an LEDC. The cultivation of rice in this region is recognised as a sustainable form of farming. Because of high population density and very low incomes, farming is very labour intensive. Make sure that you can:

1 draw a simple sketch map of the Lower Ganges Valley
2 describe the physical inputs into farming, including the distribution of temperature and rainfall over the year
3 explain the human inputs into farming
4 comment on the processes and outputs
5 discuss recent changes in farming – land reform, the Green Revolution, appropriate technology.

Case study links

This case study has links with Chapter 6, Weather and climate – the interaction between people and environments.

Update

See 'Monsoon – case study of the Ganges Plain' (GeoActive 298, September 2003).

Learn it!

a) Describe the location of the Lower Ganges Valley.

b) How have physical factors affected agriculture in the region?

c) Discuss the characteristics of subsistence farming here.

4 Agricultural change can have both advantages and disadvantages

Changes in farming

In the UK

Farming, like other industries, is dynamic and is always changing. Sometimes changes may have advantages while other changes may be detrimental to the farmer, the people who need feeding, or the local countryside (i.e. economic, social and environmental consequences).

Some recent changes in the UK include the following:

- Fields have become larger, especially in eastern England, due to the removal of hedgerows.
- Farms have increased in size as smaller, less profitable units have been taken over.
- Improvements in technology include better machinery, although this reduces the need for manual labour, and the introduction of computers.
- Before 1992, farmers were given **subsidies** which guaranteed them a minimum price for their produce. This meant that farmers tended to overproduce. Since 1992, there has been a progressive reduction in the level of subsidies paid.
- Dairy farmers can no longer produce as much milk as they would like but are given a **quota** by the EU. The quota means the UK now produces less milk.
- Farmers, especially those growing cereals, are encouraged to **set aside** part of their farm. If they wish to continue to receive subsidies they must take 15 per cent of their farmland out of cultivation – that is, they are paid not to produce crops.
- In the last few years most farmers have seen a rapid decline in their income. This has been due to a combination of factors such as the high value of the pound, a fall in the price of farm produce, a reduction in subsidies and the loss of exports due to BSE and foot and mouth. Many have had to diversify and seek income from other sources (Figure 10.5).

Key words to know

Subsidies
Quota
Set aside

Figure 10.5 Diversification of farm use

Recreation	Accommodation	Environment and wildlife
• Creation of new golf courses (possible conflict as a development on green belt land) • Mountain-bike access and motorcycle scrambling (conflict with other countryside users) • Riding stables; trout farms	• Campsites and caravan parks (conflict over visual appearance) • Holiday villages for families to stay in, surrounded by activity opportunities (conflict with local people)	• Restoration of wetland ecosystems/re-creation of ponds • Planting trees/creating new areas of woodland • Creation of nature trails, complete with information boards

In the EU

Common Agricultural Policy (CAP)

The basic aims of the CAP when it was set up in 1962 were to:

- create a single market in which agricultural products could move freely
- make the EC more self-sufficient by giving preference to EC produce and restricting imports from elsewhere
- give financial support to EC farmers which included guaranteed prices (subsidies), and therefore a guaranteed market, for unlimited production
- increase the average field size, farm size and farmers' income.

Figure 10.6 A balance sheet showing some of the achievements and some of the problems still to be faced by the EU's Common Agricultural Policy

Achievements	Problems
Achieved a larger measure of self-sufficiency. This reduces the costs and unreliability of imports.	An increase in food prices, especially in the net importing EU countries of Germany and the UK.
Created higher yields due to input of capital for machinery and fertiliser.	Creation of food surpluses – the so-called 'mountains and lakes'.
In NW Europe the average farm size has increased almost to the recommended level.	Selling of surplus products at reduced prices to East European countries (causes both political and economic opposition).
Amalgamation of fields – in parts of France the number of fields has been reduced to one-eighth of the 1950 total.	Increased gap between the favoured 'core' agriculture regions and the periphery.
Production has changed according to demands, e.g. less wheat and potatoes and more sugar beet and animal products.	Peripheral farm units still very small and often uneconomic.
Subsidies to hill farmers have reduced rural depopulation. Poorer farmers gain an opportunity to receive a second income by working in nearby factories ('5 o'clock farmers') or from tourism.	High costs of subsidies.
	'Industrial' countries such as the UK object to 70% of the EU budget being spent on agriculture.
Higher income for farmers.	'5 o'clock farmers' spend insufficient time on their farms. In France 15%, and in Germany 30% of farmers have a second income.
Subsidies have reduced the risk of even higher unemployment in such rural areas as the Mezzogiorno.	Destruction of hedges to create larger fields destroys wildlife and increases the risk of soil erosion.
Reduced reliance on crops imported from developing countries which themselves have a food shortage.	By reducing imports from developing countries the latter's main source of income is lost thus increasing the trade gap between the two areas.
A surplus one year can offset a possible crop failure in another year.	

1970s and 1980s – increasing concerns over the CAP

- 70 per cent of the EC's budget was spent supporting farming.
- Large surpluses were created – the so-called cereal, butter and beef 'mountains' and the wine and milk 'lakes'.
- Imports were subject to duties to make them less competitive with EC prices. This handicapped the less economically developed countries.
- Although EC farms became larger and more efficient, only the most prosperous farmers benefited – often at the expense both of farmers on the periphery and of the environment.

1992 – agricultural reform

Five aims were defined. These were:

1 To increase the EU's agricultural competitiveness by concentrating on quality rather than quantity and in training young farmers.
2 To stabilise markets and match supply with demand by reducing subsidies and quotas on commodities which had a surplus.
3 To ensure a fair standard of living for farmers by providing income support and early retirement to those in less favoured and marginal areas.
4 To maintain jobs on the land and reduce migration to the towns by introducing alternative forms of land use.
5 To protect and enhance the natural environment by paying farmers to 'set aside' land or change the use of their land.

Figure 10.6 summarises the achievements and the remaining problems of the CAP.

Check this!...

1 List five ways in which farms in the UK have changed in recent decades.

2 a) Why have many farms diversified in recent years?
   b) Discuss the ways in which farms can diversify.

3 Discuss the characteristics of the Common Agricultural Policy.

Back to ...

The New Wider World **pp106–107** for more information on changes in farming in the UK and the EU.

Farming and the environment

The use of chemicals

Key words to know

Pesticide
Fertiliser
Leached
Eutrophication
Organic farming

- **Pesticides** are chemicals applied to crops to control pests, diseases and weeds. Without pesticides, yields of cereal crops could be reduced by up to 45 per cent within two years. Unfortunately, pesticides can also affect non-harmful wildlife such as bees.
- **Fertiliser** is a mineral compound containing one or more of the six main nutrients needed for successful plant growth. The average soil rarely contains sufficient nutrients, especially nitrogen, phosphorus and potassium. Chemical fertiliser replaces nutrients that have been removed from the soil. There is considerable concern when nitrate is washed (**leached**) through the soil into:
  - rivers where it causes a rapid growth of algae and other plants which use up oxygen leaving insufficient for fish life – the process of **eutrophication**
  - underground domestic water supplies where it can be harmful to human health.
- Phosphate, released from farm slurry can also pollute water supplies.

The loss of wildlife habitats

The intensification of farmland during the second half of the twentieth century led to loss of important wildlife habitats such as wetlands, moorlands and hedgerows.

The removal of hedgerows

Modern farming, especially in arable areas, uses large machines that are easier to work if the fields are large. So, between 1945 and 1990 over 25 per cent of Britain's hedges were cleared to create larger fields.

However, hedgerows provide an important environment for many types of wildlife. They also reduce wind speed and their roots bind the soil, reducing erosion.

Organic farming

Since the mid-1980s a small, but increasing, number of British farmers have turned to **organic farming**. Compared with conventional farming, organic farming:

- is self-sustaining in that it does not misuse soil and water resources
- favours natural fertiliser such as animal and green manure, and mineral fertiliser such as fish and bonemeal, instead of using chemical fertiliser and pesticides. These natural fertilisers put organic matter back into the soil, enabling it to retain moisture during dry periods, allowing better drainage and aeration during wetter spells, and reducing the risk of soil erosion and exhaustion.
- is less likely to harm the environment as there are no nitrates to run off into rivers and no pesticides to harm wildlife.

However, organic farming has its problems:

- Using no chemical fertiliser means that, initially, yields are lower.
- Using no pesticide means more weeding has to be done.
- Farmers have to wait several years before they can market their goods as 'organic'.
- The extra work means organic produce is more expensive for the shopper to buy.

Genetically modified (GM) crops

GM crops were first developed for commercial production in 1996 (Figure 10.7). Two-thirds of GM crops are produced in the USA, and 99 per cent by the USA, Argentina, Canada and China. GM crops include corn (maize), oilseed rape, sugar beet and soya beans. Although seen by scientists as a solution to food shortages in developing countries, their production in the UK is being strongly opposed by conservation groups.

Irrigation

Irrigation needs careful and expensive management to avoid **salinisation** (Figure 10.8). If water, which contains salts, is channelled on to the land, it must also be drained away. If not, the soil will become increasingly saline. Estimates suggest that nearly half the former irrigated land in places like Pakistan, the Nile Valley and California is now affected by salinisation.

Check this!...

1 How has the use of farm chemicals affected the environment?

2 Describe the characteristics of organic farming.

3 What are genetically modified crops?

4 Explain the differences between well managed and badly managed irrigation.

For further information see 'Modern agricultural practices and their impact on the environment' (GeoActive, January 2001).

Genetic modification

Genetic modification involves taking genes from one species and inserting them into another to give it new qualities, such as improved resistance to pests, heat or cold. Advocates say the technique is sound, safe and can help to increase crop yields or improve animal breeds. Detractors argue that there is a risk that genes engineered in plants and animals will be transferred to species in the wild, irreversibly altering the world's ecosystems.

Figure 10.7 From *Geographical Magazine*, March 2002

Key words to know

Genetically modified (GM) crops
Salinisation
Malnutrition

Food supply and malnutrition

- **Malnutrition** is caused by deficiencies in diet, either in amount (quantity) or type (quality).
- Until the 1970s, it was believed that malnutrition resulted from the population growing more rapidly than food supplies.
- Today it is attributed to poverty, as large numbers of the world's population are unable to afford to buy an adequate diet.

Back to ...

The New Wider World **pp108–109** for more information on farming and the environment.

Figure 10.8 Salinisation

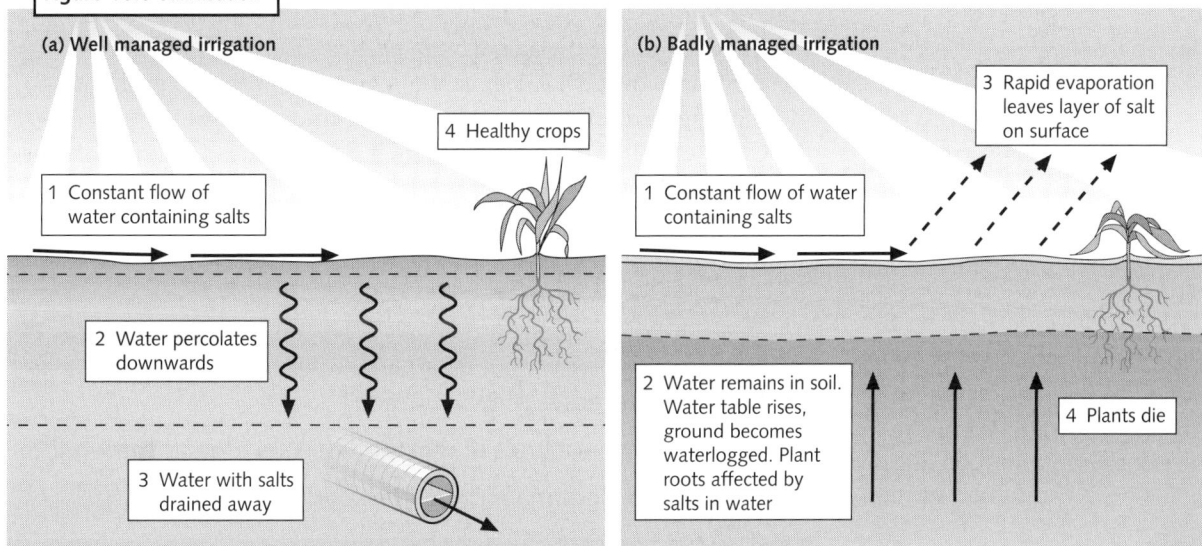

(a) Well managed irrigation

4 Healthy crops

1 Constant flow of water containing salts

2 Water percolates downwards

3 Water with salts drained away

(b) Badly managed irrigation

3 Rapid evaporation leaves layer of salt on surface

1 Constant flow of water containing salts

2 Water remains in soil. Water table rises, ground becomes waterlogged. Plant roots affected by salts in water

4 Plants die

- While malnutrition results in starvation only under extreme conditions, it does reduce people's capacity to work and their resistance to disease.
- In children, it can retard mental and physical development, and cause illness.

Dietary energy supply (DES)

DES is the number of calories per capita available each day in a country. Between 1970 and 2000 there was an increase in available food supplies per capita in every developing region except sub-Saharan Africa (Figure 10.9). It has been estimated that in most developing countries, especially those within the tropics, a person consuming less than 2350 calories per day is likely to experience chronic malnutrition. In 2000, 20 per cent of people living in these countries were suffering from chronic malnutrition. Their numbers have increased from 435 million in 1975 to 600 million in 2000. This increase is mainly due to human factors (e.g. civil wars, political instability and international debt) rather than to physical causes (e.g. natural disaster such as drought).

Key words to know

Dietary energy supply (DES)
Marasmus
Kwashiorkor

Figure 10.9 Percentage of chronically underfed, 1970–2000

Region	1970	1980	1990	2000
Sub-Saharan Africa	35	36	37	42
Near East and North Africa	23	10	5	12
Central America and Caribbean	24	15	13	11
South America	17	12	12	9
South Asia	34	30	24	22
East Asia	35	22	17	16
China	46	28	16	14
All developing regions	36	26	20	19

Malnutrition in children

Low-birthweight babies are children born weighing less than 2500 g, their low weight being attributed to maternal malnutrition. Low birthweight children are often prone to a shortened lifetime full of health problems, including retarded development and susceptibility to disease.

Children under the age of 5 are particularly susceptible to malnutrition. In 2000, 35 per cent of children in this age-group in the developing world were considered to be underweight.

Children fall ill either because their diet contains too few proteins, which are particularly important during early stages of growth, or too few calories. The two major protein deficiency diseases are **marasmus** and **kwashiorkor**.

Back to …

The New Wider World
pp110–111 for more information on food supply and malnutrition.

Check this!…

1 What are the causes of malnutrition?

2 How does the incidence of malnutrition vary around the world?

3 What impact does malnutrition have on children?

Soil erosion

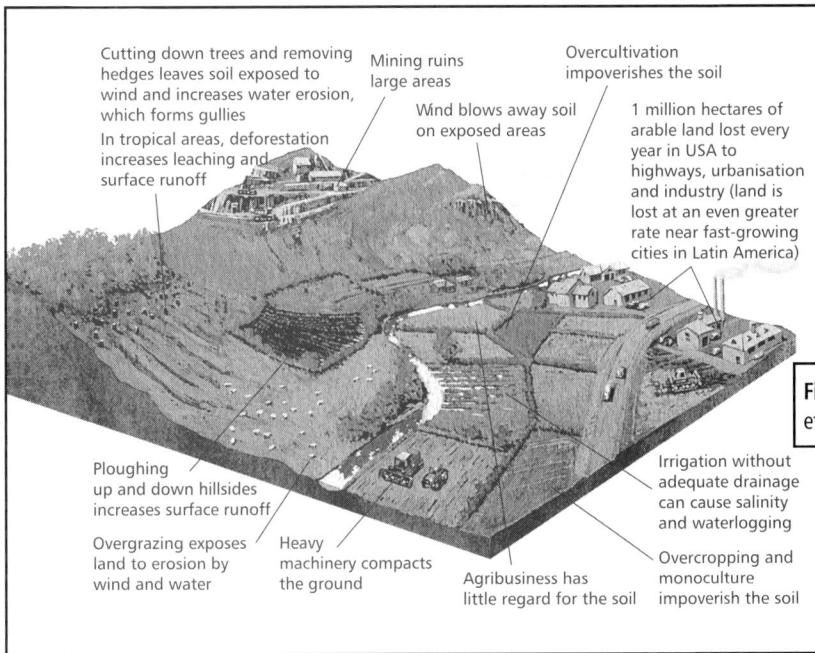

Cutting down trees and removing hedges leaves soil exposed to wind and increases water erosion, which forms gullies

In tropical areas, deforestation increases leaching and surface runoff

Mining ruins large areas

Wind blows away soil on exposed areas

Overcultivation impoverishes the soil

1 million hectares of arable land lost every year in USA to highways, urbanisation and industry (land is lost at an even greater rate near fast-growing cities in Latin America)

Ploughing up and down hillsides increases surface runoff

Overgrazing exposes land to erosion by wind and water

Heavy machinery compacts the ground

Agribusiness has little regard for the soil

Irrigation without adequate drainage can cause salinity and waterlogging

Overcropping and monoculture impoverish the soil

Figure 10.10 Some causes and effects of soil erosion

It can take up to 400 years for 1 cm of soil to form, and between 3000 and 12 000 years to produce a sufficient depth for farming. At present, only 11 per cent of the Earth's land surface is classified as prime agricultural land.

So far the increase in population has been matched by increases in food production but the capacity of the soil to produce enough food is being stretched to the limit. The problem is aggravated where human development is actually ruining this essential resource, through erosion or degradation (Figure 10.10).

Erosion is most rapid in areas where:
- the land is mismanaged
- the protective vegetation cover is removed
- there is rapid population growth
- the land is steep
- climatic conditions are extreme, especially if rainfall is seasonal, comes as downpours or is unreliable.

Removal of vegetation

Most damage to the soil results from the removal of vegetation. Where vegetation is removed there will be no:
- replacement of humus
- interception of rain by plants
- roots to bind the soil together, so the surface will be left exposed to rain and wind.

Overcultivation and overgrazing

- **Overcultivation** occurs when crops are grown on the same piece of land year after year.
- **Overgrazing** is where there are too many animals for the amount of grass available.

Overcultivation and overgrazing tend to occur mainly in developing countries where the increase in population means that the land is in constant use. Local farmers neither have the money to buy fertiliser for their land, nor the time to allow a resting (fallow) period for the soil to recover naturally.

Key words to know

Overcultivation
Overgrazing

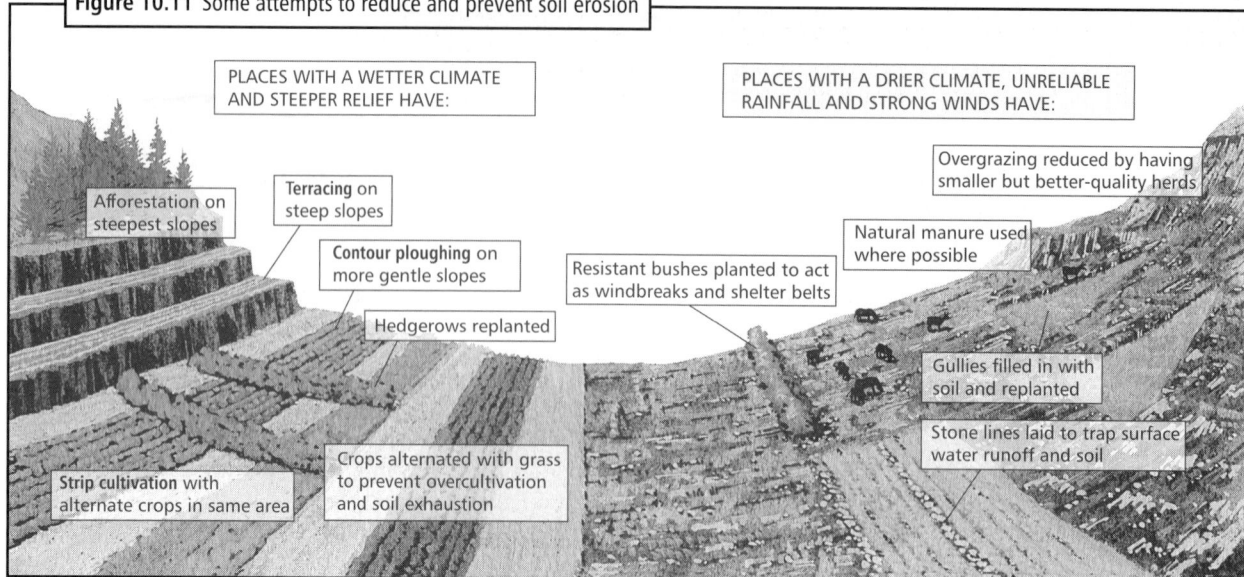

Figure 10.11 Some attempts to reduce and prevent soil erosion

PLACES WITH A WETTER CLIMATE AND STEEPER RELIEF HAVE:

Afforestation on steepest slopes

Terracing on steep slopes

Contour ploughing on more gentle slopes

Hedgerows replanted

Strip cultivation with alternate crops in same area

Crops alternated with grass to prevent overcultivation and soil exhaustion

PLACES WITH A DRIER CLIMATE, UNRELIABLE RAINFALL AND STRONG WINDS HAVE:

Overgrazing reduced by having smaller but better-quality herds

Natural manure used where possible

Resistant bushes planted to act as windbreaks and shelter belts

Gullies filled in with soil and replanted

Stone lines laid to trap surface water runoff and soil

Back to ...

The New Wider World
pp254–255 for more
information on soil erosion
and soil management.

Soil management

Soil is a sustainable resource, but only if it is carefully managed. Various techniques (Figure 10.11) can reduce soil erosion by over 50 per cent. The best protection against soil erosion is to prevent it from being exposed to wind and rain. Trees, bushes and grass can act as windbreaks, improve water retention and bind the soil together.

Check this!...

Key words to know

Contour ploughing
Strip cultivation
Terracing

1 Make a list of the main causes of soil erosion.
2 Define:
   a) overcultivation
   b) overgrazing.
3 Discuss the ways in which the soil can be managed more sustainably.

For further information see 'Soil erosion: Nepal and the Himalayas' (GeoActive, September 1999).

EXAM PRACTICE

1 a Give an example of farming that is both commercial and intensive. (1)

   b Define:
   i   subsistence farming
   ii extensive farming. (4)

2 a How do physical factors affect farming in the UK? (6)

   b Describe and explain two changes that have occurred in farming in Britain over the last 30 years. (6)

3 With reference to examples:

   a describe the main causes of soil erosion

   b explain how soils can be managed to reduce erosion. (8)

Back to ...

The New Wider World website
to check your answers to the
Exam Practice question.

EXAM TIPS

For question 2b there are two 'command' words, describe and explain. Ensure that your answer has a sensible balance between the two.

Industry

11

1 Industry as a system

The industrial system

Industry, like farming, can be regarded as a system. There are inputs into a factory (or industry), processes that take place in the factory, and outputs from the factory (Figure 11.1). For a firm to be profitable and to remain in business, the value of its outputs must be greater than the cost of its inputs. Some of the profit should then be re-invested, e.g. in modernising the factory and introducing new technology.

KEY IDEAS

1 Industry as a system.

2 Industrial activity can be classified.

3 Industrial location is influenced by many factors.

4 Industrial changes may have both advantages and disadvantages.

Figure 11.1 The industrial system

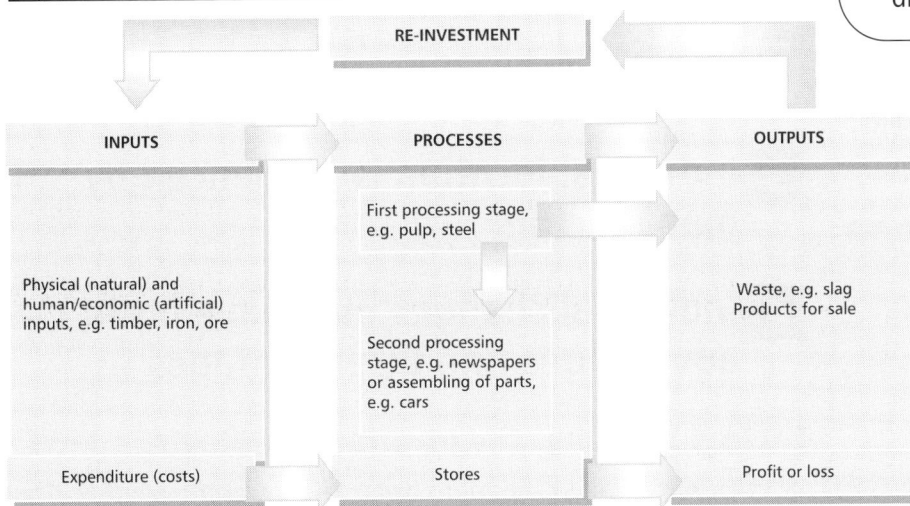

RE-INVESTMENT

INPUTS	PROCESSES	OUTPUTS
Physical (natural) and human/economic (artificial) inputs, e.g. timber, iron, ore	First processing stage, e.g. pulp, steel	Waste, e.g. slag Products for sale
	Second processing stage, e.g. newspapers or assembling of parts, e.g. cars	
Expenditure (costs)	Stores	Profit or loss

PHYSICAL FACTORS

Raw materials The bulkier and heavier these are to transport, the nearer the factory should be located to the raw materials. This was even more important in times when transport was less developed.

Power – energy This is needed to work the machines in the factory. Early industry needed to be sited near to fast-flowing rivers or coal reserves, but today electricity can be transported long distances.

Natural routes River valleys and flat areas were essential in the days before the railway, car or lorry.

Site and land Although early industry did not at first take up much space, it did need flat land. As the size of plant increased (e.g. steelworks), more land was needed. Ideally such sites should be on low-quality farmland where the cost of purchase is lower. Last century many sites were in today's 'inner city' areas whereas now they tend to be on edge-of-city 'greenfield' locations.

- In the nineteenth century it was physical factors such as the source of raw materials (e.g. iron ore) and sources of energy (e.g. coal) which determined industrial locations.

Figure 11.2 Factors affecting the location of industry in the UK

HUMAN AND ECONOMIC FACTORS

Labour This includes both quantity (large numbers in nineteenth-century factories) and quality (some areas demand special skills as technology develops).

Capital (money) Early industry depended on wealthy entrepreneurs. Now banks and governments may provide the money.

Markets The size and location of markets have become more important than the source of raw materials.

Transport Costs increase when items moved are bulky, fragile, heavy or perishable.

Economies of scale Small units may become unprofitable and so merge with, or are taken over by, other firms.

Government policies As governments tend to control most wealth, they can influence industrial location.

Improved technology Examples are facsimile (fax) machines and electronic mail.

Leisure facilities Both within the town and the surrounding countryside, leisure activities are becoming more desirable.

- By the late twentieth century, the three main factors deciding industrial location were more likely to be the nearness to a large market, the availability of skilled labour, and government policies.

2 Industrial activity can be classified

Key words to know

Primary
Secondary
Tertiary
Quaternary

Classification of economic activities

- **Primary** industries extract raw materials directly from the Earth or sea. Examples include farming, fishing, forestry and mining.
- **Secondary** industries process and manufacture the primary products, e.g. steelmaking and furniture manufacture. They also include the construction industry and the assembly of component parts made by other secondary industries, e.g. car assembly.
- **Tertiary** industries provide a service. These include education, health, office work, retailing, transport and entertainment.
- **Quaternary** industries provide information and expertise. They include the relatively new micro-electronics industries.

The proportion of people working in each of the primary, secondary and tertiary sectors is called the employment structure. There are, of course, important links between the sectors. For example, the crops produced by farms (primary) are used in food processing factories (secondary) to make the products that we buy in supermarkets (tertiary).

Check this!...

1 Why can a factory be seen as a system?

2 Name four examples of secondary industries.

3 Give two examples of the way in which the different sectors of industry are linked.

3 Industrial location is influenced by many factors

4 Industrial changes may have both advantages and disadvantages

Factors affecting the location of industry

Before a factory is built, decisions have to be made as to which will be the best site for its location. It is unlikely that any site will have all the factors that are listed as advantages in Figure 11.2. Where several sites are available, the individual or company must decide which is likely to provide the best location. In many cases this decision is determined by predicting which site will give the greatest profit.

Location of industry in the UK

Figure 11.3 shows the location and distribution of Britain's traditional heavy industries. Most of these industries were established in the nineteenth century. Their growth was based on:

- the use of coal
- the development of technology to process local and imported raw materials
- the creativity of the people
- the ability to export manufactured goods.

Consequently the major industrial areas were either on Britain's coalfields or in coastal ports located on deep-water estuaries.

The location, distribution and type of Britain's present-day manufacturing industry have changed considerably (Figure 11.4). For a variety of reasons (Figure 11.5) coal mines began to close in the 1920s, textile mills in the 1960s, shipyards in the 1970s and steelworks in the 1980s. Modern replacement industries, many of which are high-tech and connected with electronics, employ fewer people and are often located well away from the traditional manufacturing areas. They are said to be **footloose** as, not being tied to raw materials, they have a relatively free choice of location.

For further information see 'Industrial development in the West Midlands' (GeoActive, September 2002).

Central Lowlands of Scotland
Coal mining, steel, textiles, shipbuilding, engineering

Cumbria
Coal mining, steel, shipbuilding

Belfast
Textiles, shipbuilding, engineering

North Wales
Coal mining, steel

North Staffs
Pottery

West Midlands
Engineering, car assembly

South Wales
Coal mining, steel, tinplate, engineering

North-east England
Coal mining, steel, chemicals, shipbuilding, engineering

Lancashire
Textiles, shipbuilding, chemicals, coal mining, engineering

Yorks, Derby, Notts
Coal mining, textiles, steel, cutlery, footwear

East Midlands
Textiles

London
Clothing, port industries, food processing

Bristol
Food processing

0   100 km

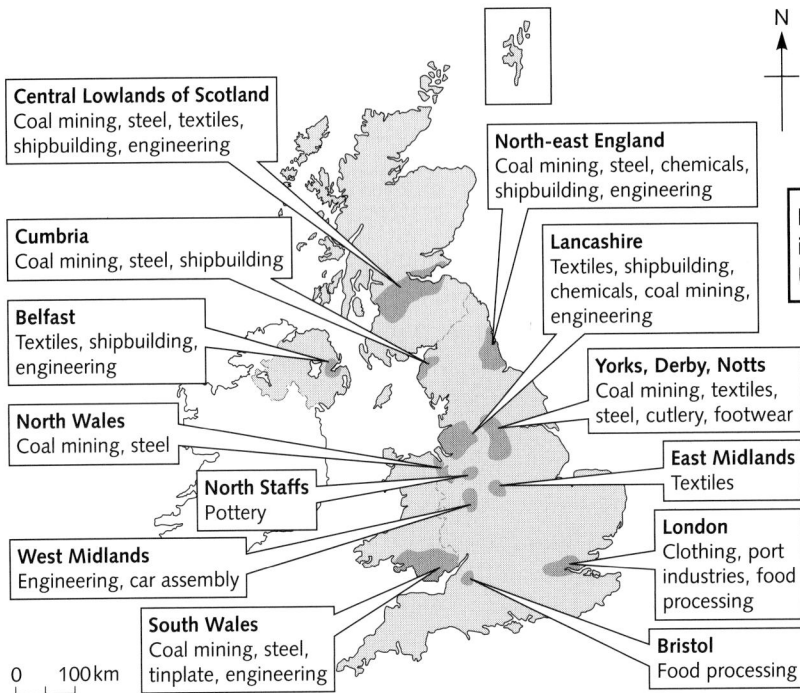

Figure 11.3 Traditional industrial areas in the UK (before 1970)

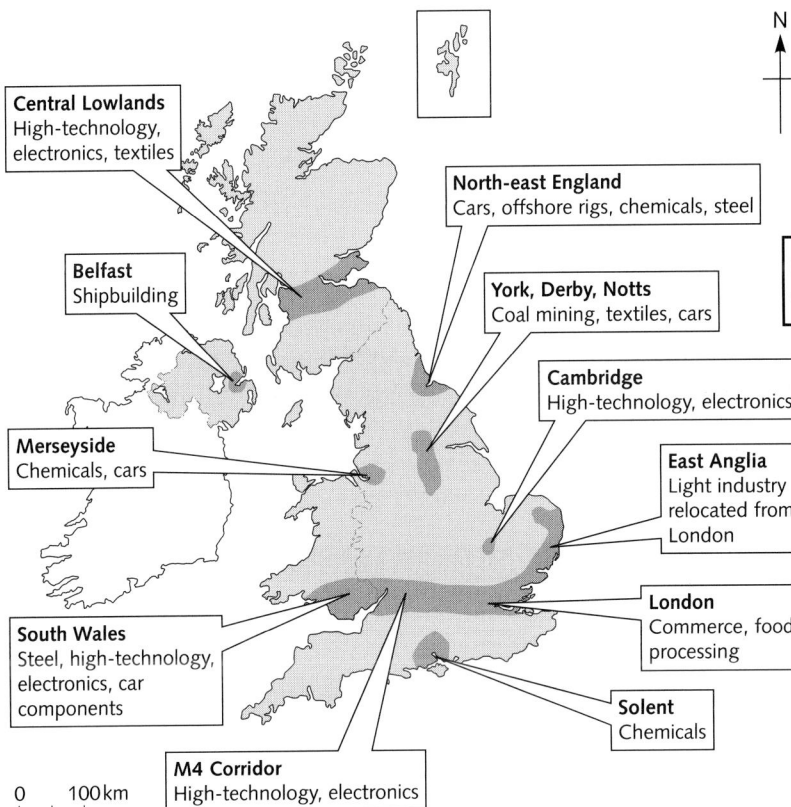

Central Lowlands
High-technology, electronics, textiles

Belfast
Shipbuilding

Merseyside
Chemicals, cars

South Wales
Steel, high-technology, electronics, car components

M4 Corridor
High-technology, electronics

North-east England
Cars, offshore rigs, chemicals, steel

York, Derby, Notts
Coal mining, textiles, cars

Cambridge
High-technology, electronics

East Anglia
Light industry relocated from London

London
Commerce, food processing

Solent
Chemicals

0   100 km

Figure 11.4 Location of present-day industries in the UK

	Reasons for job losses
•	Exhaustion of resources
•	Introduction of new machinery or new methods needing fewer workers (automation)
•	Fall in demand for product
•	Site needed for other uses
•	Large-scale redevelopment of inner city areas
•	Closure due to high costs of production – high wages, old, inefficient method or difficult conditions
•	Rationalisation of programme of a larger company
•	Competition from overseas
•	Lack of money for investment
•	Competition from rival products
•	Political decisions which deny government financial assistance to ailing companies

Figure 11.5 Reasons for job losses

Key words to know

High-technology industry

Changing location – high-technology industries

The term **high-technology industry** refers, usually, to industries developed within the last 25 years and whose processing techniques often involve micro-electronics. These industries, many of which are footloose, have been the 'growth industries' of recent years though unfortunately they employ few people in comparison with the older, declining heavy industries. Two possible subdivisions of high-tech industries are:

1 the 'sunrise industries' which have a high-technology base
2 information technology industries involving computers, telecommunications and micro-electronics.

As a highly skilled, inventive, intelligent workforce is essential, and as access to raw materials is relatively unimportant, these high-tech footloose industries tend to become attracted to areas which the researchers and operators find attractive – from a climatic, scenic, health and social point of view. Such areas include:

- Silicon Glen in central Scotland
- Silicon Valley in California
- Sunrise Strip which follows the route of the M4 from London westwards towards Newbury (locally known as Video Valley), Bristol (Aztec West) and into South Wales
- south of France behind Nice.

Case Study

Back to …

The New Wider World p140 for the case study on the M4 Corridor.

Using your case study

Use this case study as an example of the locational factors responsible for the clustering of high-technology firms. The M4 corridor is the most important region of its kind in the UK. Make sure that you can:

1 draw a simple sketch map of the M4 Corridor
2 describe the advantages of the region in terms of communications
3 explain the importance of university, government and private sector research establishments located nearby
4 discuss the advantages of the region's highly qualified labour force and industrial linkage
5 explain the high quality of life and why this is an important location factor.

Learn it!

a) List the main urban areas along the M4 Corridor.

b) What are the factors that give the M4 Corridor a high level of accessibility?

c) Discuss the environmental attractions of the region.

The Ruhr: A changing industrial region in the EU

Figure 11.6 The Ruhr

The Ruhr coalfield region is in the middle of a dramatic transformation. Most of the coal mines, steel works and the other traditional industries have closed. They have been replaced by modern enterprises such as telecommunications, computer products and service industries. The evidence of this 'structural change' can be found all across the region.

Industrialisation and deindustrialisation

Deindustrialisation is the long-term absolute decline of employment in manufacturing industry.

- The Ruhr region lies along, and north of, the Ruhr river (Figure 11.6), a tributary of the River Rhine.
- The industrialisation of the region was based on extensive coal deposits.
- Coal production reached its height in 1956 when there were almost half a million people employed in the mining industry.
- Since the 1970s, collieries, steelworks and other associated heavy industries have closed down one after another.

- The number employed in coal mining fell from 470 000 in 1955 to 53 000 in 1999. During the same period the number of working collieries fell from 136 to 9.
- Today, less than 9 per cent of the region's employment is in the coal and steel industries.
- The rapid decline of traditional industries caused unemployment to shoot up.
- Poverty is concentrated in specific urban areas.

Reindustrialisation

Reindustrialisation is the establishment of new industries in a country or region which has experienced considerable decline of traditional industries. In the Ruhr, work on creating a new economic structure began in the 1960s:

- Today 65 per cent of the Ruhr's workforce are employed in the tertiary sector. The strongest branch is the retail industry, followed by health and veterinary services, transport and communications, legal and business consultants and estate agencies. Further growth areas are computer and internet services, multimedia, advertising agencies, telecommunications and engineering consultants.
- Many businesses in the 'new economy' are clustered on modern trading estates or office parks.

Environmental improvement

- The closure of coal mines, steel works and other heavy industrial premises resulted in large areas of abandoned industrial wasteland. However, the scale of industrial reclamation has been staggering. For example, an entire region along the River Emscher has been transformed to create Europe's largest regional park.
- The Ruhr is attracting a growing number of tourists. The Route of Industrial Heritage, opened in 1999, shows 150 years of industrial history over its 400 km length. The region now boasts 300 nature conservation areas covering more than 4 per cent of the total land area.
- Deindustrialisation has meant that air quality has improved dramatically.

Deindustrialisation
Reindustrialisation

Using your case study

Use this case study as an example of a region in the EU which has undergone considerable industrial change. Make sure that you can:

1 draw a simple sketch map of the region
2 state why so much heavy industry was attracted to the Ruhr
3 suggest why heavy industry declined here
4 comment on the impact of job losses in coal, steel and other traditional industries
5 describe the reindustrialisation of the Ruhr
6 explain the environmental impact of such changes.

Learn it!

a) Why did the Ruhr become Europe's main centre of heavy industry?

b) What were the reasons for deindustrialisation in the Ruhr?

c) Describe the reindustrialisation that has occurred in the Ruhr.

Transnational corporation
(TNC)
Globalisation

Transnational (or multinational) corporations

A **transnational corporation (TNC)** is one that operates in many countries. The headquarters and main factory is usually in an MEDC with, increasingly, branch factories in LEDCs.

- TNCs are believed to directly employ some 40 million people around the world and to control over 75 per cent of world trade.
- The largest TNCs have long been car manufacturers and oil corporations but these have, more recently, been joined by electronic and high-tech firms.
- TNCs controlled one-fifth of the world's manufacturing in 1966 and over a half by the late 1990s.
- Many organisations and individuals have attacked TNCs as being exploiters of poor people, especially women and children, who live in LEDCs (Figure 11.7).

The global car industry

Car firms were amongst the first to opt for transnational operations. They found that by locating in different parts of the world they could:

- get around trade barriers
- reduce costs by gaining access to cheaper labour and/or raw materials
- be nearer to large markets.

Ford – a global car corporation

Globalisation is used to describe those TNCs that see the world, rather than the local area, as their supplier of labour, raw materials and component parts and their areas of sales.

The giant Ford Corporation originally located in Detroit. By the late 1990s it was:

- manufacturing and/or assembling its cars worldwide, although the bulk of the parts were still produced in the more industrialised parts of North America, Japan and the EU
- increasingly locating its new factories in LEDCs
- increasingly making parts in several countries (reducing the risk of strikes) so that each particular model is no longer made in one country

- working in Detroit with its previous rivals, Chrysler and General Motors, to produce a car that will use less fuel, cause less pollution and challenge the dominance of Japanese and, increasingly, Korean cars.

Figure 11.7 Advantages and disadvantages of transnational corporations

Advantages to the country	Disadvantages to the country
Brings work to the country and uses local labour	Numbers employed small in comparison with amount of investment
Local workforce receives a guaranteed income	Local labour force usually poorly paid
Improves the levels of education and technical skill of the people	Very few local skilled workers employed
Brings welcome investment and foreign currency to the country	Most of the profits go overseas (outflow of wealth)
Companies provide expensive machinery and modern technology	Mechanisation reduces the size of the labour force
Increased gross national product/personal income can lead to an increased demand for consumer goods and the growth of new industries	GNP grows less quickly than that of the parent company's headquarters, widening the gap between developed and developing countries
Leads to development of mineral wealth and new energy resources	Minerals are usually exported rather than manufactured and energy costs may lead to a national debt
Improvements in roads, airports and services	Money possibly better spent on improving housing, diet and sanitation
Prestige value (e.g. Volta project)	Big schemes can increase national debt (e.g. Brazil)
Widens economic base of country	Decisions are made outside the country, and the firm could pull out at any time
Some improvement in standards of production, health control, and recently in environmental control	Insufficient attention to safety and health factors and the protection of the environment

Check this!...

1 Define the terms:
   a) transnational corporation
   b) globalisation.

2 Suggest three reasons why large firms might want to locate factories in other countries.

3 What are the advantages to a country of attracting TNCs?

4 What are the problems that TNCs can bring to the countries in which they locate?

Back to ...

The New Wider World
pp144–145 for more
information on TNCs.

Business and science parks

Most **business parks** have grown up on edge-of-city greenfield sites. The major attractions of greenfield sites are the relatively low cost of land and a pleasant working environment with a low density of buildings. Usually over 70 per cent of the land in business parks is landscaped. Business parks form an ideal location for high-tech industries such as electronics, and research institutions. **Science parks** are similar but with the addition of direct links with universities.

Key words to know

Business park
Science park

Check this!...

1 Why do business parks and science parks frequently locate on greenfield sites in the rural–urban fringe?

2 What are the disadvantages to these areas of such new development?

Back to ...

The New Wider World **p141**
for more information on
business and science parks.

The NICs in East Asia

Governments in eastern Asia set out to improve their standards of living. They did this by investing in manufacturing industry and, early on, developing heavy industries (e.g. steel and shipbuilding). Later, they were to concentrate on high-tech industries. Manufacturing output rose most rapidly after 1960 in South Korea, Taiwan, Hong Kong and Singapore – four countries which collectively became known as the 'four tigers'. Like Japan, these four countries:

- lacked basic raw materials
- had governments that introduced long-term industrial planning
- had a dedicated workforce which was reliable and, initially, was prepared to work long hours for relatively little pay.

Economic growth in these newly industrialised countries (NICs) continued during the 1980s at a time when it was slowing down in the developed economies and world manufacturing was declining.

Since the 1980s, Malaysia, Thailand, Indonesia and, to a lesser extent, the Philippines have attempted to join the list of NICs. The next to emerge, and potentially the largest, is likely to be China.

Back to ...

The New Wider World **p147** for more information on NICs in East Asia.

Case Study

São Paulo – industry in an LEDC

Back to ...

The New Wider World pp154–155 for the case study on industry in a city in a developing country – São Paulo.

Using your case study

This case study is a good example of a newly industrialised country (NIC) which has attracted a wide range of transnational corporations (TNCs). Make sure that you can:

1 describe the location of São Paulo
2 explain the attraction of São Paulo to early industrial location
3 explain why so many transnational corporations, particularly in the car industry have located in São Paulo

4 comment on the problems, environmental and otherwise, caused by industrialisation
5 distinguish between the **formal** and the **informal sectors** of the economy.

Key words to know

Formal sector
Informal sector

Learn it!

a) Draw an annotated sketch map to show the location of São Paulo and its attractions to industrial location.

b) Why have so many TNC car manufacturers located in São Paulo?

c) Describe the differences between the formal and informal sectors in São Paulo.

Key words to know

Appropriate technology

Sustainable development in less economically developed countries

Appropriate technology is low cost and appropriate or suitable to the place in which it is used. It can contribute to a more sustainable way of life in LEDCs in particular. Appropriate technology may include:

- labour-intensive projects – with so many people likely to be unemployed or underemployed, it is of little value replacing existing workers with machines
- encouraging technology that is sustainable and fully utilises the existing skills and techniques of local people

- using tools designed to take advantage of local knowledge and resources
- developing local crafts and industries by using local natural resources and, where possible, recycling materials
- low-cost schemes using technologies that people can afford and manage
- developing projects that are in harmony with the environment.

Check this!...

1 What is appropriate technology?

2 Why is it often much more suitable for LEDCs than western style industry?

Back to ...

The New Wider World **pp150–151** for more information on sustainable development in LEDCs.

EXAM PRACTICE

1 a Look at Figure 11.8. On a copy of the diagram complete the boxes to give three physical and three human factors that can affect the location of a factory. (3)

  b Explain the importance of two of these factors. (4)

2 a Why have many traditional areas of heavy industry in MEDCs declined? (5)

  b What have governments done to try to reduce the impact of such decline? (5)

3 Describe and explain the advantages and disadvantages of TNCs to LEDCs. (8)

Physical factors

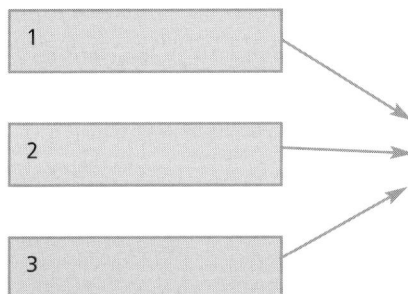

| 1 |
| 2 |
| 3 |

Factory

Human factors

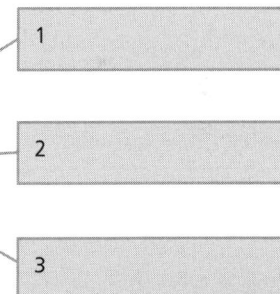

| 1 |
| 2 |
| 3 |

Figure 11.8 Factors affecting the location of industry

EXAM TIPS

You will need to plan your answer to question 3 very carefully as there are four things to do. Again, the balance between description and explanation is important. Also try to devote equal attention to the content demands of the question – the advantages and disadvantages.

Back to ...

The New Wider World website to check your answers to the Exam Practice question.

12 Managing resources

➡ *The New Wider World*, pp118–125; 160–175; 184–185; 218–221

KEY IDEAS

1 Management of resources is crucial to sustainable development.

2 Tourism in MEDCs and LEDCs and its consequences.

Key words to know

Natural resources
Human resources
Non-renewable resources
Renewable resources

1 Management of resources is crucial to sustainable development

What are resources?

Resources are features of the environment which are needed and used by people. The term usually refers to **natural resources** which occur in the air, in water or on the land. These resources include raw materials, climate, vegetation and soils. Sometimes the term is widened to include **human resources** such as labour, skills, machinery and capital (Figure 12.1).

Natural resources can be subdivided into two groups:

1 Non-renewable resources are finite or non-sustainable as their exploitation and use will eventually lead to their exhaustion.

2 Renewable resources can either be:

- a flow of nature so that, being continuous, they can be used over and over again, e.g. solar and water power
- sustainable, which means they are renewable and self-generating if left to nature, e.g. clean water, trees, fish, wildlife, soils, ecosystems and landscapes. However, if these sustainable resources are used carelessly or are over-used by people, then either:
  - they may be degraded, as when soils lose their fertility and are eroded, water supplies are polluted or trees die due to acid rain, or
  - their existence is threatened, as with overfishing, deforestation, the draining of wetlands or the development of scenic areas.

Figure 12.1 Classification of resources

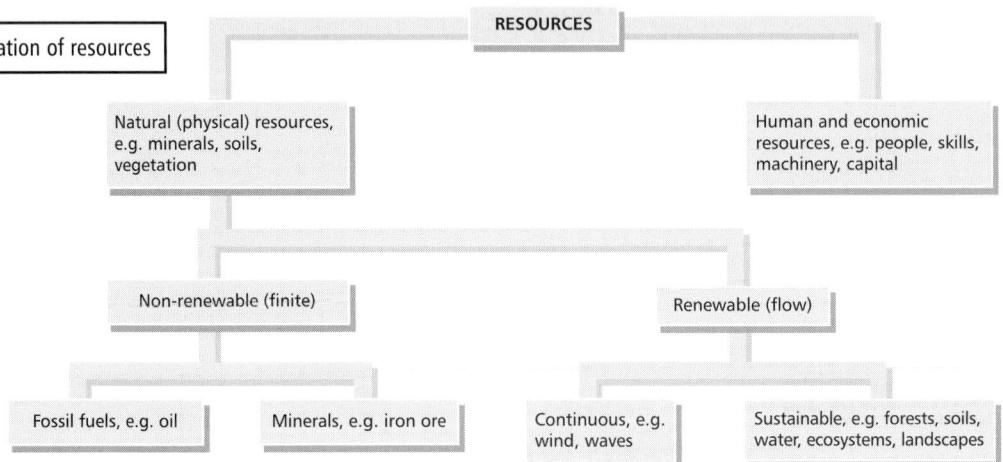

RESOURCES

Natural (physical) resources, e.g. minerals, soils, vegetation

Human and economic resources, e.g. people, skills, machinery, capital

Non-renewable (finite)

Renewable (flow)

Fossil fuels, e.g. oil

Minerals, e.g. iron ore

Continuous, e.g. wind, waves

Sustainable, e.g. forests, soils, water, ecosystems, landscapes

Why is the demand for resources increasing?

The demand for, and the use of, the world's resources continues to grow at an increasingly faster rate. This is mainly due to:

- population growth as the number of people in the world continues to increase
- economic development as more countries try to develop industrially and economically and attempt to raise their standard of living and quality of life
- increasing wealth, especially in the more economically developed countries
- technological advances.

MEDCs use a much larger share of the world's resources than LEDCs. For example, although less than 25 per cent of the world's people live in the MEDCs, they consume two-thirds of the energy produced. The USA with 5 per cent of the world's population consumes 25 per cent of world energy.

How can the Earth's resources be protected?

The combined effects of population growth, economic development, increasing wealth and technological advances mean that there is a growing need to manage and protect the Earth's resources. This might be achieved through **sustainable development** (Figure 12.2) which is improving people's standard of living and quality of life without wasting resources or spoiling the environment. This includes:

- conservation
- recycling
- greater efficiency in existing resource use
- developing renewable resources
- controlling pollution
- using **appropriate technology** (Figure 12.3).

Sustainable development in MEDCs

It is often mistakenly believed that the concept of sustainable development and the use of appropriate technology is not applicable to MEDCs. This is not the case, as it is the MEDCs that, at present:

- consume most of the world's non-renewable resources
- are the greatest contributors to global pollution.

Four important elements of sustainability in MEDCs are:

- conservation
- resource substitution
- recycling
- pollution control.

An appropriate technology can contribute to a more sustainable way of life for people who are rich or poor, living in places that are considered to be either more developed or less developed. The only difference is that for those living in MEDCs, the appropriate technology is likely to involve more capital (money) and to be high-tech.

Key words to know

Sustainable development
Appropriate technology

Back to …

p104 of this book for information on sustainable development in LEDCs (Chapter 11).

	Sustainable development	Non-sustainable development
Socio-economic	• Family planning, steady replacement rate	• High birth rate, rapid natural increase, ageing population
	• Building materials • Controlled urban growth	• Rapid urbanisation • Loss of countryside
People and resources	• Renewable energy • Soil conservation • Re-afforestation • Clean water supply • Recycling materials	• Continued use of minerals and fossil fuels • Soil erosion due to overgrazing and overcultivation • Deforestation • Pollution of water supplies • Heavy use of fertiliser in farming
People and the environment	• Ecotourism • National Parks and game reserves • Protecting scenery and wildlife habitats	• Mass tourism, especially at coastal resorts and mountain resorts

Figure 12.2 Differences between sustainable and non-sustainable development

Back to ...

The New Wider World **pp184–185** for more information on sustainable development.

Figure 12.3 Appropriate technology

Encouraging economic development at a pace a country can afford so as to prevent it falling into debt.

Using tools designed to take advantage of local knowledge and resources.

Encouraging technology that uses existing skills and techniques of local people and which can be handed down to future generations.

Developing projects that are in harmony with the environment.

Introducing labour-intensive projects as, with so many people already likely to be seeking work, it is no use replacing existing workers with machines.

Developing local crafts and industries by using local natural resources and, where possible, recycling materials.

Developing materials that use fewer resources and will last for longer.

Adopting low-cost schemes and technologies that people can afford and can manage.

Check this!...

1 Explain the classification of resources shown in Figure 12.1.

2 Why has the demand for resources increased?

3 How can the Earth's remaining resources be protected?

Key words to know

Photosynthesis
Fossil fuels

Energy resources

The sun is the primary source of the Earth's energy. Without energy, nothing can live and no work can be done. Green plants convert energy, through the process of **photosynthesis**, into a form that can be used by people.

Non-renewable resources

In the mid-1990s, coal, oil and natural gas (**fossil fuels**) accounted for 87.8 per cent of the world's commercially produced energy. These are forms of stored solar energy produced by photosynthesis in plants over thousands of years. As these three types of energy take so long to form and be replaced, they are regarded as non-renewable. Each year the world consumes an amount of fossil fuel that took nature one million years to provide. Fossil fuels have, in the past, been relatively easy to obtain and cheap to use, but they have become major polluters.

Two other non-renewable sources of energy are:
- nuclear energy which uses uranium and so is not a fossil fuel
- fuelwood – a non-commercial source of energy. It provides 14 per cent of the world's and 35 per cent of developing countries' energy requirements.

Renewable resources

Renewable resources of energy are considered to be sustainable. At present only running water (hydro-electricity) is a significant source of renewable energy on a global scale. Other sources, often more important on a local scale, are:
- the sun (solar)
- the wind
- vegetation waste (biomass)
- heat from the Earth (geothermal).

As yet, economic and technical problems tend to restrict the conversion of these sources of energy on a large scale. However, in time the world is likely to have to look to these, and other sources of renewable energy (e.g. waves and tides), as the supply of fossil fuels becomes exhausted.

A renewable energy resource: Hydro-electric power (HEP)

- Hydro-electricity generates the highest proportion of the renewable types of energy.
- Although accounting for only 6.5 per cent of the world's total commercial energy, in many countries it accounts for over 80 per cent, e.g. Paraguay, Norway, Brazil.
- It is important to both developed and developing countries – providing they have a constant supply of fast-flowing water.
- Figure 12.4 shows some of the factors ideally needed for the location of a hydro-electric power station.
- Hydro-electricity can be generated at a natural waterfall (e.g. Niagara Falls), by building a dam across a valley (e.g. the Three Gorges Dam on the Yangtze, and at Itaipù) or where water flows rapidly down a hillside (e.g. Norway).

Key words to know
Greenhouse gases

Figure 12.4 Advantages and disadvantages of hydro-electric power

Advantages	Disadvantages
Hydro-electric power is renewable	Dams are very expensive to build
Often produced in highland areas where the population is sparse	There is always the possibility of a dam collapsing
Is a relatively cheap form of electricity	Large areas of farmland and wildlife habitats may have to be flooded forcing people and animals to move
Creates only limited pollution	If an area is flooded, the decaying vegetation can release methane and carbon dioxide – two **greenhouse gases**
Dams, where built to store water, reduce the risks of flooding and water shortages	Unsightly pylons can cause visual pollution
	Silt, previously spread over farmland, will be deposited in the lake

For further information see 'Issues in dam construction' (GeoActive, September 2002).

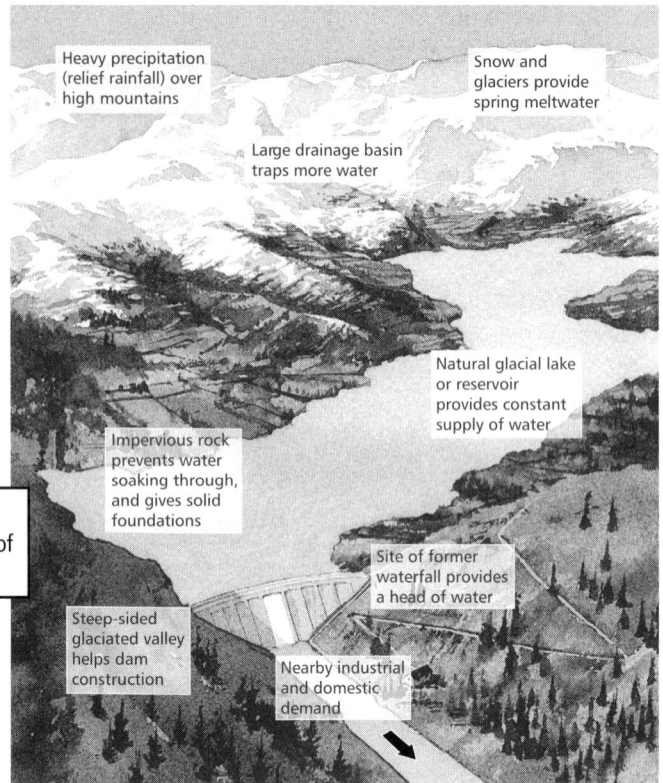

Figure 12.5 Factors involved in the location of an HEP station

Labels on figure:
- Heavy precipitation (relief rainfall) over high mountains
- Snow and glaciers provide spring meltwater
- Large drainage basin traps more water
- Natural glacial lake or reservoir provides constant supply of water
- Impervious rock prevents water soaking through, and gives solid foundations
- Site of former waterfall provides a head of water
- Steep-sided glaciated valley helps dam construction
- Nearby industrial and domestic demand

Case Study

Itaipù, Brazil

Back to ...

The New Wider World p122 for the case study on Itaipù, Brazil.

Using your case study
Use this case study as your example of renewable energy. Make sure that you can:
1 draw a simple sketch map to show the location of Itaipù
2 explain its location, including joint ownership with Paraguay
3 comment on its generating capacity and other characteristics
4 discuss its advantages and disadvantages.

Update
For up-to-date information on Itaipú use the link on *The New Wider World Coursemate* website.

Learn it!

a) Describe the location of Itaipù.

b) Why was the power plant built at this point?

c) Explain the advantages and disadvantages of the project.

Key words to know

Greenhouse effect

Global warming

The greenhouse effect
The Earth is warmed during the day by incoming radiation from the sun. The Earth loses heat at night through outgoing infrared radiation. Because there is a balance between incoming and outgoing radiation, the Earth's temperatures remain constant.

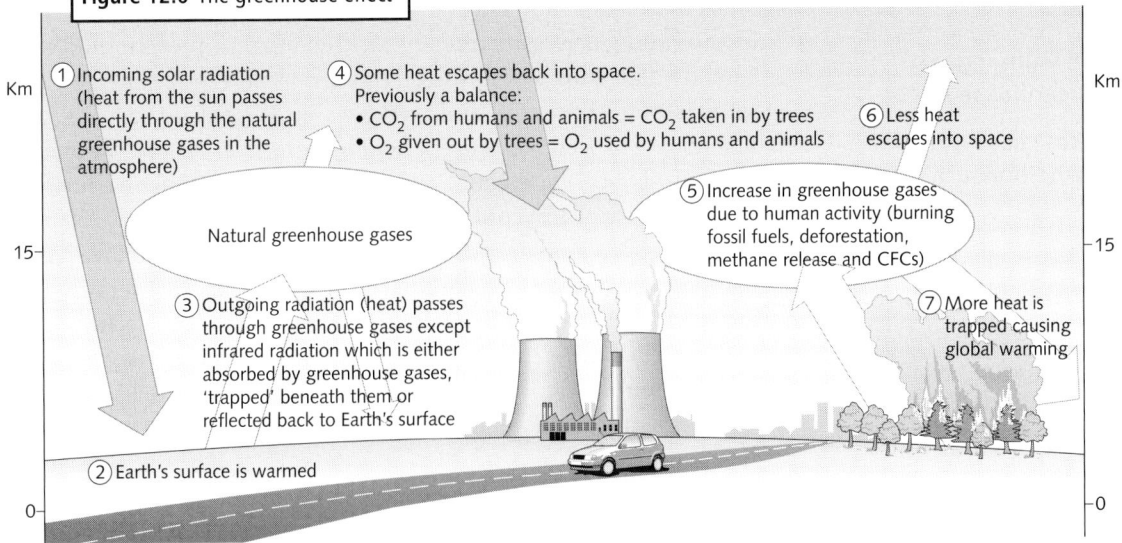

Figure 12.6 The greenhouse effect

① Incoming solar radiation (heat from the sun passes directly through the natural greenhouse gases in the atmosphere)

④ Some heat escapes back into space. Previously a balance:
• CO_2 from humans and animals = CO_2 taken in by trees
• O_2 given out by trees = O_2 used by humans and animals

⑥ Less heat escapes into space

Natural greenhouse gases

⑤ Increase in greenhouse gases due to human activity (burning fossil fuels, deforestation, methane release and CFCs)

③ Outgoing radiation (heat) passes through greenhouse gases except infrared radiation which is either absorbed by greenhouse gases, 'trapped' beneath them or reflected back to Earth's surface

⑦ More heat is trapped causing global warming

② Earth's surface is warmed

- On cloudy nights, temperatures do not drop as low as on clear nights. This is because the clouds act as a blanket and trap some of the heat. Greenhouse gases in the atmosphere also act as a blanket, as they prevent the escape of infrared radiation (Figure 12.6).
- Without these greenhouse gases, which include carbon dioxide, the Earth's average temperature would be 33°C lower than it is today.
- Recent human activity has led to a significant increase in the amount, and type, of greenhouse gases in the atmosphere. This is preventing heat from escaping into space, and is believed to be responsible for a rise in world temperatures.
- World temperatures rose by 0.6°C last century, with seven of the century's warmest years occurring in the 1990s. The process by which world temperatures are rising is known as **global warming**.

Key words to know

Global warming

Causes of global warming

The major contributors to global warming are carbon dioxide and other pollutants released into the atmosphere:

- Carbon dioxide (72 per cent of greenhouse gases) is the most important single factor in global warming. It is produced by a) road vehicles, b) burning fossil fuels in power stations, in factories and in the home and c) deforestation and the burning of the tropical rainforests.
- CFCs (chlorofluorocarbons – 13 per cent) from aerosols, air conditioners, foam packaging and refrigerators are the most damaging of the greenhouse gases.
- Methane (10 per cent) is released from decaying organic matter such as peat bogs, swamps, landfill sites, animal dung and farms.
- Nitrous oxide (5 per cent) is emitted from car exhausts, power stations and agricultural fertiliser.

Effects of global warming

The scientists on the Intergovernmental Panel on Climatic Change have made predictions which include the following:

- As sea temperatures rise, water in the oceans is expanding causing sea-levels to rise. Scientists claim that sea-level rose by 0.2

Check this!...

1 Define:
   a) global warming
   b) the greenhouse effect.

2 Which gases cause global warming and how are they produced?

3 What are the predicted consequences of global warming?

For further information see 'Global warming update' (GeoActive, January 2002).

Back to ...

The New Wider World **pp218–220** for more information on global warming.

Figure 12.7 Gas emissions

(a) UK Carbon dioxide emissions

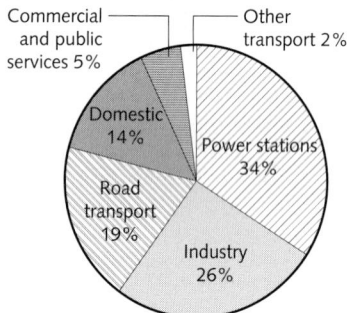

Commercial and public services 5%
Other transport 2%
Domestic 14%
Power stations 34%
Road transport 19%
Industry 26%

(b) Main greenhouse gas emitters

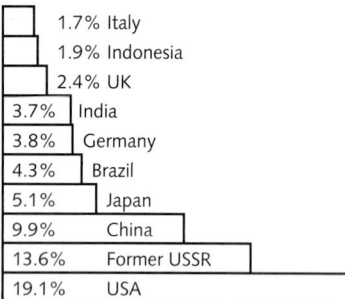

1.7%	Italy
1.9%	Indonesia
2.4%	UK
3.7%	India
3.8%	Germany
4.3%	Brazil
5.1%	Japan
9.9%	China
13.6%	Former USSR
19.1%	USA

metres during the last century, and give an average predicted rise of 0.4 metres for this century.

- Icecaps and glaciers are already melting at an unprecedented rate. Satellite data shows that, since 1960, sea-ice in the Arctic has retreated by 15 per cent and is 40 per cent less thick.
- The release of water at present held in storage as ice and snow in the hydrological cycle could raise the world's sea-level by a further 5 m. Even a rise of 1 m could flood 25 per cent of Bangladesh, 30 per cent of Egypt's arable land, and totally submerge several low-lying islands in the Indian and Pacific Oceans. At present, 40 per cent of the world's population live within 100 km of the coast – many people being vulnerable to rising sea-levels and storm surges.
- The distribution of precipitation is predicted to change. Places with:
  – sufficient rainfall are likely to get more, resulting in increased flooding
  – insufficient rainfall are likely to get less in terms of both amount and reliability, giving increased drought – a prediction which claims that the 1.7 billion people already short of water in 2000 could become 5 billion by 2025.
- Ecosystems at all levels may be subject to such a rapid change that plants and wildlife may not have the time in which to adjust. This includes coral reefs, mangrove swamps, wetlands, coniferous and tropical forests, and tropical grassland.
- Crop yields are expected to fall even further in Africa as well as in parts of Asia and Latin America, although they may increase in northern Europe and North America.
- A greater proportion of the world's population will be at risk from insect-borne and water-borne diseases.

It will be the poor who will be hardest hit. The effects will be greatest in the LEDCs – in water and food shortages, diseases and natural disasters – places where people can least afford to adapt or are unable to migrate.

The global warming debate

However, not all scientists and other interested people believe that these predictions will come true. They argue that we do not have enough evidence yet to make such predictions with accuracy. Many large companies whose operations are claimed to be helping global warming also argue that the impact of what they do is being exaggerated. This debate is set to run for many years to come.

Solutions to global warming

This problem can only be solved by drastically reducing the emission of greenhouse gases. Measures to achieve this include:
- burning less fossil fuels in power stations by increasing investment in renewable energy resources
- greatly increasing recycling and the reuse of products that we currently throw away after using once (e.g. supermarket plastic bags)
- reducing emissions from car exhausts
- technological advance to eliminate the use of CFCs.

2 Tourism in MEDCs and LEDCs and its consequences

Tourism

Recent trends and changing patterns

- Tourism has become the world's fastest-growing and largest industry.
- It is an important factor in the economy of most developed countries and many developing countries.
- It has grown rapidly in the last 50 years, mainly as a result of globalisation
  – in this context meaning the easier movement of people around the world. Travel for a privileged minority has been replaced by **mass tourism**.
- The MEDCs receive just over 75 per cent of all international tourist arrivals but destinations in LEDCs in Africa, South-east Asia, the Pacific and the Middle East have become more popular and accessible in recent years.
- Recent trends in tourism, and the changing demands made by tourists, have resulted from a wide range of factors (Figure 12.8).

Key words to know

Mass tourism
Long-haul

The United Kingdom

Within the UK the most popular tourist region is the South West with its warmer climate and wide range of attractive scenery. Abroad, Spain remains the major destination, although its importance has declined in the last twenty years as more people are prepared to take **long-haul** holidays to more distant, exotic and adventurous locations. Figure 12.9 summarises some of the factors that have influenced the development of tourism in both the UK and the world.

Figure 12.8 Recent trends in tourism in the UK

Greater affluence	– People who have employment within the UK usually earn a high salary – certainly higher than several decades ago
Greater mobility	– The increase in car ownership has given people greater freedom to choose where and when they go for the day, or for a longer period. In 1951, only 1 UK family in 20 had a car. By 2000, 74 per cent had at least one car. – Chartered aircraft have reduced the costs of overseas travel
Improved accessibility and transport facilities	– Improvements in roads, especially motorways and urban by-passes, have reduced driving times between places and encourage people to travel more frequently and greater distances – Improved and enlarged airports (although many are still congested at peak periods). Reduced air fares. Package holidays, computerised reservation systems. – Organisation of mass tourism by transnational companies
More leisure time	– Shorter working week (although still the longest in the EU) and longer paid holidays (on average 3 weeks a year, compared with 1 week in the USA) – Flexitime, more people working from home, and more firms (especially retailing) employing part-time workers – An ageing population, many of whom are still active
Changing lifestyles	– People are retiring early and are able to take advantage of their greater fitness – People at work need longer/more frequent rest periods as pressure of work seems to increase – Changing fashions, e.g. health resorts, fitness holidays, winter sun
Changing recreational activities	– Slight decline in the 'beach holiday' – partly due to the threat of skin cancer – Increase in active holidays (skiing, water sports) and in self-catering – Most rapid growth in mid-1990s has been in 'cruise holidays' – Importance of theme parks
Advertising and TV programmes	– Holiday programmes, magazines and brochures promote new and different places and activities
'Green' or sustainable tourism	– Need to benefit local economy, environment and people without spoiling the attractiveness and amenities of the places visited

Figure 12.9 Factors affecting the growth of tourism in the UK and the world

Factors	Specific examples	UK example of area or resort	World example
1 Transport and accessibility	• Early resorts (stage coach), spa towns • Water transport (18th century) • Railways • Car and coach • Plane • Cruise ships	Bath Margate Blackpool, Brighton Cornwall, Scottish highlands Channel Islands Scottish islands	Baden-Baden Amsterdam Paris, Istanbul (Orient Express) Rhinelands, Alps Florida, Ayers rock (Uluru) Norweigian Fiords, Caribbean
2 Scenery	• Sandy beaches • Coasts of outstanding beauty • Mountains, lakes and rivers	Margate, Blackpool Pembroke, Antrim, Cornwall Lake District, Snowdonia	Benidorm, Rio de Janeiro Barrier Reef Nepal, Switzerland, Rhine
3 Weather	• Hot, dry sunny summers • Snow	Margate Aviemore	Costa del Sol, Greece Alps, Rockies
4 Accommodation	• Hotels and boarding house resorts • Holiday camps • Caravan parks and campsites	Margate, Blackpool Minehead, Pwllheli National and forest parks	Benidorm, Costa del Sol Caribbean French Riviera
5 Amenities	• Culture and history (castles, cathedrals) • Active amenities (sailing, golf, water-skiing) • Passive amenities (shops, cinemas) • Theme parks • Theatres, museums, music	York, Edinburgh Kielder, St Andrews Most resorts Alton Towers, Longleat London	Athens, Florence, Paris Costal del Sol Most resorts Disney World Paris, Vienna
6 Ecotourism and sustainability	• Nature reserves and game parks • World heritage sites	Slimbridge Hadrian's Wall	Kenya Cairo, Venice, Grand Canyon

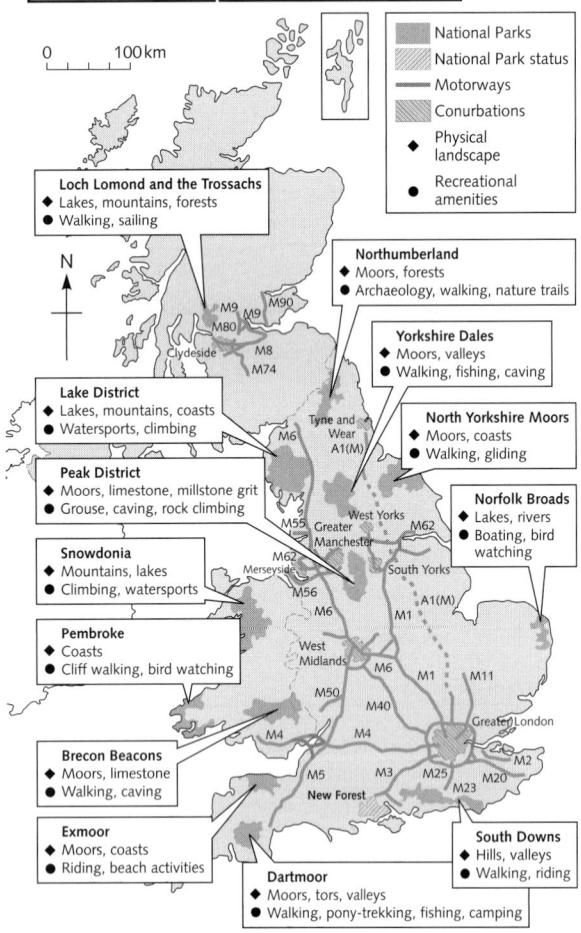

Figure 12.10 National Parks, conurbations and motorways in the UK

National Parks in the UK

- National Parks contain some of the most diverse and spectacular upland scenery in the UK.
- They are mainly in private ownership, though bodies such as the National Trust, the Forestry Commission and water authorities are important landowners (the Parks are not owned by the nation).
- Public access is encouraged, but is restricted to footpaths, bridleways, open fells and mountains.
- They support local populations who are dependent on primary (farming, forestry and mining) and tertiary (tourism) forms of employment.
- The National Parks contain a variety of scenery which in turn provides a wide range of recreational activities (Figure 12.10).

The National Parks were usually located within easy reach of the major conurbations (Figure 12.10). This enabled the maximum number of people, including those who lived in large urban areas, to escape to a quieter, more pleasant rural environment. Since then the growth of the motorway network has considerably reduced driving times and, in effect, has reduced distances between the conurbations and the National Parks.

Check this!...

1 Suggest why tourism is now the world's largest industry.

2 Describe the location of National Parks in the UK.

3 How have National Parks become more accessible in recent decades?

Back to ...

The New Wider World
pp160–162 for more information on tourism trends globally and in the UK.

Case Study

The Lake District – National Park

Back to ...

The New Wider World pp172–175 for the case study on the Lake District National Park.

Using your case study
Use this case study as your example of a named UK tourist area. Make sure that you can:
1 draw a simple sketch map to show the location of the Lake District.
2 describe the attractions of the Lake District
3 comment on the range of tourist activities
4 outline the problems created by visitors
5 discuss possible solutions to these problems.

Case study links
The Lake District National Park can be used as an example of human activity in a glacial landscape (Chapter 4).

Update
For up-to-date information on the Lake District use the link on *The New Wider World Coursemate* website.

Learn it!

a) Describe the location of the Lake District and the scenery it contains.

b) What activities do visitors undertake and where do they go to in the Lake District?

c) How important is tourism to the economy of the area?

d) Outline the problems created by large numbers of visitors.

Tourism in developing countries

Since the early 1980s, European tourists have become increasingly less satisfied with package tours to Mediterranean coastal resorts. Like tourists from North America and Japan, they have sought holidays in places farther afield where the environment and culture is very different from their own. The chief beneficiaries of this change in holiday fashion and demand have been several developing countries located within, or near to, the tropics – places such as Kenya, Egypt, Sri Lanka, Thailand, Malaysia and in the West Indies. The attraction of earning money from tourism is considerable to LEDCs, many of which see it as the only possible way to raise their standard of living. However, only a limited number of LEDCs have the potential to develop a successful tourist industry, and even then the damage to their culture and environment can, at times, outweigh the benefits (Figure 12.11).

Disadvantages of tourism

- Hotels, airports and roads spoil the visual appearance and create noise, air pollution and litter.
- Usually only 10–20 per cent of the income received from tourists stays in the country. Most hotels are foreign-owned and profits go overseas. Tourists spend most of their money in the hotels.
- Much employment is seasonal. Overseas labour may be brought in to fill the better-paid jobs.
- Local craft industries may be destroyed in order to provide mass-produced, cheap souvenirs.
- Farming economy is damaged as land is sold to developers. Much of the food eaten by tourists is imported either because local production is insufficient or to meet the demands for European-style foods (but sold at the developing country's prices).
- Local people cannot afford tourist facilities.
- Borrowed money increases national debt.
- Tourists expect unlimited water – up to 500 litres a day or ten times that used by local people. Many areas may be short of water for domestic and farming use.
- Local cultures and traditions are destroyed. New social problems of prostitution, crime, drugs and drunkenness. Lack of respect for local customs and religious beliefs (e.g. semi-naked tourists visiting mosques and temples).
- The building of hotels means that local people lose their homes, land and traditional means of livelihood (e.g. fishermen, as hotels are built next to beaches) and become dependent on serving wealthy tourists.

… Tourism is a form of economic colonialism

Advantages of tourism

- The natural environment (sun, sand, sea and scenery) is used to attract tourists and their much-needed money.
- Income from tourism is usually greater than the income from the export of a few raw materials.
- Creates domestic employment, e.g. hotels, entertainment and guides. It is labour intensive.
- Encourages the production of souvenirs.
- Creates a market for local farm produce.
- Local people can use tourist facilities.
- Overseas investment in airports, roads and hotels.
- Profits can be used to improve local housing, schools, hospitals, electricity and water supplies.
- Increased cultural links with foreign countries, and the preservation of local customs and heritage.
- Reduces migration.

… Tourism raises the standard of living

Figure 12.11 Disadvantages and advantages of tourism

Key words to know

Ecotourism

Back to …

The New Wider World
pp168–169 for more information on tourism in developing countries.

Check this!...

1 What is ecotourism?

2 Why is ecotourism increasing in popularity?

3 How can ecotourism still have a negative impact on LEDCs?

For further information see 'Ecotourism in Antarctica: Should it be allowed?' (GeoActive, April 2003).

Ecotourism

Ecotourism, sometimes known as green tourism, is a sustainable form of tourism that is more appropriate to developing countries than the mass tourism in developed countries. Ecotourism includes:

- visiting places in order to appreciate their scenery and wildlife and to understand their culture
- creating economic opportunities (jobs) in an area while at the same time protecting natural resources (scenery and wildlife) and the local way of life (culture).

Compared with mass tourists, ecotourists usually travel in small groups and share specialist interests (bird watching, photography). They are more likely to merge and live with local communities and to appreciate local cultures rather than 'stop, take a photo and move on'. They often visit National Parks and game reserves where the scenery and wildlife that attracted them there in the first place, are carefully protected and managed. Even so, ecotourists:

- usually pay for their holiday in advance (meaning they spend relatively little in the developing country)
- are not all environmentally educated or concerned
- can cause land prices to rise
- congregate at prime sites (honeypots)
- may still cause conflict with local people.

Case Study

Kenya

← **Back to ...**

The New Wider World pp170–171 for the case study on tourism in Kenya.

Using your case study

Use this case study as your named tourist area in an LEDC. Make sure that you can:

1 draw a simple sketch map to show Kenya and some of its National Parks
2 explain why Kenya is one of the main tourist destinations in Africa
3 describe the impact of tourism
4 suggest how the impact of tourism could be minimised in the future.

Update

For up-to-date information on Kenya use the link on *The New Wider World Coursemate* website.

Learn it!

a) Name and describe the location of two of Kenya's National Parks.

b) What does a 'safari' holiday involve?

c) How has tourism impacted on:
   i   the environment
   ii wildlife
   iii local people?

EXAM PRACTICE

1 What is the difference between a renewable and a non-renewable resource?   (2)

2 a Explain the location factors which apply to one renewable source of energy.   (4)

   b Briefly discuss the disadvantages of this source of energy.   (3)

3 a Name two greenhouse gases.   (2)

   b Discuss three ways in which global warming could change the global environment.   (6)

4 Using one or more examples, explain the advantages and disadvantages of tourism to LEDCs.   (8)

← **Back to ...**

The New Wider World website to check your answers to the Exam Practice question.

EXAM TIPS

For question 3b try to ensure that there are clear differences between the 'three ways' you select. Repetition could cost you marks.

13 Development

KEY IDEAS

1 Contrasts in development are related to economic, environmental, social and political conditions.

2 Trade and aid in MEDCs and LEDCs and its consequences.

Key words to know

Gross national product (GNP) per capita

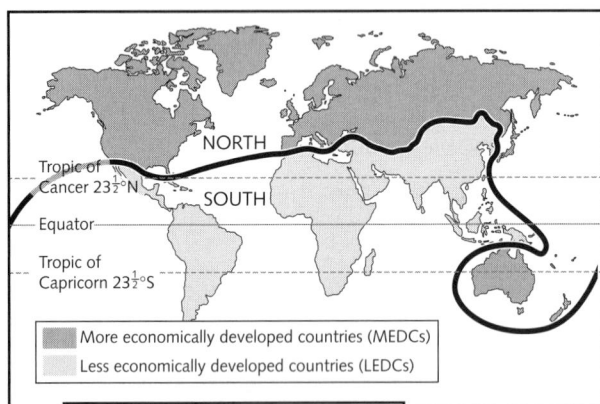

Figure 13.1 Pattern of development

1 Contrasts in development are related to economic, environmental, social and political conditions

Patterns and characteristics of development

Patterns

The most commonly used map to show differences in development is that of Figure 13.1. Here, the world is divided into two groups:

1 The more economically developed countries (MEDCs) of the developed 'North'.

2 The less economically developed countries (LEDCs) of the developing 'South'.

Characteristics

Geographers have suggested several methods by which they can measure development.

1 Economic wealth

The wealth of a country is measured by its **gross national product (GNP) per capita**. The GNP per person is the total value of goods and services produced by a country in a year, divided by the total number of people living in that country. To make comparisons between countries easier, GNP is given in US dollars (US$).

Figure 13.2 includes the GNP per capita for selected countries at different levels of development.

Figure 13.2 Indicators (measures) of development, 2000	Country	Economic wealth	Social indicators						Other indicators			
			Population			Health			Literacy	Nutrition	Employment	Energy consumption
		GNP per capita (US$)	Birth rate	Death rate	Natural increase	Infant mortality	Life expectancy	Population per doctor	% Adult literacy	Calories per person per day	% in agriculture	Tonnes coal equivalent per year
MEDCS	Japan	39 640	9	8	1	4	81	600	99	2932	7	4.74
	USA	26 980	15	9	6	7	77	420	99	3699	3	10.74
	Italy	19 020	9	10	−1	6	79	211	98	3507	9	4.02
	UK	18 700	12	11	1	6	77	300	99	3276	2	5.40
Middle-income LEDCs (NICs)	Malaysia	3 890	25	4	21	8	73	2 564	87	2977	27	1.80
	Brazil	3 640	22	7	15	34	68	1 000	84	2974	25	0.44
	Mexico	3 320	24	5	21	27	75	621	91	3097	28	1.89
Low-income LEDCs	India	340	26	9	17	70	61	2 439	85	2496	64	0.35
	Kenya	280	34	14	20	76	48	10 000	80	1976	80	0.11
	Bangladesh	240	28	8	20	58	59	12 500	60	2085	65	0.08
	Ethiopia	100	44	15	29	118	52	33 000	64	1858	86	0.03

2 Social indicators

Figures 13.2 and 13.3 show possible links between development and a range of social measures.

In general, the MEDCs have lower birth rates and a slower natural increase than LEDCs. Population structures show that the MEDCs have a smaller proportion of children aged under 15 and a higher proportion of people aged over 65 than developing countries. Similarly, MEDCs have a lower infant mortality rate, a longer life expectancy and fewer people per doctor than the LEDCs.

3 Other indicators

These include measures related to **adult literacy**, diet, employment structures and energy consumption (Figure 13.2). Notice, however, that many of these criteria are themselves related to the wealth of a country. The more wealthy and, therefore, economically developed a country is, the more it can spend on health care, education, energy provision and providing other services.

Human Development Index (HDI)

In 1990, the United Nations replaced GNP as their measure of development with the **Human Development Index (HDI)**. The HDI is a social welfare index measuring three variables: life expectancy (health), adult literacy (education), and real GNP per capita (standard of living).

- Life expectancy is regarded by the UN as the best measure of the health and safety of a country.
- Education attainment is obtained by combining adult literacy rates and the primary, secondary and tertiary student enrolment rate.
- Real GNP per capita is the GNP adjusted to the actual purchasing power (PPP in US$), i.e. what the average income will actually buy in a country.

Each variable is given a score ranging from 1.000 (the wealthiest) to 0.000 (the poorest). The HDI, which is the average of the three scores, in 2000 put Norway top with a score of 0.939 and Sierra Leone bottom with a score of 0.258.

Figure 13.3 Differences between MEDCs and LEDCs

Indicators/measures		MEDCs	LEDCs
Economic (GNP)		Majority over US$5000 per capita. 80% of the world's income.	Majority under US$2000 per capita. 20% of the world's total income.
Social	Population	Low, steady birth rate partly due to family planning. Slow natural increase – takes 100 years to double. 18% of world's population.	High birth rate, partly due to limited family planning, but falling. Relatively high death rate but falling except in sub-Saharan Africa. Rapid natural increase – doubling population in 30 years. 82% of world's population.
	Health	Low infant mortality rate, long and increasing life expectancy. Mainly due to vaccines, large number of doctors and hospitals, and high standard of health care.	High, though falling, infant mortality rate, shorter life expectancy, especially in poorest countries. Relatively few doctors and hospitals. Little money available.
Others	Education	Majority have full-time education, many have 16+ education. Most adults, including women, are literate.	Limited numbers get full-time education, and few go on after 16. Low adult literacy rate, and women are disadvantaged.
	Diet	Balanced. Several meals per day. High protein intake.	Unbalanced. 35% of children under 5 are underfed. Low protein intake.
	Employment	Few jobs in primary sector, more in secondary, most in tertiary sector. Mechanisation and technology.	Most in primary sector, few in secondary and tertiary sectors. Limited mechanisation and technology.
	Energy	High levels of consumption – mainly coal, oil, natural gas and nuclear power. Use 70% of world's energy.	Low levels of consumption – often only fuelwood. Only use 30% of world's energy.
	Trade	Large volume and value – mainly manufactured goods.	Small volume and value – mainly unprocessed raw materials.

Causes of inequality

There are numerous factors that may lead to inequalities in development. For example:

- *Economic*   Countries with mineral deposits and energy resources were more likely to have been the first to develop industrially. As they accumulated wealth through the sale of manufactured goods, they were able to buy resources either because their own became exhausted or because they did not possess them. They were able to provide numerous jobs, improve transport systems and develop new technologies as well as imposing trade restrictions on less developed countries.
- *Social*   The more a country develops, the more money it has to spend on education, health and better-quality housing.
- *Political*   Countries were likely to develop more quickly if they had a government that was stable, invested in the economy and avoided civil war. Former colonial powers developed at the expense of their colonies.
- *Environmental*   Countries were also likely to develop more quickly if they were unaffected by frequent and severe natural hazards, disease and illness, pests, and if they were able to provide a reliable supply of clean water.

Back to …

The New Wider World
pp180–183 for more information on contrasts in development.

Check this!…

1   Look at Figure 13.1. Which parts of the world are in the North and which are in the South?

2   Describe the differences in social indicators for the countries shown in Figure 13.2.

3   Suggest two other indicators of development that are not shown in Figure 13.2.

4   Justify the indicators that are used in the Human Development Index.

Case Study

Japan and Kenya

Back to …

The New Wider World pp192–193 for the case study on 'Japan and Kenya: Levels of development'.

Using your case study

Use this case study to show the extent of the development gap between an MEDC and an LEDC. Make sure that you can:

1   compare the two countries in GNP per capita
2   describe and explain the differences in employment structure
3   comment on differences in population and social indicators.

Update

For up-to-date information on Kenya use the link on *The New Wider World Coursemate* website.

Learn it!

a) What is the GNP per capita in:
   i   Japan
   ii Kenya?

b) Briefly discuss the relationship between employment structure and GNP per capita.

c) Make a list of the differences in population figures between the two countries.

d) Why are social conditions much better in Japan compared with Kenya?

Water supply in developing countries

Differences between the availability and cleanliness of water supply between MEDCs and LEDCs has a major impact on development. An estimated 1500 million people lack a satisfactory or safe water supply. In developing countries, water supplies may be contaminated:

- in rural areas where rivers and streams are used for drinking, washing and the disposal of sewage
- in urban areas where, especially in shanty settlements, the absence of drains means that sewage may pollute water supplies
- in many shanty settlements which either lack clean water or where large numbers of people are forced to share the same tap
- due to a lack of government, legislation and implementation.

Water that is dirty or polluted is no longer a renewable resource and often leads to outbreaks of diseases such as cholera, typhoid, dysentery and diarrhoea.

50 per cent of people in rural areas now have an adequate supply compared with only 30 per cent in 1980. However, the rapid growth in population and urbanisation meant that 500 million more people lacked sanitation in 2000 than in 1980. The improvements in rural water supplies were mainly due to international charity organisations like Oxfam which have helped local communities to introduce appropriate technology. These included self-help schemes such as:

- digging wells to reach permanent underground supplies
- lining the sides of the well with concrete (to prevent seepage) and adding a cover (to reduce evaporation)
- using modern pumps.

Check this!...

1 Why are many people in LEDCs unable to gain access to clean water?

2 What are the consequences of people using dirty or polluted water?

3 How have non-governmental organisations (NGOs) tried to improve access to clean water in LEDCs?

Back to ...

The New Wider World **p225** for more information on access to clean water.

Food supply and malnutrition

There are considerable differences in the quality and quantity of **food supply** between MEDCs and LEDCs. Very poor countries are lacking in both the quantity and quality of food. This hinders development which in turn makes it more and more difficult to solve the food problem.

- **Malnutrition** is caused by deficiencies in diet, either in amount (quantity) or type (quality).
- It is attributed to poverty, as large numbers of the world's population are unable to afford to buy an adequate diet.
- While malnutrition results in starvation only under extreme conditions, it does reduce people's capacity to work and their resistance to disease.
- In children, it can retard mental and physical development, and cause illness.

Between 1970 and 2000 there was an increase in available food supplies per capita in every developing region except sub-Saharan

Key words to know

Food supply
Malnutrition

Africa. It has been estimated that in most developing countries, especially those within the tropics, a person consuming less than 2350 calories per day is likely to experience chronic malnutrition. In 2000, 20 per cent of people living in these countries were suffering from chronic malnutrition.

Back to ...

The New Wider World
pp110–111 for more information on food supply and malnutrition.

Check this!...

1 What is meant by the terms:
   a) food supply
   b) malnutrition?

2 Suggest why food supplies decreased in sub-Saharan Africa between 1970 and 2000.

3 How does an inadequate food supply hinder development?

Key words to know

Sustainable development
Appropriate technology

Sustainable development and appropriate technology

Sustainable development should, according to the UN:
'...meet the needs of the present without compromising the ability of future generations to meet their own needs.'
   It should lead to an improvement in people's:
   ● quality of life – allowing them to become more content with their way of life and the environment in which they live
   ● standard of living – enabling them, and future generations, to become better off economically.
   This may be achieved in a variety of ways:
   ● By encouraging economic development at a pace that a country can afford and manage so as to avoid that country falling into debt.
   ● By developing technology that is appropriate to the skills, wealth and needs of local people and developing local skills so that they may be handed down to future generations.
   ● By using natural resources without harming the environment, developing materials that will use fewer resources, and using materials that will last for longer.
   Sustainable development needs careful planning and, as it involves a commitment to conservation, the co-operation of different groups of countries adopting global agreements.

Back to ...

The New Wider World
pp184–185 for more information on sustainable development.

Check this!...

1 Define the terms:
   a) sustainable development
   b) appropriate technology.

2 Why is sustainable development desirable?

3 Discuss the ways in which appropriate technology can be used in LEDCs.

For up-to-date information on appropriate technology in an LEDC look at WideWorld September 2003 (Appropriate Technology in Tanzania).

2 Trade and aid in MEDCs and LEDCs and its consequences

World trade and interdependence

- No country is self-sufficient in the full range of raw materials and manufactured goods that are needed by its inhabitants.
- To try to achieve this, countries must **trade** with one another.
- Trade is the flow of commodities from producers to consumers, and it is important in the development of a country.
- Countries that trade with other countries are said to be **interdependent**.
- Raw materials, goods and services bought by a country are called **imports**, and those sold by a country are **exports**.
- The difference between a country's imports and exports is known as its **trade balance**.
- Some countries will have a **trade surplus**, allowing them to become richer, while others will have a **trade deficit**, making them poorer and likely to fall into debt.

> **Key words to know**
>
> *Trade*
> *Interdependent*
> *Imports*
> *Exports*
> *Trade balance*
> *Trade surplus*
> *Trade deficit*

Patterns of world trade

There is a wide imbalance of trade between the LEDCs and the MEDCs (Figure 13.4). This is mainly because:

- the LEDCs provide primary goods which are usually sold to the MEDCs at low and often fluctuating prices
- the MEDCs process primary goods, which they either possess themselves or obtain from LEDCs, into secondary goods. These are sold at high and usually steady prices.
- the MEDCs that export manufactured goods earn increasingly more than the LEDCs which have only primary goods to sell. The result is a widening trade gap between the MEDCs and the LEDCs.
- although 82 per cent of the world's population lived in LEDCs in 2000, the LEDCs only contributed 24 per cent to the world's trade. Over time, the MEDCs have steadily increased their share of world trade.

Figure 13.5 gives some of the advantages and disadvantages of this pattern of world trade to LEDCs and MEDCs.

Figure 13.4 Differences between trade of LEDCs and MEDCs

Trade of less economically developed countries	Trade of more economically developed countries
A legacy of former colonial economies where a mineral once mined, or a crop once grown is exported in its 'raw state'. Most exports are primary products.	Mainly manufactured goods are traded, as these countries have become industrialised. Cereals also exported.
Often only two or three items are exported	A wide range of items are exported
Prices of, and demand for, these products fluctuate annually. Prices rise less quickly than for manufactured goods.	Prices of, and demand for, these products tend to be steady. Prices have risen considerably in comparison with raw materials.
The total trade of these countries is small	The total trade of these countries is large
Most exports come from transnational companies which tend to send profits back to the parent company	Profits are retained by the exporting country
Trade is hindered by poor internal transport networks	Trade is helped by good internal transport networks
Trade is severely hit at times of world economic recession	Trade is badly affected at times of world economic recession

Figure 13.5 International trade

	Advantages	Disadvantages
Richer countries (MEDCs)		
Socio-economic	Cheap imports of foodstuffs and raw materials. Expensive exports of manufactured goods. Trade surplus.	Often obtainable from considerable distances: high transport costs.
Environmental	Limited mining and deforestation. Money to improve environment.	Manufacturing goods can create air, water, noise and visual pollution.
Political	Can exert pressure on LEDCs	
Poorer countries (LEDCs)		
Socio-economic	Raw materials have a ready market in MEDCs. Source of work.	Limited range of exports. Trade deficit as imports costs more than exports.
Environmental		Problems created by mining, deforestation and overgrazing
Political	May be able to obtain overseas aid	Often tied to/dominated by MEDCs

A further problem for many LEDCs is that they rely upon just one or two major commodities for export (Figure 13.6):

- The price paid for these commodities is often fixed by the MEDCs.
- If there is a world recession, an overproduction of a crop or mineral, a change or a fall in the demand for a product, a crop failure, or the exhaustion of a mineral, then the economy of the producing country can be seriously affected.

Figure 13.6 Countries where one or two products account for more than half of all exports

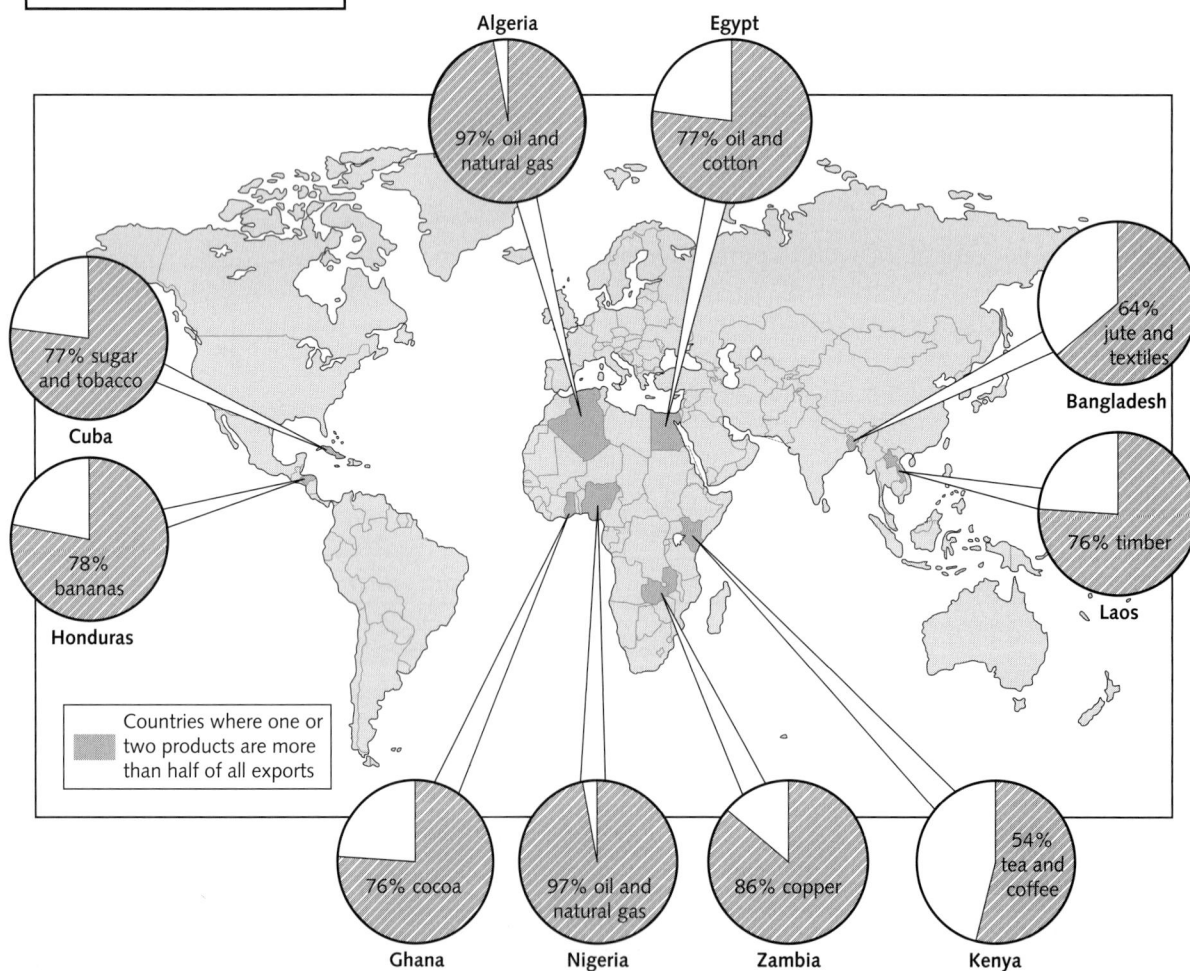

Algeria — 97% oil and natural gas

Egypt — 77% oil and cotton

Bangladesh — 64% jute and textiles

Cuba — 77% sugar and tobacco

Honduras — 78% bananas

Laos — 76% timber

Ghana — 76% cocoa

Nigeria — 97% oil and natural gas

Zambia — 86% copper

Kenya — 54% tea and coffee

Countries where one or two products are more than half of all exports

Back to ...

The New Wider World
pp186–187 for more
information on world trade
and interdependence.

1 Define:
   a) exports
   b) imports
   c) trade balance.

2 What do you understand by the term 'interdependence'?

3 Describe the pattern of trade between MEDCs and LEDCs.

4 Why do many LEDCs feel that the MEDCs gain most of the benefits from world trade?

Free trade, tariffs and quotas

Free trade is when there are no government restrictions on trade, although this rarely happens. Virtually all governments, and especially those of the MEDCs, use trade barriers to protect jobs and industries within their own country. There are two common ways of affecting the levels and patterns of international trade:

1 **Tariffs** are taxes or customs duties paid on imports. The exporter has to pay a percentage of the value of the goods to the importer.

2 **Quotas** limit the amount of goods that can be imported.

Trading groups

- The European Union (EU) is one example of a trading bloc where several countries group together for the purpose of trying to increase the volume and value of their trade.
- By eliminating customs duties (tariffs), the EU was able to reduce the cost of products sold between member countries.
- The EU also created restrictions (trade barriers) which protected goods made in the EU from those imported from the LEDCs.
- This meant that developing countries found it even harder to sell their products in the world market, increasing the trade gap between themselves and the MEDCs.

World trade – a measure of development

Figure 13.2 includes several indicators that are used to try to measure differences in levels of development between countries. Trade is also a suggested measure. Figure 13.7 shows that the MEDCs have the highest trade per capita, followed in turn by the NICs, the middle-income LEDCs and, finally, the lower-income LEDCs.

Key words to know

Tariff
Quota

Figure 13.7 Trade per capita (US$) for selected countries

MEDCs		NICs		Middle-income LEDCs		Lower-income LEDCs	
Germany	7506	Singapore	32 018	Mexico	1516	Kenya	93
UK	6485	Taiwan	5914	Chile	1216	India	60
Italy	4882	Malaysia	3808	Argentina	804	Bangladesh	52
USA	3809	South Korea	3357	Brazil	346	Sierra Leone	25
Japan	3378	Thailand	1004			Ethiopia	21

Japan and Kenya

Back to ...

The New Wider World pp194–195 for the case study 'Japan and Kenya: Trade and interdependence'.

Using your case study

Use this case study to illustrate the contrasting trade patterns of an MEDC and an LEDC and the trade links between the two countries. Make sure that you can:

1 describe the main imports and exports of Japan and Kenya
2 comment on the main trading partners of both countries
3 explain the relationship between Japan and Kenya.

Update

For up-to-date information on Japan use the link on *The New Wider World Coursemate* website.

Learn it!

a) Why does:
   i   Japan import large volumes of raw materials?
   ii Kenya export many raw materials?

b) Suggest reasons for Kenya's pattern of imports.

c) Comment on the economic relationship between the two countries.

Making trade fair

Oxfam is a major critic of the way the present world trading system operates. In 2002 it launched its Make Trade Fair campaign. Its policies include:

- giving poorer countries a stronger voice in the World Trade Organisation
- paying LEDCs a higher and fairer price for their products so that living standards can be improved
- reducing the barriers (tariffs, quotas, etc.) that MEDCs put up to reduce imports from LEDCs.

Aid

Key words to know

Aid
Donor country
Recipient country

Aid is the giving of resources by one country, or by an organisation (known as the **donor**) to another country (the **recipient**). The resource may be in the form of:

- money, although this may be given as a grant or a loan that has to be repaid
- goods, food, machinery or technology aimed at short-term relief or long-term benefit (Figure 13.8)
- people who have skills and knowledge, e.g. teachers, nurses and engineers.

LEDCs require aid for different reasons:

- Because they have a large and often increasing trade deficit. They need to borrow money in order to buy goods from richer, industrialised countries. Unfortunately, by borrowing money, the LEDCs fall further into debt. This aid is often long-term.
- To try to improve their basic amenities and infrastructure.

- To encourage self-help schemes and to promote sustainable development.
- Because either they are prone to natural disasters or they suffer as a result of human-induced disasters. This aid is often needed in an emergency and may only be short-term.

Aid is often complex and controversial as it does not always benefit the country to which it is given (Figure 13.8). Figure 13.9 describes how the traditional and often unsatisfactory trade–aid cycle may be improved. Many people believe that, as we all live in the same world, we must help each other and try to improve the quality of life for everyone – the concept of **global citizenship**.

Key words to know

Global citizenship
Tied aid

Figure 13.8 Advantages and disadvantages of aid

Type of aid	Definition	● Disadvantages / ○ Advantages
Government (Bilateral)	Given directly by a richer country (donor) to a poorer country (recipient) – often tied with 'strings attached'	● 'Tied', meaning LEDC has to buy goods from the donor, e.g. arms manufactured goods ● Money often has to be spent on prestigious schemes such as dams and international airports ● Large schemes take up land belonging to local people ● Aid often encourages corruption – money rarely reaches poorer people living in more remote areas ● LEDC unable to repay money – gets further into debt ● LEDC becomes increasingly dependent on donor country ○ Can provide grants for students to study in MEDCs
International organisations (multilateral)	Given by organisations such as the World Bank and the IMF (International Monetary Fund)	● Not meant to be tied, but less likely to be given to countries with unfavourable economic and political systems ● Encourages farming and industry but products are sent to MEDCs rather than consumed in LEDCs ● LEDCs become increasingly dependent on aid, and often fall increasingly into debt ○ Helps LEDCs to develop new crops, raw materials and industry
Voluntary	Non-governmental organisations such as Oxfam and ActionAid which collect money and receive gifts for people in LEDCs	○ Not tied ○ Deals with emergencies ○ Encourages low-cost self-help schemes ○ Money more likely to reach poorer people in more remote areas ● Dependent on charity's ability to collect money ● Annual amounts uncertain – requires longer-term planning
Short-term/emergency	Needed to cope with the effects of environmental hazards such as earthquakes and tropical storms	○ Immediate help – provides food, clothes, medical supplies and shelter ○ Goes to places and people most in need ○ Not tied, and less chance of corruption ○ Also helps refugees
Long-term/sustainable	Organisations such as Intermediate Technology Development Group that help people in LEDCs to support themselves	○ Encourages development of local skills and use of local raw materials ○ Trains local people to be teachers, nurses, health workers ○ Helps equip schools and development of local agriculture and small-scale industry ○ LEDCs do not fall into debt

However, other people question whether aid should even be given, as they believe it discourages development within LEDCs and makes them dependent upon richer countries and organisation.

Figure 13.9 The trade–aid cycle

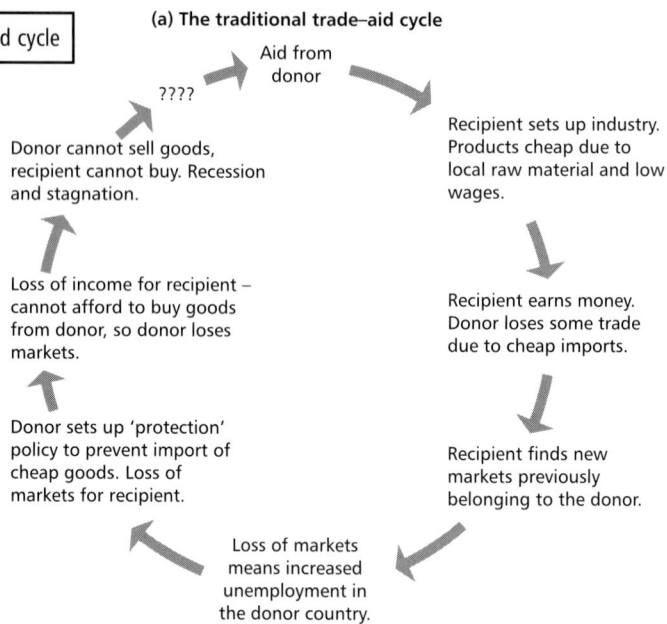

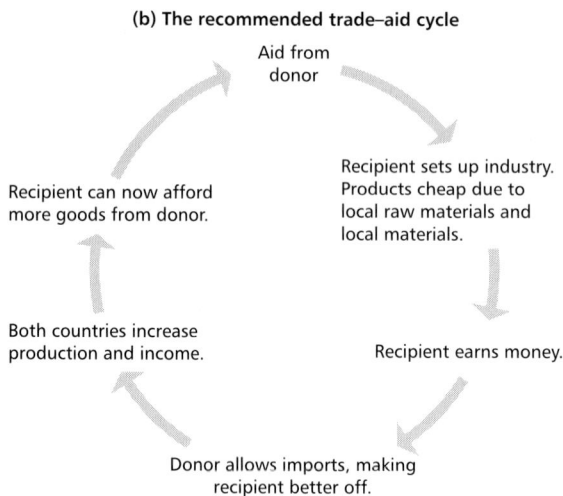

(a) The traditional trade–aid cycle

Aid from donor

????

Donor cannot sell goods, recipient cannot buy. Recession and stagnation.

Recipient sets up industry. Products cheap due to local raw material and low wages.

Loss of income for recipient – cannot afford to buy goods from donor, so donor loses markets.

Recipient earns money. Donor loses some trade due to cheap imports.

Donor sets up 'protection' policy to prevent import of cheap goods. Loss of markets for recipient.

Recipient finds new markets previously belonging to the donor.

Loss of markets means increased unemployment in the donor country.

(b) The recommended trade–aid cycle

Aid from donor

Recipient can now afford more goods from donor.

Recipient sets up industry. Products cheap due to local raw materials and local materials.

Both countries increase production and income.

Recipient earns money.

Donor allows imports, making recipient better off.

1 What is 'aid'?

2 Why do LEDCs need aid?

3 Discuss the advantages and disadvantages of the different types of aid.

4 Explain the difference between:
   a) the traditional trade–aid cycle
   b) the recommended trade–aid cycle.

For up-to-date information on Oxfam use the link on *The New Wider World Coursemate* website.

Back to ...

The New Wider World **pp190–191** for more information on aid.

EXAM PRACTICE

1 Look at Figure 13.1.

   a Describe the part of the world labelled as the South (LEDCs). (3)

   b Suggest why the division of the world into just two parts (North and South) is very simplistic. (3)

2 a Give three indicators that could be used to compare the level of development in different countries. (3)

   b Explain why these indicators are good measures of development. (6)

3 Define sustainable development. (2)

4 Describe and explain the advantages and disadvantages of aid to LEDCs. (8)

EXAM TIPS

For question 3 it is very easy just to pick up one of the two marks available for a definition. Try to make two good points in your answer if possible – an 'introductory' point and an 'elaboration' point.

Back to ...

The New Wider World website to check your answers to the Exam Practice question

14 Skills

1 Map skills

Map scales

All maps should include a scale. This shows how distance on the map (in cm or mm) relates to real-life distance on the ground.

On a map, scale is shown in two ways (see Figure 14.1). Whenever you use a map you should try to use the scale to get an idea of the real-life distance between places.

Figure 14.1 Map scales

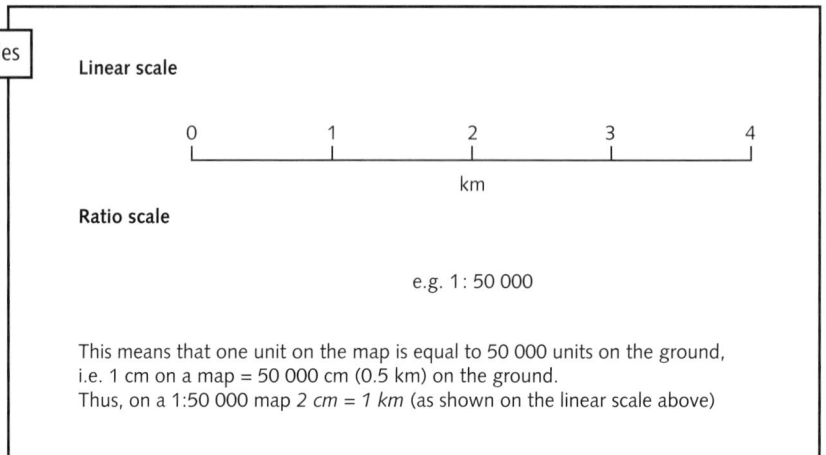

Linear scale

| 0 | 1 | 2 | 3 | 4 |

km

Ratio scale

e.g. 1 : 50 000

This means that one unit on the map is equal to 50 000 units on the ground,
i.e. 1 cm on a map = 50 000 cm (0.5 km) on the ground.
Thus, on a 1:50 000 map *2 cm = 1 km* (as shown on the linear scale above)

Back to ...

The New Wider World **pp41, 292 and 320** for examples of 1:50 000 OS maps.

There are many different scales of map. The larger the scale (e.g. 1:10 000), the more detail is shown; the smaller the scale (e.g. 1:1 million), the less detail is shown. **Large-scale** maps can show road layouts in towns, individual buildings and fields. **Small-scale** maps, like country maps in atlases, cover huge areas but give very little fine detail.

At GCSE you are most likely to come across two scales of Ordnance Survey (OS) maps: the 1:50 000 (2 cm = 1 km) and the more detailed 1:25 000 (4 cm = 1 km). You should take time to learn how to use both of these scales.

Back to ...

The New Wider World **inside back cover** to see a copy of the 1:50 000 OS map key.

Ordnance Survey map symbols

Maps contain a huge amount of information. This is made possible by using symbols instead of written labels, which would take up far too much space. Many symbols are clear in their meaning but they are always explained in a key. The key is usually found at the base or to the side of a map.

Finding grid references

Key words to know

Large-scale
Small-scale
Eastings
Northings
Four-figure grid reference
Six-figure grid reference

Ordnance Survey (OS) maps have gridlines drawn on them to enable locations to be given. The lines that run 'up and down' and increase in value from left to right (west to east), are called **eastings**. Those that run across the map and increase in value from bottom to top (south to north), are called **northings**.

To locate a grid square on a map, we use a **four-figure grid reference**. The first two digits refer to the easting value and the second two digits to the northing value.

To locate a point rather than a grid square, each grid square is split into 'tenths' to give a **six-figure grid reference**.

When giving a grid reference it is perfectly reasonable to estimate the 'tenths' but you can always use a ruler to be more precise. Exam mark schemes often allow one-tenth either side.

Giving compass directions

Figure 14.2 shows the compass directions. Usually on a map the direction north is 'straight up', but it is very important that you check the key when examining maps and diagrams. This is why it is also good practice to include a north point on all maps and diagrams that you draw.

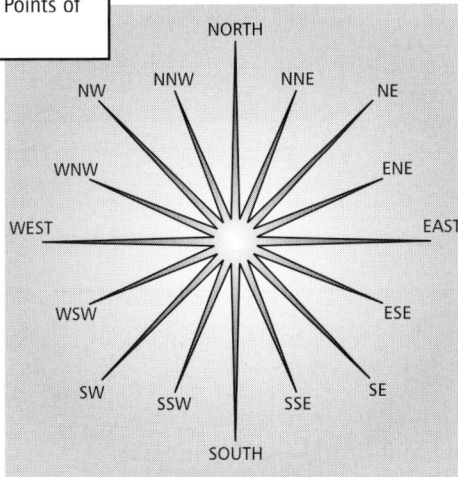

Figure 14.2 Points of the compass

Measuring distances

Every map should have a scale, usually in the form of a measured line (called a *linear scale*) with distances written alongside. To calculate a straight-line distance, you simply measure the distance on the map between the two points in question, using a ruler or the straight edge of a piece of paper. You then line up your ruler or paper alongside the linear scale to discover the actual distance on the ground in kilometres or miles.

A curved distance takes rather longer to work out. The best technique is to use the straight edge of a piece of paper to mark off sections of the curved line, effectively converting the curved distance into a straight-line distance. Look at Figure 14.3 to see how this technique works.

Remember to always give the units, for example kilometres, when writing your answer.

Back to ...

The New Wider World **p41** Figure 3.18: find the village of Thorngumbald. Most of the village is in grid square 2026.

Back to ...

The New Wider World **p41** Figure 3.18: locate the Post Office (P) in the village of Thorngumbald. Its six-figure grid reference is 208266. Notice how the eastings value is represented by the three digits 208 and the northings value is represented by the digits 266. It is the third digit of each set that is the 'tenths' value. Thus, the eastings value is 20 and 8/10ths and the northings value is 26 and 6/10ths.

Back to ...

The New Wider World **p41** Figure 3.18. When answering an exam question, be sure to express a compass direction carefully and precisely. For example, on this OS map Thorngumbald is to the south-east of Hedon, and Hedon is to the east of Salt End.

Figure 14.3 Measuring a curved distance

1. Place the straight edge of the paper alongside the route. Mark on the start (S). Look along the edge of the paper and mark off the point where the curved line no longer runs alongside the paper.

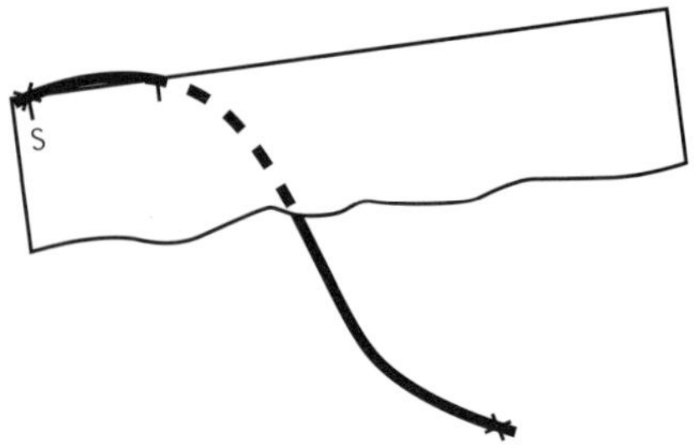

2. Carefully pivot the paper at this point until the curved line once again runs alongside. Continue along the curved line marking off the straight segments until you reach the finish. Mark this on the paper (F).

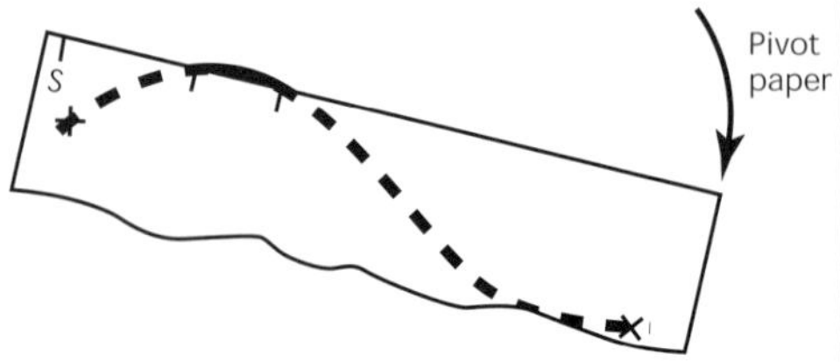

Pivot paper

3. Measure the total straight-line distance using a ruler and convert to kilometres using the linear scale on the map.

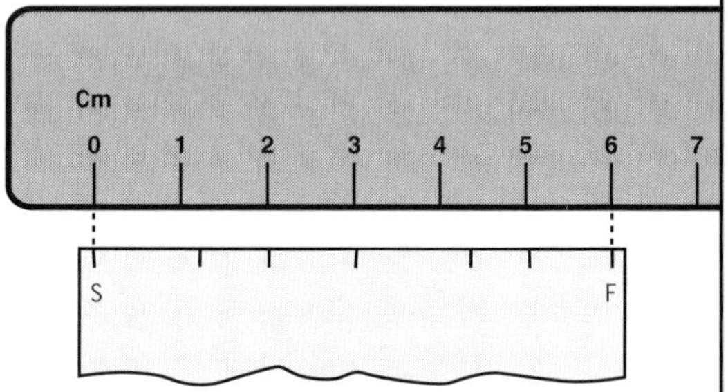

Cm

0   1   2   3   4   5   6   7

S   F

Key words to know

Sketch map

Drawing sketch maps

A **sketch map** is a simplified map that is not drawn absolutely to scale. However, it is important to add a scale even if it is just an approximation.

A sketch map is very useful because the person drawing it can decide what to include and what to leave out. It may be that only information about the physical landscape is needed or, alternatively, just the settlements and roads.

A sketch map can be drawn from any kind of map, including OS maps, maps taken from atlases, or those based on maps seen on the internet.

To draw a sketch map you should follow these steps:

- Start by drawing a frame. Make sure that the shape of the frame matches the shape of the area on the original map. It might be a square or a rectangle. Make your frame bigger or smaller than the original if you want to enlarge or reduce it.
- Now carefully transfer the information that you require from the original map on to your sketch map. You could use grid lines to help you – this is easy if your original map is an OS map – or simply draw one or two major guiding features, such as roads or rivers.
- Once complete, you can use colour and shading if you wish, although black-and-white sketches are often the most successful.

● Label and annotate as required (see below), and don't forget to include an approximate scale, a north point and a title.

Labels

Labels are often single words identifying, for example, physical features or names of places.

Annotations

Annotations are usually short sentences giving a description or explanation. They are more detailed and often more useful than labels.

Remember that most of the credit for a sketch map will relate to your labels and annotations, which show your ability to interpret the map.

Drawing a cross-section

A **cross-section** is an imaginary slice through a landscape. It is very useful because it helps you to visualise what a landscape actually looks like.

To draw a cross-section you need a piece of scrap paper, a sharp pencil, a ruler and an eraser. The stages of construction are shown in Figure 14.4.

Key words to know

Labels
Annotations

Key words to know

Cross-section

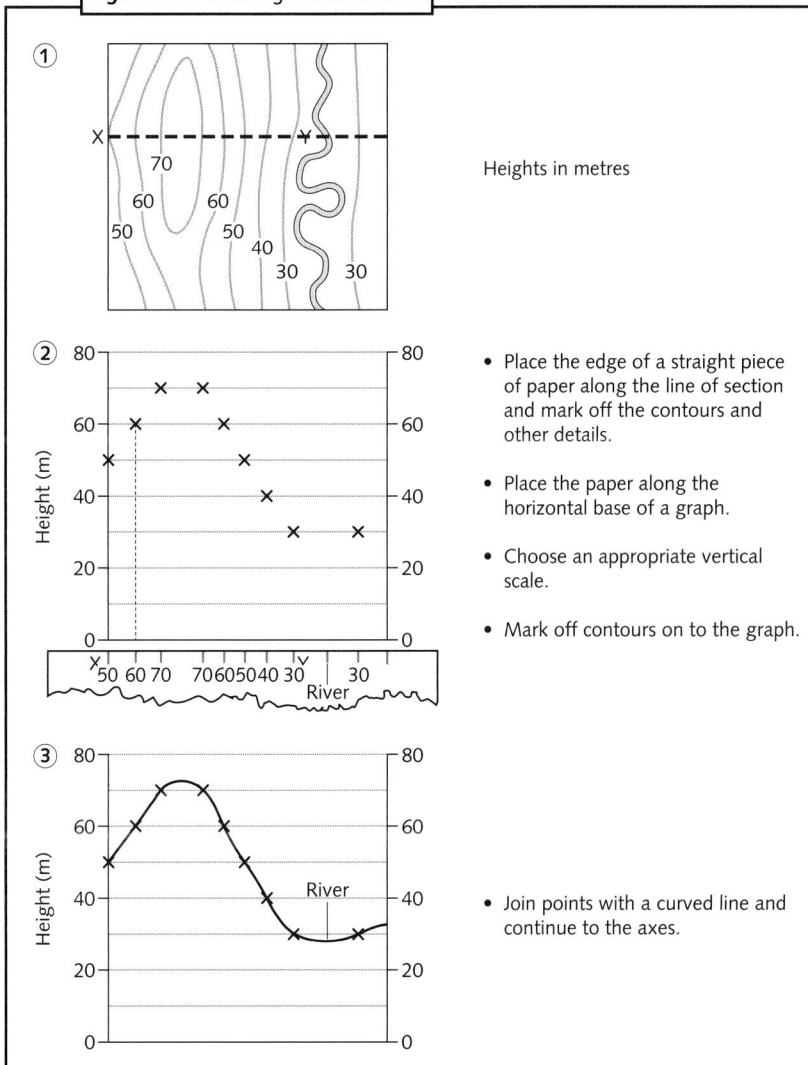

Figure 14.4 Drawing a cross-section

① Heights in metres

② • Place the edge of a straight piece of paper along the line of section and mark off the contours and other details.

• Place the paper along the horizontal base of a graph.

• Choose an appropriate vertical scale.

• Mark off contours on to the graph.

③ • Join points with a curved line and continue to the axes.

As you complete your cross-section, bear in mind the following points:

- double-check that you have written down the correct height values
- make your vertical scale as realistic as possible – don't exaggerate it so much that you create a totally unreal landscape
- complete the cross-section to both vertical axes by carrying on the trend of the landscape
- label any features
- complete axes labels and give grid references for each end of your cross-section
- give your cross-section a title.

A *long profile* is very similar to a cross-section, although it usually involves marking off contour values along a curved distance (see 'Measuring distances' on p131). Long profiles are most commonly drawn to show changes down a river valley.

Key words to know

Relief
Drainage

Describing the physical landscape

It is very likely that you will be asked to describe aspects of the physical landscape on an OS map. Mostly this involves describing the relief and drainage.

Relief is the geographical term used to describe the lie of the land. To gain the most marks in an exam you should comment on:

- The height of the land, using actual figures taken from contours or spot heights to support your points. Using words like 'high' and 'low' is fairly meaningless, without the use of actual figures. Refer to different areas or parts of the map using compass directions to enable you to be precise.
- The slope of the land – is the land flat, or sloping? Which way do the slopes face? Are the slopes gentle or steep? Are there bare cliffs exposed? Again, it is important to give precise supporting information such as grid references, compass directions, etc.
- The presence of features such as valleys, dry valleys, escarpments, etc. Refer to names and use grid references.

Drainage is all about the presence (or absence) of water. When describing the drainage of an area try to comment on the following:

- Are there rivers on the map and which way are they flowing (look at the contours)? Is there a dense network of rivers?
- Are the rivers single or multi-channelled? Give names of the rivers, and use distances, heights and directions to add depth to your description.

Back to ...

The New Wider World **p278**
Figure 17.2: the River Exe drainage basin is a very dense network.

- If there are no surface rivers, it may well be that the rock is permeable and that water has passed underground. If this is the case look for evidence of springs or wells.
- Can you see a pattern to the rivers (see Figure 14.5)?
- Are there any lakes, artificial or man-made?
- Is there evidence of the influence of people on drainage channels, for example straightened channels, built embankments, etc? Straight channels are rare in nature and usually indicate human intervention.

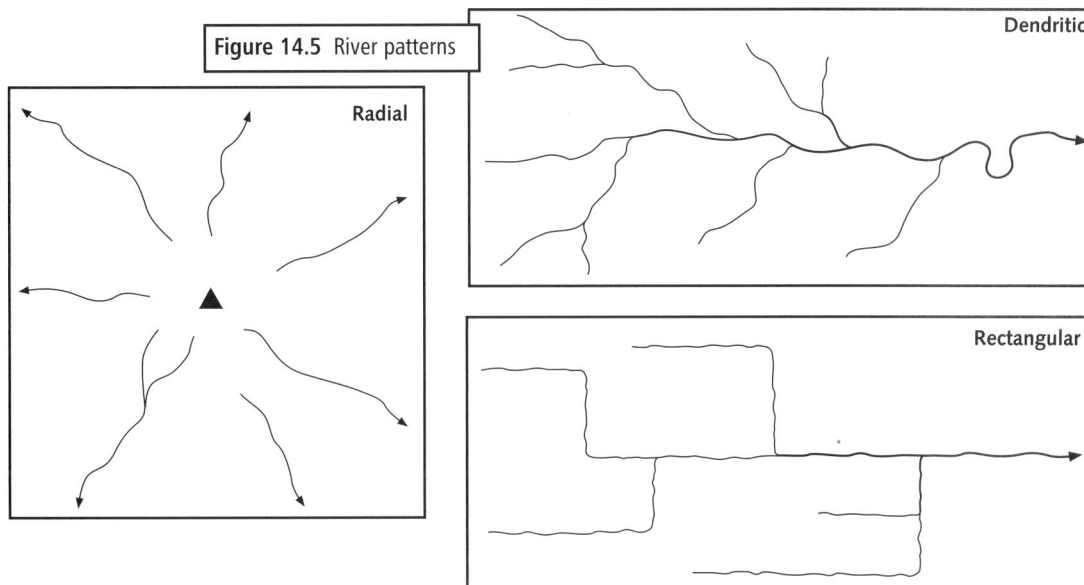

Figure 14.5 River patterns

Radial

Dendritic

Rectangular

Describing the human landscape

Ordnance Survey maps contain a lot of information about aspects of human geography, for example roads, settlements, functions and industry.

- **Roads** Different colours are used to show the various types of road. When describing road networks, refer to the type of road and use road numbers whenever possible. For example, the main road passing through Thorngumbald (2026) is the A1033. Use compass directions when describing the pattern of roads. Look out for roads that might be intended to act as by-passes, such as the A1033 to the south of Hedon. Road networks are clearly visible in settlements and it is possible to identify patterns. Notice how in grid square 1430 the roads tend to form a regular grid pattern, suggesting that they are probably part of an older terraced housing area. A more modern housing area, with curved roads and cul-de-sacs, can be found in grid square 1432.

- **Settlements** The pale pink/brown colour on the map shows the extent of the built-up areas. This is where the houses and shops are. The white spaces in between are areas of open ground, such as parks. Some important buildings such as schools – you can see several of these on the outskirts of Hull – are shown separately. The shapes of settlements (for example, whether they are nucleated or linear) can be readily identified.

- **Functions** There are several functions and services shown on the map. In Preston just to the north of Hedon, there is a Post Office, a public house, several places of worship, a school and a sports centre. The number and type of functions can be used to suggest a settlement hierarchy, though it is important to remember that not all functions, particularly shops, are shown on OS maps.

- **Industry** Industrial buildings are usually large and are often arranged in a regular pattern. A good example is the Works to the south of Salt End in grid squares 1627 and 1628. Notice how, in

Back to ...

The New Wider World **p291** Figures 17.36 and 17.37 which show what happens when rivers are artificially straightened.

Back to ...

The New Wider World **p41** Figure 3.18: study the roads, settlements, functions and industry.

common with many industrial sites, this is on the outskirts of the main town where there is plenty of relatively cheap land available. It has easy access to main roads and, in this case, has a jetty into the river. You can see other industrial buildings alongside the A1033 to the west of Salt End.

Describing patterns on specialist maps

In addition to OS maps, there are many specialist maps, e.g. geological maps, weather maps, etc.

- Geological maps show the different types of rock below the ground surface.
- Soil maps show different types of soil.
- Weather maps (synoptic charts) show weather information.

To interpret specialist maps you should make good use of the key, which will tell you the meaning of the symbols. In describing what the maps show, apply all the principles of good practice described above. Refer to specific locations, give facts and figures, refer to distances and compass directions, etc. You may be asked to relate a specialist map to an OS map.

2 Interpreting photographs and observing landscapes

Interpreting ground photographs

Ground photographs are photographs taken by someone standing on the ground. They show what a place looks like as we would see it if we were standing on the ground.

To interpret a ground photograph you need to look at it closely and look for clues to help you understand what is happening. For example, if trees are in leaf and people are wearing shorts then it was probably taken in the summer.

Interpreting aerial photographs

Aerial photographs give us much the same view of an area as we would see when looking out of an aeroplane window. Vertical aerial photographs look directly down on an area much as a map does. Oblique aerial photographs look down at an area at an angle.

Aerial photographs are excellent in showing what an area looks like. They can help us understand and bring to life the detail shown on a map.

You may well be required to relate an aerial photograph to a map extract. Usually you will be asked to work out which way the photograph is looking. To do this, you first need to locate on the map extract some of the features shown at the bottom, middle and top of the photograph. This gives you a line of sight. Then use the compass directions on the map to help you work out which way the photograph is looking.

Interpreting satellite photographs and images

Satellites can provide us with very accurate and detailed photographs often covering large areas of the Earth's surface. Many modern maps are produced using satellite photographs because they are so accurate and up to date.

Back to ...

The New Wider World **p305** Figure 18.18 which is an example of a geological map.

The New Wider World **pp205–206** Figures 12.13, 12.15 and 12.16 which are all examples of weather maps.

The New Wider World **p305** Figures 18.17 and 18.18. A geological map appears alongside an OS map. In an exam you may be asked to relate the rock types to the landscape. In this case, notice, for example, that The Foreland (a geographical feature known as a headland) corresponds with the resistant rock chalk.

The New Wider World **p150** Figures 9.33–9.34, which show some features of recycling and appropriate technology in LEDCs. In an exam, you could be asked to describe in detail what the people are doing.

The New Wider World **p88** Figure 5.26, which is an oblique aerial photograph of the new town Barra di Tijuca near Rio de Janeiro.

Computers can create satellite images that use false colours to help identify features of interest, for example, green crops, surface water or settlements.

Drawing a sketch from a photograph

It is important to realise that the purpose of a **sketch** is to identify the main geographical characteristics of the landscape. It is not necessary to produce a brilliant artistic drawing; clarity and accuracy are all that is needed. The majority of marks awarded in an exam are given for accurate labels and annotations.

To draw a sketch, you first need to draw a frame to the same general shape of the photograph. Then draw one or two major lines that will subsequently act as guidelines for the rest of your sketch. You could draw the profile of a slope or a hilltop, or a road or river, for example. Consider what it is that you are trying to show and concentrate on these aspects; it may be river features or the pattern of settlements. Don't take time drawing a lot of detail that is not required and only serves to confuse.

Always use a good sharp pencil and don't be afraid to rub things out as you go along.

Finally, remember to label or annotate (detailed labels) your sketch to identify the features, and give your sketch a title.

Back to …

The New Wider World **p216**
Figure 13.13, which is a satellite photograph of a hurricane to the west of Florida.

Key word to know

Aerial photograph
Sketch

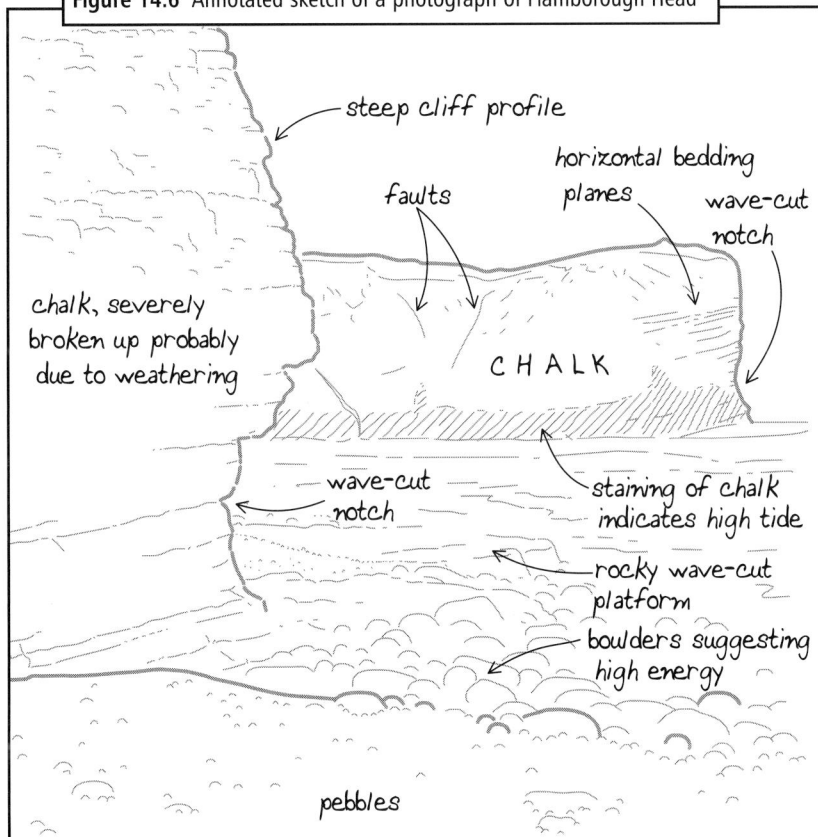

Figure 14.6 Annotated sketch of a photograph of Flamborough Head

- steep cliff profile
- faults
- horizontal bedding planes
- wave-cut notch
- chalk, severely broken up probably due to weathering
- CHALK
- wave-cut notch
- staining of chalk indicates high tide
- rocky wave-cut platform
- boulders suggesting high energy
- pebbles

Back to …

The New Wider World **p300**
Figure 18.5, which shows several features of coastal erosion. Figure 14.6 is an annotated sketch of this photograph.

Drawing field sketches

A **field sketch** is a sketch drawn outside (in the field) to show a particular view. Field sketches are often used to show aspects of the physical landscape, for example a waterfall or cliff. However, they can

Key words to know

Field sketch

also be used to show features of the human landscape, for example aspects of village architecture or farming land use.

To draw a field sketch, you should follow the guidelines in 'Drawing a sketch from a photograph' on p137. Decide how large an area you wish to sketch and draw a frame to the appropriate size and shape. Take time to represent the landscape accurately within your frame but avoid the temptation to strive for a work of art! It is the labels and annotations that are most valuable.

3 Graphical skills

Drawing line graphs

A **line graph** shows continuous changes over a period of time, for example stream flow or population change. It is a very common and effective technique to use, but it is important to remember that time, which is shown on the horizontal axis, must have an equal spacing, for example from year to year.

Drawing bar graphs and histograms

Bar graphs and histograms are one of the most common methods used to display statistical information. However, they are not exactly the same.

- A **bar graph** or chart is used to show the frequency or amount of a number of different categories, such as types of goods bought from a supermarket. The bars are drawn with a gap between them and they are coloured or shaded differently because they are unconnected (see Figure 14.7).

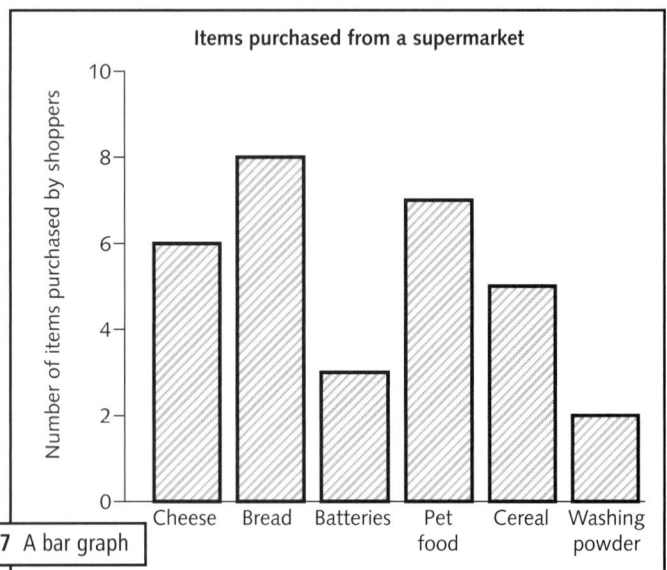

Figure 14.7 A bar graph

- A **histogram** also uses blocks but with no gaps between them. This is because a histogram is drawn when there is continuous data (such as daily rainfall values over a period of a month) or the values are all part of a single survey, for example the sizes of particles in a sediment sample. As the bars are effectively connected, a single colour or type of shading is used.

It is possible to use multiple bar charts and 'split' or composite bar charts to show two or more pieces of information at the same time.

Key words to know

Line graph
Bar graph
Histogram
Pie chart
Triangular graph
Rose diagram
Proportional circle
Scattergraph
Best-fit line

Back to ...

The New Wider World **p10** Figure 1.10, which is a line graph showing the growth in world population since 1800. Notice that the points have been joined up with a freehand curve, which is usually the case with such graphs.

Back to ...

The New Wider World **p164** Figure 10.15, which is a rainfall climate graph and is an example of a histogram. The monthly rainfall values form part of the total annual rainfall, so they can be drawn as 'touching' bars.

Back to ...

The New Wider World **p14** Figure 1.17 which is a composite bar chart showing the differences between male and female life expectancy in selected countries.

Drawing pie charts

A **pie chart** is quite simply a circle divided into segments, rather like slicing a cake! It is usually drawn to show the proportions of a total, for example the number of shoppers visiting a supermarket each day during one week. Pie charts work best when they have between 4 and 10 segments; pie charts with only one segment are a waste of time and those with many segments become too confusing.

When drawing a pie chart, remember to convert your values into degrees (for percentages multiply by 3.6).

Drawing triangular graphs

A **triangular graph** enables three values to be plotted at the same time to produce a single point. The values take the form of percentages that add up to 100. They are commonly used to show soil texture, employment and types of mass movement.

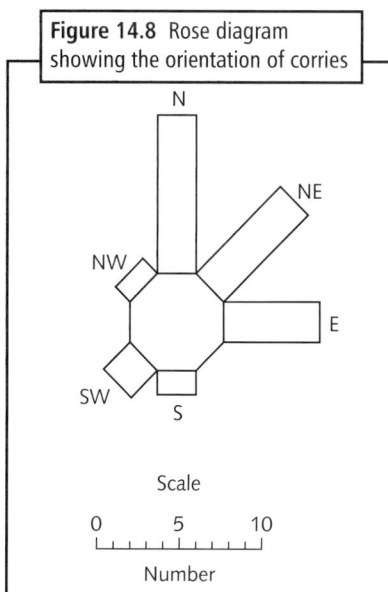

Figure 14.8 Rose diagram showing the orientation of corries

Drawing rose diagrams

A **rose diagram** shows the orientation of observed data, for example wind direction or the orientation of corries (Figure 14.8). Bars are drawn from an octagonal central shape to represent the number or frequency of each direction.

Drawing proportional symbols

Proportional circles are very effective ways to show data, particularly on a base map where spatial variations can be seen. However, they are rather tricky to draw and you will need to choose your scale carefully.

Select a scale for the radius of your circle. As it is the *area* of the circle that needs to be proportional, you must use the square root value as your radius distance.

Drawing scattergraphs

If you think that two sets of data are related, then the information can be plotted on a graph called a **scattergraph**. To complete a scattergraph you should do the following:

- Draw two graph axes in the normal way, but try to put the variable that is thought to be causing the change in the other (called the *independent variable*) on the horizontal (*x*) axis. In Figure 14.9, the wealth of a country (GNP) is thought to be responsible for the number of doctors.
- Use each pair of values to plot a single point on the graph using a cross.
- Use a **best-fit line** to clarify the trend of the points if there is one (see Figure 14.9). Your best-fit line should pass roughly through the centre of the points so that there is approximately the same number

Back to ...

The New Wider World **p173** Figure 10.36 which uses pie charts to show statistics for the Lake District National Park.

The New Wider World **p186** Figure 11.11 which compares types of trade for a number of different countries.

The New Wider World **p93** Figure 6.4 which shows how employment structure data can be displayed on a triangular graph.

The New Wider World **p93** Figure 6.3: proportional circles are used very effectively to show regional variations in employment structures in the UK. Notice how the circles are also used as pie charts to show the different types of employment. This complex method of data presentation will score highly in any coursework that you undertake.

Figure 14.9 Drawing a scattergraph

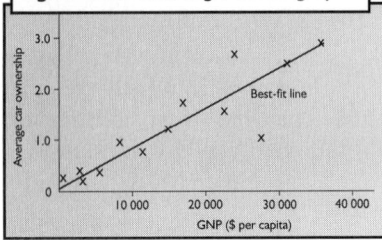

of points on either side of the line. Use a ruler to draw a straight line. The best-fit line does *not* need to pass through the origin. The resultant pattern can now be described.

Drawing flow lines

Flow lines are an excellent way to show movement, for example where people visiting a particular country have come from. Each line is drawn with its width proportional to its value, for example 1 cm = 10 million tourists. Flow lines are most effective when drawn on a base map.

Drawing choropleth maps

A **choropleth map** is a map that uses different colours or density of shading to show the distribution of data categories.

Notice the following key features in Figure 1.2 on p5 of *The New Wider World*:

- The base map shows regions or areas, in this case countries.
- Data is divided into a number of groups or categories. Ideally there should be between four and six categories. Notice that the category values do not overlap.
- The darker the shading, the higher the values.
- The map has a powerful and immediate visual impact; it is an effective form of mapping.

Drawing isopleth maps

An **isopleth map** is a map that uses lines of equal value to show patterns. Contours are a good example of isopleths, and are usually drawn at intervals of 10 metres.

Some of the most common isopleth maps are drawn to show aspects of weather and climate, e.g. isobars show pressure, and isotherms show temperature.

Whilst isopleth maps are rather difficult maps to draw, they are very effective at showing patterns, particularly when they are superimposed on a base map.

To draw an isopleth map, you need to mark your observed data on to a base map or sheet of tracing paper/acetate. You then need to consider how many lines to attempt to draw and at what intervals you will draw them. This decision is largely 'trial and error' and you may need to have a go in rough first.

Look at Figure 14.10 to see how isopleths are drawn. Notice how they pass between values that are higher and lower than the value of the line. Just remember that all values to one side of a line will be higher, and all those to the other side will be lower.

There is a degree of individual determination and decision-making, so do not worry if your map turns out to be slightly different from those of your neighbours.

Drawing topological maps

A **topological map** is a map that is not drawn to a true distance scale. Whilst it shows where places are relative to each other, it often appears distorted.

Figure 14.11 shows the Newcastle Metro system. Whilst stations are located correctly according to their links, no attempt has been made to draw the map to a true distance scale.

Back to ...

The New Wider World **p178** Question 4 which includes a flow map showing the numbers of tourists travelling to Spain. Notice that the largest number of tourists come from France.

Back to ...

The New Wider World **p201** Figure 12.3 which uses isotherms to show average July temperatures in the UK. Figure 12.4 on the same page uses isotherms to show January temperatures.

Back to ...

The New Wider World **p201** Figures 12.3 and 12.4, in which the isotherms have been drawn at 1° intervals.

Figure 14.10 An isopleth map showing a pedestrian count

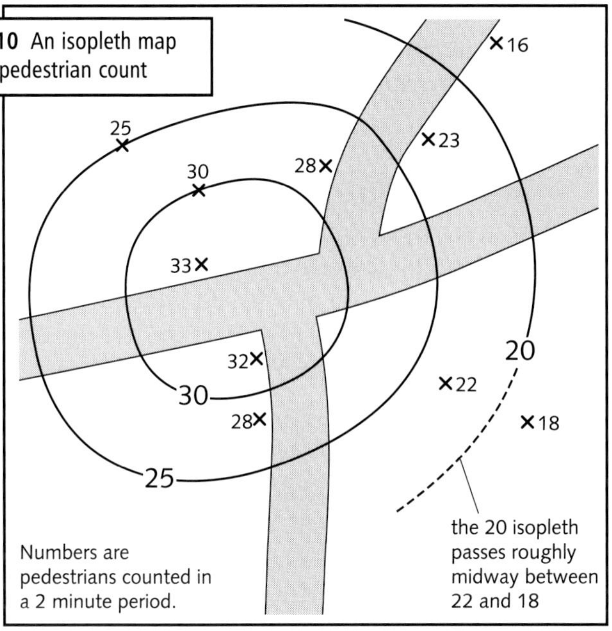

Numbers are pedestrians counted in a 2 minute period.

the 20 isopleth passes roughly midway between 22 and 18

Figure 14.14 Newcastle Metro system

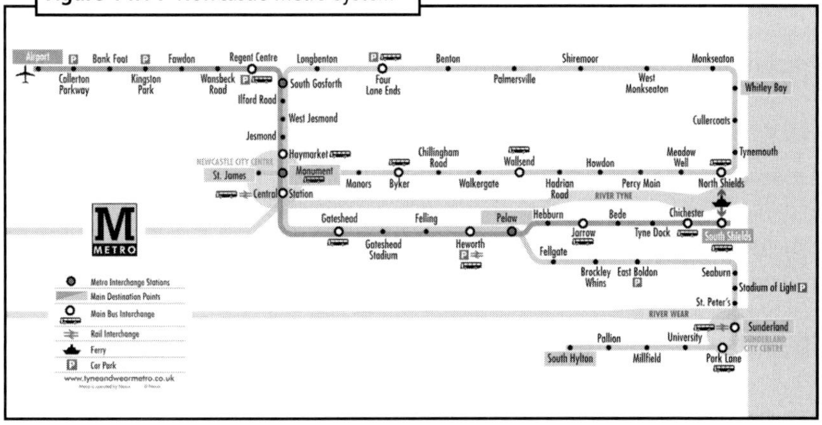

Metro Interchange Stations
Main Destination Points
Main Bus Interchange
Rail Interchange
Ferry
Car Park
www.tyneandwearmetro.co.uk

Topological maps can be very effective and can stimulate discussion, such as those drawn to a scale of time taken rather than distance.

4 Looking for patterns

How to 'describe'

To **describe** a map, photograph or diagram you need to put into words what it shows. Start by describing the overall picture or pattern. Refer to the information available on the map, photograph or diagram and give actual facts and figures to support your statements. Then, if appropriate, look for any exceptions (called *anomalies*) to the general pattern. The most important thing is to be as precise and detailed as you can. Also, avoid giving reasons unless you are specifically asked to 'explain'.

How to 'compare' and 'contrast'

To **compare** or **contrast**, you need to write about similarities and differences, for example between two areas on a map. It is essential to make comparisons all the way through your answer, so you should use

Key words to know

Describe
Compare and contrast

Back to ...

The New Wider World **p4**
Figure 1.1: a description of the distribution of world population as shown here might be as follows:

'World population is unevenly distributed. In some parts of the world, for example north-west Europe, India, eastern China and south-east Africa, there is a dense population distribution. However, large parts of the world have a relatively low population density, for example Canada, much of the Russian Federation, north Africa and much of Australia.'

Back to ...

The New Wider World
pp268–269: a comparison between the two volcanic eruptions shown in these photographs might read as follows:

'In Figure 16.20 the volcano is erupting large quantities of red-hot lava, whereas the volcano in Figure 16.22 is erupting dense black clouds of ash and pyroclastics. An ash cloud is rising into the atmosphere from the volcano in Figure 16.22, whereas there is no ash cloud in Figure 16.20. Both eruptions look very dramatic and dangerous.'

Key words to know

Explain
Analyse
Synthesise

Back to ...

The New Wider World **p81**
Figure 17.8: an analysis of this complex hydrograph is given in the Case Study box. Notice that it involves a detailed study of the graph together with an interpretation of the effects of drainage basin characteristics on river flow.

Back to ...

The New Wider World
pp272–273: the case study of the Afghanistan earthquake of 1998 is a good example of a synthesis. Several different pieces of information, including tectonic details, the physical geography of Afghanistan, and economic and social characteristics of the population, are used to account for the impact of the earthquake.

words like 'whereas' or 'compared with'. Avoid the temptation to write separate paragraphs on the two areas under discussion.

As with making a description, you should refer to places and data wherever possible.

How to 'explain' or 'give reasons'

To **explain** patterns on maps or diagrams you need to try to think of reasons why they exist. This is much more difficult and will test your understanding of geography. You may need to refer to other maps and diagrams to help you. For example, to explain the hydrographs in Figure 17.6 on p280 of *The New Wider World* you could write:

'The main reason why the hydrograph for drainage basin A has a higher peak and more rapidly rising and falling limbs than the hydrograph for drainage basin B is because there is a much higher drainage density in basin A than in B. In basin A, water passes quickly into river channels and then it flows rapidly to the gauging station resulting in a dramatic hydrograph. In basin B, the lower drainage density means that it takes far longer for water to pass through the system hence the longer time lag and the flatter hydrograph.'

You will often be awarded marks for suggesting a reasonable explanation even if it is not absolutely accurate; an examiner will give you credit for making a reasonable suggestion.

How to 'analyse'

An **analysis** is very similar to an explanation except that it usually involves more detail and a much greater use of facts and figures. When conducting your coursework you will probably be required to **analyse** your data.

How to 'synthesise'

A synthesis involves the 'pulling together' of a variety of different forms of information to give a general overview. It is a kind of conclusion, pulling together all the different aspects that have been studied. Whilst you are unlikely to be asked to **synthesise** in an exam, it is possible that you will be required to do so in your coursework.